THE FOOD
CHILDREN EAT

How to Get Children to Like Good Food

....

Joanna Blythman

FOURTH ESTATE • London

First published in Great Britain in 1999 by
Fourth Estate Limited
6 Salem Road
London W2 4BU

10 9 8 7 6 5 4 3 2 1

The right of Joanna Blythman to be identified as the author of this work has
been asserted by her in accordance with the Copyright, Designs and Patents
Act 1988.

A catalogue record for this book is available from the British Library.

ISBN 1-85702-936-4

Typeset by Rowland Phototypesetting Limited,
Bury St Edmunds, Suffolk
Printed in Great Britain by The Bath Press Limited, Bath

CONTENTS

PART THREE: THE GENTLE ART OF PERSUASION

PART FOUR: GETTING IT RIGHT WITH BABIES AND TODDLERS

PART EIGHT: NITTY-GRITTY IDEAS AND RECIPES FOR INSPIRATION

This book is written for my mother, Marion Blythman, and my grandmother, Marion Paterson, who taught me effortlessly how to love good food

I would also like to thank the following people, who helped make this book happen.

Amy and Zoe inspired me by offering the living proof that modern children can eat well.

Nick met writer's block with patience, good humour and logic.

Lynda Brown, Mary Contini, Carolyn Czoski, Matthew Fort, Sue Lawrence, Charlotte Mitchell and Nigel Slater all provided ideas, clear thinking and enthusiasm.

Louise Haines edited the text wisely and supportively and her twins put their small stamp on it too. Jane Middleton plugged the gaps with creative but practical suggestions.

Lizzie Vann and Michelle Barker of Baby Organix, Professor Tim Lang of Thames Valley University and Jack Winkler of Action and Information on Sugar all gave useful information.

McCance and Widdowson's Composition of Food provided essential reference.

A FEW PAGES TO READ FIRST

This is a book for people who want their children to become adults with wide-ranging food tastes, adults who select a good diet for themselves and find pleasure in the process of eating.

Achieving such an outcome ought to be a straightforward matter, but these days children who fit this bill are something of an endangered species. Children no longer eat what adults eat. We now live in a world that assumes children must be catered for separately, from a repertoire of special 'children's foods' designed to please their distinctive palate.

In the new millennium, perhaps sociologists and social historians will look back on the second half of the twentieth century and point to the emergence of this separate diet as a curious phenomenon. When you stop to think about it, it's a huge watershed. For centuries children all over the world have been brought up to eat what their parents ate.

Traditionally, children's food has always been inextricably linked with adult diet, right from day one. Children were breastfed – even if that meant finding a wet nurse.

Graduating on to more complex foods, they were fed ground-down, pulverised versions of what the extended family was eating. As soon as they had teeth and had become more independent, they ate whatever was produced in the kitchen in whatever form it emerged.

Now in many industrialised countries, and in the UK in particular, it's more likely that children are tucking into a restricted number of specifically 'children's foods'. We are all too familiar with them. The working title 'junk' fits them as well as any other. But if we wanted to analyse that loaded term a little further, we might describe it as consisting of a small selection of highly processed, long-life foods – many technological interventions removed from their raw-food roots – heavily loaded with fat, sugar and salt.

Enter the 'modern' child and a typical food day. This might start with a bowl of highly refined cereal stuck together with sugar in one form or another, followed by a sweet drink and a packet of crisps for morning snack. Chips and custard might be the most popular canteen choice at lunchtime, or a protein and fat-based, vegetable-free sandwich in the lunch box, accompanied by sweets, a token apple (if you're lucky) and often yet another packet of crisps. In the starving after-school interval, biscuits and more crisps fill the gap until an early 'children's teatime', when out come the frozen Kievs, fish fingers, pizzas and burgers, destined to be scoffed with chips and copious amounts of ketchup and washed down by something sweet and fizzy. For pudding, there's the sickly-sweet 'kiddie' yogurt with its lovable cartoon characters and child-friendly synthetic flavours. Not surprisingly, by bedtime they're hungry again and it's time for supper. That packet of cereal beckons once more, as do the biscuits.

The consequences of this change in our attitude towards child nutrition are so enormous that they are hard to grasp. We are embarked on an experiment with our children's health that is unprecedented. This is a radical departure from the tried and tested way of nourishing children that societies have adopted since history began.

You don't have to be a paediatrician to figure out that this sort of eating defies the laws of nutrition. Nearly every item has been processed out of its natural form. It is top-heavy on ingredients we know cause health problems long-term and notoriously short on those that keep the human body healthy: whole, unprocessed plant foods, especially fruit and vegetables. So we are living through a strange irony. Instead of being given the best food available, as they ought to be, children are being given the worst.

It is going to take time for the impact of this major change in eating patterns to show through but initial indications are not good. Worrying tales have emerged from the US, where doctors have been shocked by the premature furring up of arteries that has inadvertently come to light when children have been admitted to hospital as road casualties.

Teachers complain that their pupils' concentration span is not what it should be because they are going from one quick sugary snack to another and simply don't have the stamina that a long, slow release of nutrients from a balanced diet would give them. According to the World Health Organisation, 'The prevalence of overweight and obesity is increasing worldwide at an alarming rate . . . Moreover, as the problem appears to be increasing rapidly in children as well as adults, the truth health consequences may only become fully apparent in the distant future.'

Knowing how far this modern children's diet is from any concept of good food, let alone healthy eating, an outside observer might assume that it is the prerogative of a poor and disadvantaged underclass that can't afford to feed its children properly. But junk food is the great leveller. These days children from affluent backgrounds often eat as badly as their less privileged counterparts. The nation's youth, it seems, is united in its attachment to junk.

Many parents recognise that they are not feeding their children the way they themselves were fed when young and they worry about this. But our anxieties are soothed by the overwhelming cynicism that surrounds the whole subject of feeding children. The fact that most children in the UK eat extremely badly has become institutionalised. Though new parents set out with good intentions, puréeing wholesome foods and vowing to be different, there's a prevalent feeling that it's only a matter of time till children graduate on to the modern crisps-and-cola, burgers-and-turkey-nugget repertoire. After all, they encounter it everywhere – at school, at friends' houses, at the corner shop, on television.

The pressure on children to eat junk is so strong and so widespread that many parents simply throw in the towel. Why fight the inevitable, especially when no one else seems to be bothered? And there's succour to be had from the feeling of safety in numbers, too. If all those freezer cabinets are full of pre-fried, re-formed bits of cheap animal protein targeted at children, surely they can't be *too* bad? If the neighbourhood crèche recommends crisps as a morning snack because fruit makes too much mess, who are we to stick out our necks and say differently? So many children live on this typical 'children's diet' that surely it must be the norm?

Thus we live in hope that sooner or later, as though by magic, our offspring will be transformed miraculously into sensible adults with wide-ranging, sophisticated food tastes. We fondly imagine that burger-and-biscuit-addicted Kevin or Holly will turn into a marvellous eighteen-year-old who adores spinach salad, or stir-fried squid, aubergine and anchovies.

If you find those rationalisations comforting, then you may not want to read on. This book is for people who have the gut reaction that, however ubiquitous and common it might have become, the typical children's diet is unacceptable. First, because it drastically limits children's food horizons and therefore their ability to get pleasure from the delicious diversity of foods available, not to mention the sociable rituals that surround eating. Second, because it deviates so much from any notion of good nutrition that it stores up problems for their long-term health.

The core is that we need separate and different children's food about as badly as we need a fatal illness. Instead, we should abandon the whole concept and reintegrate children into mainstream eating.

The ideas and strategies in this book are designed to help parents who want their children to eat better and who are prepared to put some effort into achieving that goal. The basic approach can work with children of all ages, even those who have already become accustomed to eating the typical children's junk food. It is based on my knowledge as a specialist food journalist and my experience as a parent. The first has given me the conviction that we cannot afford to be passive about children's junk because it amounts to a modern brand of malnutrition. The second has shown me that children can come to appreciate and actively desire a wide range of good, wholesome unprocessed food if the adults who feed them are committed to that idea.

My children, aged fourteen and ten, do not eat absolutely everything that I might as an adult, but they will eat, or at least try, most things. They have their likes and dislikes, as do adults. Mushrooms and aubergine get the joint thumbs-down. One refuses tomatoes but adores avocado; the other leaves the avocado and wolfs down the tomatoes. Nevertheless, they both eat a wide range of different foods from all food groups and there are no complete categories of food – such as vegetables – that are no-go areas. What pleases me most is that they actively enjoy eating. Meals aren't just a refuelling exercise. They are enthusiastic eaters who approach even new foods with a positive and open attitude.

Some people wonder how they came to be this way. '*What did you do with them?*' they ask. '*Mine won't eat that way, your kids are different,*' they remark. It's an interesting cultural shift to see how children who eat reasonably widely and well have become the exception rather than the rule.

The answer is that there is absolutely nothing complicated, or even particularly demanding, about producing children who eat well. I have done nothing with my children that hasn't already been done by generations of parents. The approach amounts to little more than common sense. It is just that these days, children's junk food is so prevalent that parents think that the old laws of nutrition no longer apply. We need to be reminded of them.

So this book offers a common-sense strategy for getting children to eat better – one that also makes the job of feeding children easier, not harder. There are workable and effective strategies for every testing situation but, in essence, the approach is terribly simple.

HOW TO GET YOUR CHILDREN TO EAT WELL

- Feed children the same food you yourself eat.

- Socialise children into good eating habits by eating with them as much as you possibly can.

- Consciously open up children's food horizons by introducing them to a wide range of tastes.

- Keep on presenting them with a wide range of foods even if they resist them at first: they will learn to like what they are given.

- Give them the freshest, most nutritious and best-quality food you possibly can.

This is the opposite of how many modern children eat.

HOW TO GET YOUR CHILDREN TO EAT BADLY

- Give them different food from that which you yourself eat.

- Feed them separately most of the time.

- Stereotype them as having narrow food horizons and therefore offer them only a limited number of foods.

- When they reject a food, do not offer it to them again consistently.

- Give them the most processed, least satisfying and least nutritious food around, otherwise known as 'children's food'.

The underlying assumption in the points above is that there is only one kind of food suitable for children – good food – and that the best way to deliver that is to socialise them into adult eating patterns and tastes from the time they are weaned. I firmly believe that the modern idea of separate children's food, which assumes that children have different requirements from adults, is the enemy of good eating in the long term. By going down that 'separate' and 'different' road, food manufacturers have got away with transforming children's food into a junk-food ghetto.

For this reason, I have deviated from other children's eating guides by not including recipes for separate 'children's' dishes. This book does, however, include recipes and meal ideas that should appeal to both adults and children alike; to my mind this is much more useful. It seems to me that children need to, and can, eat the same as everyone else.

Why? Because it's much less time-consuming for the person preparing the food if there is just one meal on the go. Who can dream up and prepare two different sets of good meals each day for any length of time? If you adopt this way of doing things, then something has to give. What happens more often than not is that one 'real' meal is prepared for the adults and the children end up with reheated processed junk. So it seems to me that if we want children to eat well in the long run, we need to get them accustomed to eating the same as everyone else as early as possible rather than feeding them differently.

This book also asks you to question the modern habit of feeding children on their own, not alongside adults at communal mealtimes. If we accept that children need ultimately to pick up eating patterns that will stand them in good stead for the rest of their lives, the quickest and most effortless way to achieve that is for them to share mealtimes with adults as often as possible. I am not saying that it is impossible for children to learn to eat well when they are eating on their own, just that it is considerably more difficult.

These days, as I discovered in the process of researching and writing this book, any insistence on some commitment – however small – to communal household eating is controversial. Although many parents want their children to eat well in the long term, in the short term they find it easier and more practical to feed them earlier and apart. Modern lifestyles have changed. The nuclear family no longer sits down around the table at five o'clock.

Please believe that, as a parent who has always worked, I am not suggesting we turn the clock back to the 'good old days' when Mummy was perpetually in the kitchen baking and didn't go out to work. I do not want any parent – male or female – to feel a failure or traumatised with guilt because they do not bake their own bread or make their own pasta in the frantic 'happy hour' after they get in from work and attempt to deal with everything from seven-times tables to endlessly ringing phones. But I do still think that, although communal mealtimes may not be possible every day of the week, even if you can manage it some nights and not others it will help socialise children into liking and appreciating a wide variety of good food and provide an important model for eating which challenges the pressure to eat junk.

So, while advocating communal eating as the goal to try for, this book also recognises the stresses faced by busy, modern parents and offers practical strategies for making successful compromises. It offers a positive long-term philosophy which allows lots of room for individual variation, not a rigid set of rules which are broken at the first deviation from theory. Believe me, it is designed to make life easier for those looking after children, not harder.

You will notice that this book is not presented as a 'healthy-eating' manual for children. There are no recommendations to switch your kids on to skimmed milk, lower-fat crisps or diet yogurt, or to read nutrition labels or count calories.

Why? Obviously, one of the main reasons most parents want their children to eat better is that this will make them healthier, but if we are overly concerned with health there is a danger of becoming almost hung up about what we eat. We stop eating certain things because they are 'bad' for us and food becomes all about prohibitions and 'what is good for you'. Even for adults, this type of thinking is a pleasure-killer and for children that feeling is more intense.

What's more, this thinking is pointless because children can learn to enjoy fresh, wholesome, healthy food when it is presented to them in a positive way, mainly because it smells and tastes good in a way that junky children's food never can. So the main rationale we give children for eating natural, wholesome food as opposed to junk has to be that it tastes better, not because it is 'good for you'.

The concept of healthy eating is also much abused and often reinforces the paralysing modern notion that parents do not know how to feed their children any longer and so need help from 'experts' who provide 'special foods'. But often these 'experts' are backed by powerful industry interests whose 'advice' is highly suspect. A lot of junk and heavily processed food these days can be presented as 'healthy' simply because it is low fat, despite the fact that it contains almost no useful nutrition. Thus a diet cola drink can actually come over as a healthy alternative to regular cola. But no cola drink has a place in any common-sense understanding of a wholesome diet.

The philosophy behind this book is that if you give your children food prepared from fresh raw materials in their natural, nutritious, unprocessed form, and encourage them to eat a wide selection of foods from all the major food groups, they will be eating healthily – end of story.

Most modern children do not eat this way. Their diet is top-heavy with protein, fat, refined carbohydrates, salt and sugar – a consequence of their dependence on processed foods. Their consumption of fresh fruit and vegetables is almost invariably far too low. 'Eat more fresh fruit and vegetables' is the one positive food message on which most nutritionists can agree and it's the only modern health message on which parents really need to focus. So this book provides plenty of positive and effective strategies for getting children to like fruit and vegetables and increase their consumption of them.

But that is as far as conscious 'healthy-eating' guidance goes. The typical unbalanced children's diet is a consequence of feeding children on a separate range of highly processed foods, which have been manufactured for profit rather than to retain their nutritional integrity. By drastically reducing the processed foods given to children and replacing them with wholesome unprocessed ones, parents can embrace healthy eating without getting embroiled in often-contradictory nutritional guidance.

So if you follow the real-food approach described in Part Two, you won't get bogged down in whether that margarine has 15 or 50 per cent polyunsaturates. Instead, you'll be concentrating on stimulating your children's palate so that they enjoy a wide variety of fresh, unprocessed food, where pride of place is given to fruit and vegetables. If you do that, then you can afford to be laid-back about 'healthy eating'.

This book is organised so readers can home in on the sections they find most useful. Part One examines the nature of the general problem we have on our hands now that so many children live on junk. You may find that it makes disquieting reading. Skip it, by all means, if you prefer, and move on to the rest of the book. Part Two, Breaking the Mould at Home, explains the general strategy for getting children to eat well. Part Three, The Gentle Art of Persuasion, is a troubleshooting section for when the general strategy doesn't seem to work. Part Four explains how feeding babies can dovetail with this overall approach. Parts Five and Six offer practical strategies for sticky situations. Part Seven suggests ways of reinforcing your efforts, while Part Eight offers ideas to inspire you when you can't see beyond the difficulties.

This book is an empowering one which offers parents the conviction that over time, and with a little bit of commitment, you can produce children who actively enjoy good wholesome food. Such a goal is both desirable and attainable. It will strengthen your resolve to trust your own common sense and good judgement and to be different from the pack, but it will also arm you with devices to cope with the 'real world' challenges faced by parents who want their children to eat well.

The motivation is not just the well-being of our children but the satisfaction that we parents can get from knowing that our children share with us a love of food and the pleasure of eating. When we are older and greyer, what a delight to drop in to a son or daughter for a home-cooked meal prepared from fresh, wholesome, unprocessed ingredients. And if there are grandchildren sitting around the table, too, all the better. If they learn, as their parents did, to appreciate real food, then our food chain will be so much safer in their hands.

PART ONE
....
THE GHETTO OF 'CHILDREN'S FOOD'

THE MODERN 'CHILDREN'S DIET'

Let's look at those distinctive foods that have become the mainstay of the modern British children's diet. It won't take long, because they are so very limited.

The backbone foods and drinks of the very restricted diet and their shortcomings

BREAKFAST CEREAL AND MILK

The typical 'children's cereal' favourites consist of highly processed and over-refined grains stuck together with sugar in one form or another, and many are also high in salt. Prominent added vitamins give an aura of health but are only an attempt to replace the goodness that has been refined out of the processed grain. These are overwhelmingly sugary foods. The nutritional goodness of the milk (protein, calcium and vitamins) can't compensate for that.

BURGERS

Mass-produced burgers of the type aimed at children have a very different composition from ones you might make at home. They tend to contain much more fat, and include a number of chemical additives to improve flavour and consistency. They are generally made with meat that represents the lowest common legal denominator in terms of cuts allowed and the source of the animals.

SAUSAGES AND SAUSAGE ROLLS

Similar objections to burgers except that the amount of meat is often lower and there are more chemical additives. Sausage rolls have an additional layer of fatty pastry which makes them even less healthy. They are often served inadequately reheated from frozen and this, combined with the poor quality of the meat, makes them a likely food poisoning source.

POULTRY OR FISH IN BREADCRUMBS

Any food in breadcrumbs is automatically much fattier than its unbreaded equivalent because the coating holds fat, even when it is grilled rather than fried. Apart from whole fillets of poultry or fish, the minced poultry meat in products such as Kievs and nuggets represents a very low-grade mulch of intensively produced meat, held together with chemical additives. They seem cheap but they represent poor value for money given the ingredients used.

FISH FINGERS

Many contain just a fish and additive sludge. Some more expensive fish fingers do contain only fish fillets – even if this is at a vastly inflated price – but they are a less healthy alternative to a plain fillet because of the coating.

CHIPS

A very fatty food, even oven or lower-fat chips. Processing can result in a loss of vitamins.

TINNED BAKED BEANS

Beans offer useful fibre, some protein and beneficial vitamins. But tinned versions usually contain surprisingly large amounts of sugar and salt. This makes them less healthy than we might think.

TINNED TOMATO SOUP

The healthy nutrition offered by the tomatoes is outweighed, or at least cancelled out, by the unhealthy amounts of sugar. Another 'savoury' food that is usually surprisingly sweet.

PIZZA

A disc of highly refined bread dough with a very thin smear of sweetened tomato concentrate and some rubbery processed cheese, most kid's pizzas are temporarily filling but low on any positively beneficial ingredients.

SWEETS

Children's chocolate confectionery is basically a mixture of chemically hardened vegetable fats, vast amounts of sugar and small amounts of cocoa solids, with chemical flavourings. Fruity sweets consist mainly of sugar, mixed with sometimes natural but mainly chemical flavourings, colourings and other additives.

BISCUITS

Typical children's biscuits consist overwhelmingly of highly refined flour, generous quantities of sugar and chemically hardened vegetable fat. Healthier-seeming versions prominently featuring ingredients such as oats and dried fruits often contain even more sugar than the standard biscuit and surprisingly large amounts of fat.

CRISPS AND EXTRUDED SNACKS

Crisps are both fatty and high in salt. Flavoured ones nearly always contain chemical additives and sweeteners in various forms, too. They are not filling and offer little good nutrition, so they will leave a hungry child dissatisfied and most probably thirsty, too.

Extruded snacks come in shapes such as hoops, flying saucers or wafers, not slices. They are called extruded because they are made from a mixture of dehydrated potato, starches, emulsifiers and a number of chemical additives which is forced out (extruded) in a particular shape. They tend to contain even more additives than crisps.

FIZZY DRINKS

These are basically water that has been carbonated and then flavoured with artificial – or occasionally natural – flavourings. They also contain other chemical additives such as colourings and huge amounts of sugar or smaller amounts of chemical sweeteners. The routine presence of certain chemical preservatives and flavourings is now being linked to allergic reactions of all sorts, but particularly oral disease causing puffy lips, mouths and swollen jaws. These drinks contain nothing that is beneficial for health; instead they include ingredients that are known to attack good health. A typical can of cola contains the equivalent of seven teaspoons of white sugar. Drinks with sweeteners may have fewer calories and won't attack tooth enamel but some scientists believe sweeteners may pose a risk to health.

SQUASH

Squash in its many forms often presents a healthy image based around the goodness of fruit. Some do contain real fruit juice in very small quantities but otherwise their ingredients are similar to fizzy drinks, just without the carbon dioxide, and the same objections apply. Even when considerably diluted, they can acustom children to a level of sweetness that makes 'real' drinks seem unpalatable by comparison.

ICE CREAM

The more expensive 'premium' ice creams contain a lot of fat in the form of cream and a lot of sugar but there is some nutritional goodness to be had from the non-sugar ingredients and they are fairly naturally made. Cheaper ice creams aimed at children, however, are highly synthetic concoctions of air, water, milk powder, hardened vegetable fat and lots of sugar blended together with chemical emulsifiers, stabilisers, colourings and flavourings.

The slightly wider range of popular children's foods and their limitations

APPLES AND BANANAS

These are really nutritious foods and it is good that children eat them but they are the only fruits that many children eat. If they are given them all the time, they may get bored with them and decide they don't like fruit in general.

FROZEN PEAS AND SWEETCORN

Frozen vegetables are a useful and nutritious stand-by. But peas and sweetcorn both taste quite sweet. Children need to get used to a range of vegetables with different flavours, such as the tartness of a fresh tomato, the refreshing quality of cucumber and the pepperiness of watercress.

TOAST

Toast is only as good as the quality of the basic bread and what you put on it. Most mass-produced British bread is pappy, light and insubstantial. It takes many slices of this sort of bread to fill you up because it fails to satisfy. Children may be spreading fats or jams on each slice, so when several slices are being eaten, the fats and sugars in the spreads can easily dwarf any goodness to be had from the bread.

YOGURT AND FROMAGE FRAIS

A straightforward natural yogurt or fromage frais, flavoured with fruit purée, is a healthy and nutritious food but most children's versions have so much sugar or artificial sweetener in them that they need to be thought of as puddings. A thick fruit compote layer can be surprisingly sweet, and it's now common for crunchy, sweet additions to be sold as part of a yogurt or fromage frais dessert. Cheaper types often contain no fruit, just chemical fruit flavours. Some that do contain fresh fruit routinely include chemical preservatives, which are not beneficial for health (see page 120).

If we let children eat almost exclusively from this typical range of children's food, what does their diet amount to? We can sum it up as consisting overwhelmingly of processed foods composed of:

- lots of protein
- lots of refined carbohydrate or starchy food
- lots of fat, sugar and salt.

Fruit and vegetables are almost entirely missing or under-represented.

This is more or less the opposite of what children should be eating for good health. Though there is still surprisingly little consensus on what constitutes a 'healthy' diet, most nutritionists would agree from various perspectives that this classic children's diet is a disaster.

With its almost total absence of fruit and vegetables – the key category of food that all nutritionists think is healthy – and its heavy reliance on refined carbohydrate, sugar and fat, not to mention the excessive amounts of protein, the typical children's diet seems to be incompatible with long-term good health.

This modern form of malnutrition, learned in childhood and very likely carried on into adulthood, is clearly implicated heavily in the growing prevalence of obesity. It is also increasingly viewed as a strong contributory factor in a surprisingly wide range of illnesses, from heart disease to cancer. If our children continue to eat this way, the prognosis for the nation's health looks very gloomy.

For parents who feel they can't live with that thought, Parts Two to Four of this book concentrate on practical ways to break out of the children's junk-food ghetto. Healthier Look-alike Alternatives to Common 'Children's Foods' (pages 114–19) points you in the direction of foods that have the appeal of junk for children but are healthier and more natural.

'PICKY-EATER' CULTURE

These days, more adults than ever before seem to have inordinate difficulty getting their children to eat a reasonably wide range of good, wholesome food. Why do we live in a land where children seem drawn only to food that is bad for them?

It's a curious modern phenomenon. British and American children seem to be bonded by a common culture that fosters resistance to good food. They stand out from children in other parts of the world with more traditional food cultures, even Europe. Most Italians would throw up their hands in horror at the very idea of a child who would not eat vegetables. In the UK we shrug our shoulders and say, reluctantly, that this is normal. In France, sales of crisps rely on adults serving them with drinks as an aperitif. It would be an eye-opener to most French people to witness the hordes of UK schoolchildren walking to and from school with bags of crisps and fizzy drinks. In fact it seems that wherever Anglo–American food culture becomes strong, a liking for junk food and a problematic attitude towards good food follow. Within this type of food culture there has been a population explosion of 'picky eaters'. When once the infamous picky eaters were the exception, now they are the rule.

How can this be? There are lots of theories ploughing both sides of the nature–nurture divide. One belief is that junk food is basically so appealing that once children have tasted it that is all they will want: it is just a matter of time until those other traditional food countries follow suit.

Listen to the powerful transnational companies that run the food industry and you might believe that it had absolutely nothing to do with creating those modern legions of picky eaters. They say that they are simply servicing a need for popular food. If children are eating badly, then that is their parents' fault for not balancing their diet. There is no such thing as an unhealthy food, they tell us, just an unhealthy diet.

Working mothers are another 'usual suspect', often asked to carry the can for children's deteriorating food habits. We are told that because women now work (in three out of every five families where the parents are married, women have jobs), this has led to the erosion of family meals and real food in favour of more convenient processed food. So grazing has taken over from three square meals, leading to ever more reliance on anything that is quick to prepare and comes in single units of food that can be eaten as required. Junk food fits the bill.

All these theories are basically fatalistic about children's suscepti-bility to junk and treat it as a fact of modern life – no turning the clock back. When forced to face up to the consequences of this thinking in the form of the millions of children who now fit the picky-eater description, there is a general wringing of hands. Helpful responses come in the form of quick techno-fixes. Okay, your chil-dren don't want to eat breakfast, so we have created breakfast bars. The fact that they are stuck together with sugar is neither here nor there.

This sort of logic is invidious and, in the long term, does nothing to help either children or the adults trying to feed them. The reality is that nowadays we live in a culture where the prevailing conditions are all going against children eating well, and the dominant expec-tations lead children to conform to a depressingly limited food stereo-type – whether or not their parents go out to work.

The existence of major structural factors described elsewhere in this book, like rapacious advertising targeted at children and an absence of real food education, means that parents (working or other-wise) who want their children to eat well are up against it. No surprise that many of us just go with the flow and give in to negative thinking. We almost expect to have problems feeding our children before we even begin.

Despite these very tangible structural obstacles, however, there is still considerable scope for winning back children to the delights of good food. The prospects for feeding children in a better, more wholesome way are nowhere near as bleak as made out.

Yes, all children are different and there is the odd child – even a significant minority of children – who does seem to conform naturally to that picky-eater stereotype. But there is also a huge middle ground of children who, if the conditions are right, will eat something approximating to a wide-ranging and basically wholesome diet. Some children will even actively seek it out, surprising us with their adventurousness and ability to revel in the pleasures of food and the rituals of eating.

For adults who do not want to give in to the prevailing determinism that writes off children's food prospects, Parts Two to Six of this book give workable strategies for creating the conditions in which children can learn to eat well.

PARENTS' ATTITUDES

Some older parents realise that their children's diet is very different from what they ate when they were young and feel anxious about that. Other younger parents think it's normal for children to live on junky processed foods because that is how they were brought up. Either way, separate 'children's food' is so ubiquitous that many parents find ways of rationalising the misgivings they might have. Let's examine some commonly expressed points of view and consider more positive and optimistic alternatives.

The 'concerned and worried *but*' parent

'I'm worried that the kids eat such a limited and unhealthy diet but I let them get into bad habits years ago and now they are a lost cause.'
It's true that it is harder to wean children on to good eating habits when they already have bad ones but it is perfectly possible. All the strategies mentioned in Part Two, Breaking the Mould at Home, can work with older children provided they are introduced gradually. Pages 61–6, Getting the Message Across, suggest tactics (bad-mouthing junk, cashing in on concern over appearance) that work, especially with older children.

'I am relying on childcarers to feed my child on weekdays. It's hard to control what the children eat.'
This is not an insurmountable problem. Read What You Can Expect from Childcarers, pages 169–75.

'I'd like the children to eat better but when I try, I find it hard to keep it up.'

Like anything else you really want to do, encouraging children to have good, wide-ranging eating habits does require some staying power and commitment. Parts Two and Three outline various ways to overcome common pitfalls and hurdles.

'Even if my children eat well at home, I meet a brick wall at school/ nursery where junk is accepted as normal.'

The food that children eat at home is going to be the most formative type they get and you can largely control that. Don't worry too much about what goes on outside the house but read Part Five, Influencing What Children Eat When You're Not There, for solutions in outside situations.

'How can I make my kids eat well without making both them and myself stand out as weird and awkward?'

Explain to children from an early age why they eat some food and not others so that they understand and feel confident about that. Prepare them diplomatically for situations outside the house where they will be making a different choice from other children in the group. Part Five, Influencing What Children Eat When You're Not There, suggests how you can do that.

'If I take a tough line on junk and restrict it, won't that make them react and go the wrong way?'

There's so much commercial pressure on children to eat junk that if you don't take a stand they will almost certainly conform to that pressure. Children need to hear an overt 'real-food' message. However, it is important not to get involved with 'banning' foods or appearing to deprive children of treats. Part Two, Breaking the Mould at Home, Part Three, The Gentle Art of Persuasion, and pages 91–5, Sweets, Treats and Bans, all explain how to get that balance.

'No matter how hard I try, my children reject food and I can't stand the fights any more.'

Head-on confrontations are a no-no. Perhaps you're going about it in the wrong way. Read Part Three, The Gentle Art of Persuasion.

The philosophical parent

'Children are picky eaters naturally, it's to be expected.'

A self-fulfilling prophecy that has been promoted by the food industry, which makes a mint out of selling children junk. Children in most parts of the world eat what adults eat. It's mainly in the UK and North America that children are considered to need a different diet. If you keep on presenting them with real food they will learn to like it. If you stereotype them as picky eaters, then that is what they will become.

'Better the kids eat junk than nothing at all.'

This is very short-term thinking. The more you offer children junk, the less likely they'll be to accept real food in the long term. Part Three, The Gentle Art of Persuasion, suggests how to encourage children to eat something decent without having head-on fights. Children won't starve; they will eventually eat something worthwhile if you adopt the approach outlined in Part Two, Breaking the Mould at Home.

'It's okay to eat junk as long as they exercise.'

Children can burn up a lot of energy and work off an unhealthy diet to a certain extent, but however fit and active they might appear, they are being deprived of vital nutrients if they live on junk. Children brought up on junk will very likely turn into adults who may be less physically active. These unbalanced eating habits will catch up with them in later life. They need to learn wide-ranging and wholesome eating patterns which will see them through into a ripe old age.

'Surely in moderation junk is okay?'

In theory, if a child eats well generally then the odd packet of sweets or crisps is not a problem. But it is very easy for the proportion of junk to creep up so that it is actually much more significant in their total diet than parents realise. And how do you draw the line between moderate amounts of junk and too much? A better approach is to say that, in general, children aren't given junk foods except on the very odd occasion and that they are always offered an attractive alternative. For ideas read Part Eight, Nitty-Gritty Ideas and Recipes for Inspiration.

The parent who accepts junk food

'I'm not worried. The kids will learn to like better food as adults. After all, I did.'

It is theoretically possible that a child will spontaneously find a love of good food as an adult but it is much more likely that he or she will simply become an adult who lives on junk. It's true that parents generally eat more adventurously than their children, but adults with sophisticated tastes may have forgotten that their diet as children, though limited, was nowhere near as limited as the modern child's, and that they ate with adults, not apart.

'Good food is wasted on children.'

Another self-fulfilling prophecy. Children learn to like what they are given. If they are given only junk, then this is what they will learn to like and expect. If you follow this approach to its logical extreme, you will only ever feed your children on processed junk. Is that what you really want? Besides, it's vital that children learn to like real food if they are to be properly nourished – so rather than being wasted on them it's a priority that they have it.

'I don't have time to feed my kids on anything but processed children's foods, and communal eating doesn't fit in with our lifestyle.'

Fine, but can you live with the fact that your children will end up living on an imbalanced diet which will not provide the nutrients they need? It isn't necessarily any more time-consuming to give them real food in any case.

'It's normal for children to eat junk. They nearly all do and they aren't dead yet.'

This phenomenon is widespread only in the UK and North America. Children in other countries still overwhelmingly eat real food. A large body of scientific research now suggests that a diet high in fat, protein, salt and sugar and deficient in fruit and vegetables (the typical 'children's diet') is implicated in health problems that attack us in adult life – cancer, heart disease, diabetes etc.

THE ROT BEGINS WITH THOSE LITTLE JARS

When we try to trace the origins of how children's diet became the junk-food ghetto that it is today, the trail starts with the modern idea that their food should somehow be separate from the general food supply. This mindset kicks in with baby food.

Baby-food manufacturers assure parents that their products are 'specially formulated for your baby', but such foods would be more accurately described as 'specially formulated to con parents into believing that they can't feed children by themselves'. This hidden agenda, of course, is never made explicit.

Nowadays, manufacturers realise that they must pay lip service to the idea that their baby foods are not intended to replace home-prepared food and that they are just a safe, handy convenience for the 'busy mum'. But by clever labelling, which first raises anxieties then appears to allay them, they implicitly perpetuate the false idea that parents somehow lack the nutritional knowledge to prepare baby food themselves. They undermine our confidence about feeding our babies on variations of the household food supply that we ourselves eat, even though this was, after all, the common-sense and highly practical way that parents fed their children until quite recently.

How does this work?

We start to make decisions about how our children will eat from day one. The first issue is whether to breastfeed or use formula milk in a bottle. On this one there is widespread agreement: try to breastfeed if you can but, failing that, it's fine to fall back on formula milk.

When breastfeeding goes well, it is simple, natural and rewarding.

There are no worries about sterilising teats and bottles, no tricky temperature judging, no need to work your way through the formula milks on sale to find the one your baby accepts.

When breastfeeding doesn't work out, the routine preparation of formula and all that it entails can seem like light relief after sore nipples, frustration and a dissatisfied baby. Parents who actively choose formula milk or who just end up using it know that this milk has been specially formulated to be as similar to breast milk as possible. We have been told that it is not good enough simply to give our offspring any old milk, be that cow's, goat's, sheep's or even soya, because in its standard form it has not been adapted for the sensitive digestive systems of human infants.

Such advice is, of course, sensible and accurate. If we can't feed babies on nature's intended breast milk, we must rely on commercial companies, their scientists and nutritionists, to devise formulas that give them all they need to grow and won't upset them or spark off allergies. It's a complicated business and we must leave it in the hands of the experts.

But thereafter, if we want our children to grow up to be adults who eat well – adults with wide-ranging tastes who enjoy food and self-select nutritious food – we need to draw a line under the food industry's scientific 'advice'. From the time that we introduce the first weaning foods, usually in that critical and often challenging time when our baby is four to six months old, we do not need to rely routinely on commercial baby foods any more than we need to employ a food taster to check that our food hasn't been poisoned. Instead, we need to view all those little jars and packets with a healthy cynicism.

Why? Like formula milk, many weaning foods give the impression that there is something special about them, that they are foods devised by knowledgeable nutritionists and doctors. Obviously, manufacturers have a direct interest in fostering this impression. In 1998 the British baby-food market was worth almost £164,000 million, and it is growing each year. So food manufacturers make a lot of money supplying parents with foods they think they cannot make themselves.

But unlike formula milk, which is a carefully devised product, commercial baby foods are nothing special. Though there are a few high-quality exceptions, most commercial baby foods represent nothing more than bulk-bought ingredients that have been heavily processed.

So when we buy '*baby* apple' for example, naive and lacking in confidence as many parents are, we may fondly think that the apples therein are somehow superior to apples that we might use ourselves. Just because the jar contains apples *for babies*, it seems safer and more trustworthy than any apple equivalent we might prepare ourselves. The very existence of *baby-food* apples may even make us feel, quite wrongly, that we are not capable of producing our own version.

Yet the reality is that, with the exception of organic brands, most commercial baby-food apples are sourced in bulk from the general supply of apples destined for processing. Far from being the pick of the crop, they might just as well be turning up in a commercial apple pie or a ready-made apple sauce. The poor little baby consumers didn't get any special deal here.

This example highlights the main shortcomings of most commercial brands of baby foods, which are:

- The raw ingredients are nothing special; they are sourced from undistinguished bulk ingredients destined for processing.

- These ingredients will be processed on an industrial scale to extend their shelf life. This destroys much of the natural goodness in them and makes it necessary to introduce additives, such as synthetic vitamins, that would not be necessary in home-made versions.

- Heavy processing and the adulteration of raw ingredients with industrial additives produce food that is bland, samey and lacks the palette of flavours found in real, home-produced foods. Babies who start out on this limited range of flavours may find it hard to make the transition to the flavour of fresh food.

- They represent poor value for money. Commercial baby foods work out infinitely more expensive than home-made equivalents. You pay a high price for the convenience and the ingredients will definitely be less fresh and often of lower quality than those you might use at home.

But what about all those reassuring 'tick lists'? Don't they promise nutritional standards far above anything that can be produced at home?

The answer is no. The purpose of these lists is to inspire confidence in the adult buying the food. On typical commercial baby foods, the strategy is to dazzle you with ticks that make a virtue of the obvious by simply stressing the basic qualities that all baby food should have anyway.

A classic tick list, on those baby apples again, might read, 'No added sugar, no artificial flavours, no artificial colours, no added preservatives, no added salt, suitable for vegetarians, gluten-free, milk-free'. You don't have to be a nutritionist to figure out that you don't normally put salt in apple purée any more than you would include any of the other tick-listed items.

Although tick lists seem to be helpful and to offer more information about the product, a tick list like this on baby apples is, viewed charitably, beside the point. Sometimes it is downright confusing. Take the question of prominent added vitamins. Some parents actually stop making food for their babies because they worry that it won't have as many vitamins as commercial brands. In fact, home-made baby food is likely to retain more vitamins than over-processed commercial gloop, and these will be in a natural form which is much better for babies on wider health grounds.

On the more complicated multi-ingredient foods, the actively misleading effect of tick lists is to inspire confidence while drawing attention away from the ingredients (usually industrial bulking ingredients and water) that shouldn't be there in the first place. Other apparently confidence-inspiring claims still give baby-food manufacturers plenty of room for manoeuvre. For example, a 'No artificial colours/flavours/thickeners' claim still allows for the inclusion of natural colours, flavours and thickeners. Though these may be preferable in some ways to their synthetic equivalents, they cannot be taken as positively beneficial. If the food was good quality and made from excellent ingredients to start with, such additives – natural or synthetic – would not be necessary. Similarly a prominent 'No added sugar' claim can still go on a food that contains sweet ingredients such as fruit juice.

To put it bluntly, babies who start out life on these foods are simply eating very ordinary processed food – with all the short-comings that has – packaged so as to play on our confusion about healthy eating and our anxieties about how best to feed our children. That's precisely the kind of product that babies and parents can live without. If we want our babies to grow into children, then adults, who appreciate a wide range of wholesome food, the regular use of commercial baby food is a block to that process. So if you don't want your children to go into the black tunnel that leads from processed baby food to processed children's junk, Part Four, Getting It Right with Babies and Toddlers, tells you all you really need to know about preparing your own (which can be as simple as mashing a banana or grating an apple). It also explains how to read between the lines on food labels and select the best ready-made baby food when you need it as a back-up for home-made.

STAGGERED EATING

Family mealtimes, we are told, are rapidly becoming a thing of the past. Gone are the days when Mum was at home all day to cook and Dad waltzed in just in time to carve the meat. Nowadays, family meals are being replaced by a new phenomenon – staggered eating, where everyone eats at different times. At the extreme, we hear of households where adults and children take it in turns to use the microwave so they can reheat an individual meal of their preference, selected from a stock of ready meals and convenience foods which is replenished at the supermarket every week or ten days. The less extreme, but increasingly common, phenomenon is the two-shift mealtime, where the children are fed earlier, usually between 5 and 6 pm, and the adults eat together later, any time from 7 pm onwards.

We are not just talking about babies here. Obviously they have to be put down to sleep when they are tired and are just too small to wait for food without becoming desperate. But according to a survey carried out by the *Observer* newspaper in 1998, almost half of children aged seven to fourteen do not eat a regular evening meal with the adults in their household either.

Separate children's meals are a major departure from tradition, a relatively recent phenomenon that has probably developed out of modern working patterns. Modern adults are tired after a long day out at work, or worn out by an even longer day looking after progressively more grizzly children without the backup of an extended family. Most people eat their main meal in the evening, but longer working days for those in employment dictate that they get home late and it can be difficult or impractical to keep fractious children up and waiting for food that long. And, of course, we positively yearn for quiet adult time, to enjoy some food and a drink with a little peace and quiet – and who can blame us?

But imagine the dispiriting solitariness of separate children's meal-times from a child's point of view. Children's tea or supper generally takes place at their rattiest time of day, the infamous 'happy hour' between 5 and 6 pm. They are presented with food by an adult who is generally hurrying to get on to the next chore. It is likely to be served in a fast-track manner – at a table, if the adults still have traditional leanings, or more commonly on a plate on the lap in front of the television. The table is not set as it would be to mark the ritual of communal mealtimes and the expectations that go along with that, and the adults don't sit down with the children to share the experience.

Children who eat on their own are the most isolated of the lot, while those with brothers and sisters can at least keep each other company. But in the absence of adults who would otherwise act as socialising centrepoints, almost like a master of ceremonies, the whole business is not a lot of fun.

And then there's the food itself. If adults are basically focusing on something more interesting and 'adult' to be consumed after the children have eaten, it's obvious that the children's meal is at best secondary in their efforts and, very often, an irritating afterthought whose necessity, day after day, becomes somewhat oppressive.

The results are all too familiar. Put bluntly, when staggered eating becomes the norm it is highly likely that the children of the house will end up eating poorer-quality, less wholesome and healthy food than the adults. This is because thinking up two different evening meals a day is soul-destroying and so adults almost invariably fall back on a repertoire of recognised 'children's foods' which can be served earlier. These tend to rely on ready-prepared processed foods, the freezer and the microwave, and lack the 'feel-good' qualities of freshly prepared real food that might lead the child by the nose to eat what's on the plate.

For the child, food becomes routine and dull and eating it is pretty unrewarding. Because there is no special ritual around serving it – such as setting the table, or the gathering together of everyone in the house – the meal is indistinguishable, from a child's point of view, from casual snacks. So it's very easy for the child to view it as just more 'take it or leave it' food. It may even simply come over as an annoying distraction from other more involving activities such as playing, doing homework or fighting with siblings. The net effect is that the child eats unsatisfactorily: quickly and without pleasure.

For the adult, the whole interaction becomes more and more problematic and emotionally highly charged, as she or he reaches the conclusion that this is not just a picky eater but a child who eats hardly anything. That makes the prospect of ever integrating the child into more adult eating patterns even more bleak, and the apparent impossibility of doing so becomes a self-fulfilling prophecy. Guilt and frustration build up in equal measure in the adult, until the only 'escape' is a retreat into cynicism of the 'all kids eat junk and that is just normal' variety.

If we want children to eat well, staggered eating is a total block to achieving that goal. So once we get beyond the baby and toddler stage, when they are too tired at the end of the day to wait up to eat, it is important to try to hold on to some notion of communal eating and family mealtimes. We may not be able to do that at every meal, or even every other meal, but every bit helps.

Yes, women do work and people arrive home later than in the past, but it is still possible to establish the principle that children and adults mainly share the same food. In the long term, if we want children to like good food, eating together is the easiest way to achieve that, saving us fights, frustration and guilt. For ideas about making this work in practice, see Eating Together and Why It Matters (pages 74–7).

SWEETS AS FOOD

Children have been eating sugary and chocolaty sweets for as long as any of us can remember. A love of sweet snacks in all forms is a regular feature of childhood.

Many adults remember with great fondness the thrill of having money to spend in the sweet shop and the lure of everything from penny caramels to sherbet flying saucers.

However, the way we think about sweets has changed. We used to think of them as a different category of edible – a treat, perhaps, a bit of frivolous window-dressing after the main business of eating had been concluded. Very few people would have considered them to be a substitute for a child's mainstream nutrition. Nowadays, however, sweets are increasingly considered the main event. It is not uncommon, for example, for children to be given a chocolaty candy bar in their lunch boxes, often as an alternative to a pudding such as yogurt or fresh fruit. In 1998 when the caterer Gardner Merchant surveyed children's eating habits, it found that 39 per cent of children brought a chocolate bar to school in their lunch box.

It seems that sweet confectionery is increasingly being given to children as a staple part of their diet. We no longer expect them to fill up on 'proper' food, offering sweets as an add-on, but often rely on confectionery as food itself. The survey mentioned above also found that one in four children substituted sweets, crisps and savoury snacks for their traditional hot evening meal.

This shift in thinking has a lot to do with the power of advertising, particularly on television. Sweets are ruthlessly hyped to children through advertising which makes them desire them. Once they taste sweets, they do like them because the hefty serving of sugar, salt, and fat they offer can be irresistible, encouraging a palate that seeks that instant fix in other foods. Judged against this craving, real, natural, unprocessed foods just don't taste right and, unlike the commercial might of the confectionery industry, they don't have any powerful interests promoting them.

Most people know that, eaten in significant quantity, sweets and chocolate confectionery are bad for children's health. If parents don't intervene, the sheer weight of commercial pressure on children to eat confectionery is so strong that they will end up eating much more than the relatively harmless quantity of 'add-on' sweets we often associate with our own childhood.

The dilemma for worried parents is how to discourage consumption of sugary confectionery without appearing to ban or proscribe it, especially because it is such a big component of the ubiquitous children's diet. However, despite the pressure on children to want confectionery – and to replace other more wholesome foods with it – they can be influenced to restrict or severely limit consumption of their own volition.

How can parents achieve this?

We need to start approaching the problem not in a futile '*Sweets are bad, you aren't allowed them*' way but as part of an overall strategy towards eating, outlined in detail elsewhere in this book, that will encourage children to select food that is nutritious and good for them. The objective – a surprisingly achievable goal – is to produce children who will happily eat their clementine or yogurt when the rest of the class is munching away on fatty-sugary sweets.

Parents can achieve this by using the general approach outlined in Part Two, Breaking the Mould at Home, which is aimed at producing children who, of their own accord, will enjoy a wide range of food and select a diet that is broadly wholesome and good for them. Part Three, The Gentle Art of Persuasion, is a troubleshooting section to help parents who find it hard to make the approach in Part Two stick. Part Seven, Nitty-gritty Ideas and Recipes for

Inspiration, lists wholesome foods that can be offered in specific situations as an alternative to confectionery and other junk food. Finally, for a strategy that tackles the vexed question of sweets head-on, see pages 91–5, Sweets, Treats and Bans.

CRISP CRAZY

Just as sweets have become a significant part of many children's diet, so consumption of crisps and crunchy, puffy 'extruded snacks' amongst children has grown to unprecedented levels.

Children eat crisps on the way to school, at breaktime, for lunch, for afternoon snack, instead of tea or at supper. No school playground, high street or urban green space is free from discarded crisp packets blowing in the wind. Many children will eat at least a packet each day.

When the caterer Gardner Merchant surveyed children's eating habits in 1998, it found that 20 per cent of schoolchildren bought crisps or savoury (extruded) snacks on their way home from school each day. Crisps and savoury snacks were also *the* most common item in a packed lunch box: 57 per cent of children ate them for packed lunch while the more traditional meat or cheese sandwich trailed at 38 and 37 per cent respectively. Such habits are regarded as normal.

Ironically, crisps seem to have taken on a misleadingly 'healthy' profile amongst some parents and children. They are commonly seen as a healthier option than sweets because they are savoury and are made from potatoes or corn – both wholesome starchy foods. For many children who won't accept other savoury food such as a sandwich, filled roll or salad, crisps are routinely offered as an acceptable alternative. But the reality is that although potatoes – and, to a lesser extent, corn – are a wholesome food that children can be encouraged to eat in some quantity, crisps, and even more so extruded snacks, are not.

Here's why:

- They are fatty:
  100 grams of boiled potato contain only 0·1 milligrams of fat.
  100 grams of regular crisps contain 37·6 milligrams of fat.
  100 grams of 'low-fat' crisps contain 21·5 grams of fat.
  'Low-fat' crisps are a contradiction in terms: crisps and extruded snacks are *always* fatty foods.

- They are salty:
  100 grams of boiled potato contain 7 milligrams of sodium.
  100 grams of regular or 'low-fat' crisps contain 1,070 milligrams of sodium.
  No wonder they make children extremely thirsty.

- They are sweet:
  Although saltiness is the first flavour that hits you when you eat crisps, all but the most basic salted crisps contain sugar or artificial sweeteners to give flavour. Children eat too much of the former anyway and there are health concerns over the safety of the latter (see pages 6–7).

- They often contain undesirable additives:
  Many extruded snacks contain monosodium glutamate, for example, a chemical flavour enhancer that has been widely linked to allergic reactions in sensitive people. Acidity regulators are routinely used to balance the other chemical flavourings in crisps. Additives such as these have no benefits for health whatsoever and increase the total intake of unnecessary chemicals that children eat – an intake that many health experts would like to see reduced.

- They usually contain chemical flavourings:
  These totally synthetic flavourings are presumed safe on very thin scientific grounds because there is, as yet, no evidence that they cause harm. However, the long-term toxicological effects on

modern children – who may nowadays get a surprisingly large cocktail of them – have not been studied.

- They may contain chemical or natural colour. These can cause allergic and other reactions in some people.

To sum up the nutritional contents of all those bag snacks, they represent a large dose of everything you don't want children to eat and a very small amount of anything you might want them to eat. The nutritional goodness of any reasonably wholesome ingredient – such as potatoes, corn or wheat – is totally dwarfed by fat, salt, sweet flavourings and undesirable industrial additives.

But as well as being nutritionally unbalanced, the larger-than-life, mouth-mugging qualities of crisps and extruded snacks have a pernicious effect on young tastebuds, accustoming them to hefty servings of that all-too-familiar fat/salt/sugar trilogy so omnipresent in junk food. A taste for this will certainly distort the palate and reduce a child's ability to appreciate real, natural food that lacks these heavy-handed artificial tastes. Just as we would find it unpleasant to drink orange juice after brushing our teeth, so children accustomed to the taste effect of crisps and other junk food will find it harder to like or appreciate a wider range of more subtle, straightforward, untampered-with flavours.

Despite the poor nutrition they offer, and the junk-food palate they are likely to encourage, crisps and extruded snacks have become the ubiquitous 'savoury' convenience foods for children. They are cheap, though not necessarily good value for money, and they keep for ages. Pre-wrapped and easily opened, they are the lazy alternative to a more wholesome snack that might need to be prepared at home. When we are tired or under pressure, it's very easy just to pop that bag of crisps into the schoolbag rather than filling a roll or even washing an apple.

However, if we want our children to grow up to be adults who like wholesome, natural food and appreciate a wide range of flavours, crisps and extruded snacks are one significant category in the modern 'children's diet' they are much better off without. An occasional bag of crisps is not a cause for concern. But if children are eating them every day, sometimes twice a day, and eating them in preference to good food, then they can become a problem.

That is why it is best to strike these bag snacks off your routine shopping list and turn instead to Twenty-five Good Snacks (pages 237–8), which lists alternatives that appeal to many children. For alternative packed lunch ideas, see Ten Good Packed Lunches (pages 259–62).

THE FLICKERING SCREEN

We are tired, the children are crotchety and we need to get on with some essential tasks, so we switch on the television to give us some breathing space. But as we buy ourselves some peace and relative quiet we may, without knowing it, be storing up problems when it comes to getting our children to eat a decent, wholesome diet.

We may begin to find that, even from the youngest age, when we try to give them water the children start demanding a sweetened fizzy drink. No matter how tempting the contents of our fruit bowl, we may see them gravitating towards the biscuit tin or demanding money to visit the sweet shop. We find ourselves wondering why they won't eat anything made with fish, unless it's coated in crispy crumb or formed into a special marine 'shape'. When we buy the more traditional, unsticky breakfast cereals, we find them campaigning for the latest brand that's stuck together with sugar and other sweet ingredients. Where do these demands come from?

Before you subscribe to the prevalent attitude that all children just naturally and spontaneously want to eat junk, consider first the pressure that emanates from that flickering screen. We need look no further than the diet of food ads served up on children's prime-time television, which consists of little more than what some researchers call 'an onslaught of junk-food hype'.

In 1996 the independent watchdog, Consumers International, surveyed the type of food advertising during peak children's television hours in thirteen countries: eleven in Europe plus the USA and Australia. In the UK it found that children see seventeen adverts each hour and ten of these are for food or drink – the highest number of food and drink ads in any European country.

A massive 95 per cent of these ads were for unhealthy foods, high in fat, sugar or salt. Top of the food ad pops in the UK came confectionery, with breakfast cereals following a close second. By comparison, ads for foods that most people would agree should be encouraged, such as fruit and vegetables, were almost non-existent. The only remotely healthy ads that British children are likely to see on television are for frozen peas.

Consumers International's survey confirms the findings of another carried out in 1995 by the National Food Alliance. This also concluded that advertising during programmes appealing to children presented a grossly unbalanced nutritional message with fatty and sugary foods predominating.

This imbalance matters particularly because children are less able than adults to understand the intent of advertising or its persuasive techniques and are therefore less able to treat it with scepticism. The younger the child, the more vulnerable she or he is to swallowing an advertising message uncritically. A 1996 UK government report reiterated what other researchers have found – that children have difficulty distinguishing television advertisements from the programmes surrounding them. At the most television-dependent age of three to four, when it is a boon to plonk down your offspring in front of the television while you get on with other things, it is unlikely that they can differentiate between the two. It is now thought that it is only after the age of ten to twelve that children realise that the purpose of advertisements is to persuade you to buy things. This confusion is compounded by the use of characters or personalities popular with children which appear to endorse the product in the child's eyes. Whether it's cuddly, collectable free gifts with characters from the latest cartoon blockbuster or a cute little familiar face on that pot of fromage frais, such images exploit children's gullibility.

Obviously advertising isn't the only message that influences what children eat. The advertising industry says that its critics ignore the role of families and education in helping children make healthy choices. When that familiar 'Can we buy that?' plea follows the ad, the advertising industry expects us to take the time to explain patiently to our children how that sticky cereal or fatty snack isn't very healthy unless it's part of a 'balanced diet'. And surely public health campaigns and education at school should be pointing the nation's youth along the right path too?

But there is a lot of research to suggest that television advertising is the single most important factor influencing what children eat. In the US researchers have found that even when allowing for factors such as sex, reading level, ethnic background, parents' occupation and educational level, television viewing correlated with bad eating habits and faulty understanding of the principles of nutrition.

In Sweden and Norway the pressure has been taken off parents because no advertisements at all are allowed during children's programmes. In Denmark and Finland sponsorship of children's television isn't allowed either.

In the UK, however, there are no such restrictions on advertising directed at children. So unless parents try actively to correct distorted perceptions, the junk-food message from television ads will constantly undermine our effort to get our children to eat well.

How can we react to this? There's always the off switch, of course, but it takes a resolute spirit to keep children away from the box. More realistically, we need to recognise that children will pick up a junk-food message when watching television and that if we do nothing we are simply letting that process run its course.

On the other hand, we can decide that we are going to combat it with counter-propaganda for a wider and more wholesome range of food consistent with the real-food approach outlined in pages 55–60. This involves instilling cynicism about the taste, quality and long-term effects of eating junk and a certain determination that we aren't going to give in to the predictable demands generated by advertising.

If you want some effective strategies for doing this, turn to Getting the Message Across on pages 61–6 and The Fun and Skill of Food

Shopping on pages 221–4. For ideas about how to deal with pestering demands for junk directly, see Sweets, Treats and Bans on pages 91–5.

GIFT-WRAPPED JUNK

Having difficulty getting your child to eat? Never fear, the processed food industry's marketing team is here to help. It has devised some super products, designed to be snapped up by the nation's kiddies and make shopping easy for poor old driven-to-distraction 'Mum'. Lest she should miss these on her desperate dash round the supermarket, many chains now have helpful signs such as 'Children's Desserts' on those prominent end-of-aisle locations to make them stand out.

Not that these tailor-made products for kids are easy to ignore, either for 'Mum' or for her arm-tugging companions. They sing out with brightly coloured images of jolly cartoon characters or the latest collectable toy. And because these familiar images intrigue children – after all they see them over and over again on children's TV – trying to take a toddler or small child past them without being put under pressure to buy is about as easy as convincing them to walk past a playpark without going in.

The packaging that the images adorn is a triumph of technical wizardry. Anything straightforward is out – after all, we all *know* that kids have to be bribed into eating food, don't we? So packaging takes over and generates an endless stream of novelties designed to capture that gullible junior market.

The straightforward old yogurt pot, for example, is out. Now yogurt must come in rigid two-compartment plastic containers with a dinky-doo addition to mix in. Anything goes, from multi-coloured sprinkles to chocolate polka dots or crunchy mini-biscuits – with the caveat that it must be sweet.

If two compartments already seem old hat, then bored children can be further tempted by that little fromage frais that comes with its own toy or handy little spoon. Worried about the environmental impact of all this moulded plastic? Then plump for that reusable container which can be broken down and then remodelled into a constructable toy.

Finding those rolls and sandwiches coming home uneaten in the lunch box? Why not give the kids a miniaturized box so that they can have the fun of assembling their own lunch, sandwiching processed ham and cheese with salty crackers as perfectly as any dovetail joint?

Cheese getting the thumbs-down? What about letting them make their own self-service selection of pick 'n' mix miniaturised cheeses or trying them out with a runny cheese and dipping biscuits ensemble?

All right, no one these days seriously expects children to eat a bit of whole fish anyway, but what do you do if they begin to reject even fish fingers? Try out fishy shapes with special tails for them to hold as they dip them into that essential ketchup, of course. Dinosaur-shaped Kievs, reconstituted potato with cute little arms and legs or funny faces, condensed milk, fromage frais or yogurt drinks in squeezy tubes to suck at playtime, triangular milk shakes, mini cup cakes topped with a rice-paper image of their favourite cuddly character . . . so continues the litany of food products targeted at children.

You have to give these products credit for being both ingenious and inventive – as far as food manufacturers are concerned, that is. This endlessly novel repertoire of 'children's' specialities allows them to take heavily processed junk food, gift-wrap it in images guaranteed to appeal to children, then sell it at a tidy profit.

There's a limit, of course, to how much they can charge for a basic frozen potato shape, fish finger, fromage frais or processed cheese. But once they have succeeded in packaging it for children they can simply sit back and listen to those cash registers ringing. There's nothing wrong with profits, of course, and manufacturers insist that they are only giving parents a helping hand. What despairing parent with an infamous 'picky child' would not be prepared to pay that little premium if these products get him or her to eat something he or she would not otherwise? But the price parents and children pay is quite high if we consider the quality of the food on offer. Real potatoes don't have arms and legs – to give them these, they need to be moulded together with chemical additives. Cheese doesn't squirt naturally – a range of chemical emulsifiers and cheap dairy by-products needs to be incorporated first. It seems that the food industry has ordained that all those yogurts and fromage frais prominently featuring images of the latest desirable 'collectable' just have to have chemical preservatives and flavourings. In order to process that ham into its easy-to-handle shape, it has to have lots of added water, polyphosphates and the standard flavour enhancers. Not to put too fine a point on it, if we wanted to home in on products stiff with chemical additives, then we need look no further than these gimmicky offerings.

Most of us know that when we buy these children's novelties we are paying over the odds for something that isn't that healthy. But we feel desperate. Better they eat something than nothing, we think. And as far back as any of us can remember, there's been a deep-seated belief that by taking basic ingredients and repackaging them in forms that appeal to children, we can get them to eat what they might otherwise reject.

But is presentation really the best long-term tool to get children to eat? Does every food we offer them have to be disguised with amusing little ears or sugary sprinkles? If you have your doubts and would rather your children ate real food, not gift-wrapped junk, then turn to pages 86–90, Presentation, Boredom and the 'Yuck' Reaction, for ideas.

GOODBYE DINNER LADY, HELLO CASH CAFETERIA

From time to time we hear about a school that serves healthy lunches to its children, or another that has taken the huge step of banning sweets and crisps as snacks at break, asking pupils to bring fruit instead. Such schools generate media attention because they are so rare. The overwhelming bulk of food on offer from school catering services is over-processed, low-grade stuff from which it is almost impossible to make a wholesome selection even supposing you were an adult nutritionist, let alone a confused seven-year-old, trying to see through the queue ahead, all the time concentrating on holding your tray and not dropping your money.

Traditionally school meals have never been gastronomic experiences, but at least in the past each school employed its own cook and a good part of the food was real and unprocessed, however limited in range. Water was the standard drink. Nowadays the dinner ladies and cooks of the past have mainly been made redundant and the dinner hall has been replaced with a vastly reduced staff operating the 'cash cafeteria'. Their task consists of reheating or assembling a specified number of portions of ready-prepared items, targeted at what the food industry euphemistically calls 'young consumers', for which a more candid description might be 'consumers of junk'.

This is a consequence of the 1980 abolition of any nutritional standards for school meals and the introduction of a policy called 'Compulsory Competitive Tendering' (CCT), which was widely implemented in the 1980s. It obliged local authorities to choose the most 'competitive' (for which read cheap) catering on offer. In-house, labour-intensive school meals were widely axed in favour of cheaper,

large-scale outside catering operations. Those that were retained had
to match the lowest commercial tender.

Later in the 1980s, cuts in entitlement to free school meals
reinforced the damage done by CCT. Fewer children qualified for
free meals and this reduced the total demand. Less uptake means
fewer economies of scale and makes it even harder to provide wholesome meals on a low budget. While in 1979 some 64 per cent of
children ate school meals, by 1996 that figure had dropped to 43
per cent.

The end result is that there is basically no real cooking going on
in the vast majority of schools. On the hot front, bought-in, ready-
prepared Kievs, pizzas, even baked potatoes are simply reheated.
Burgers and sausages are cooked briefly. Everything is 'portion-
controlled' to eliminate waste and must consist of a single or small
number of units of food which can be stored for some time, preferably frozen. Even the apparently healthy and wholesome option of
soup is characteristically straight out of the packet – just add water.

In certain areas, local authorities are trying to make school meals
more profitable by converting cafeterias into 'food courts' which ape
fast-food chains. The usual burgers, pizzas and fizzy drinks are
served from US-style food counters with illuminated displays of
the food on offer – just like high-street chains – by staff wearing
baseball caps. These 'initiatives' are sponsored by manufacturers of
junk food and fizzy drinks whose corporate logos are emblazoned
over the eating area, on polystyrene plates and cups and on staff
uniforms. This trend means that children get no respite from junk-
food advertising even at school.

Other schools now have no hot food whatsoever, a consequence
of further local authority budget cuts. They tend to serve only the
very worst sort of mass-produced sandwich which even makes its
petrol-station forecourt equivalent seem gourmet. Many schools have
been told to offer salads because nutritionists advocate these as a
healthy choice. Once again, a child will be lucky to see a simple
sliced tomato, cucumber disc, carrot baton or lettuce leaf. Instead,

it's plastic tubs filled with bought-in offerings, conspicuously short on vegetables and instead loaded up with starchy, stodgy offerings of rice, corn, pasta, pulses or egg, all slathered in commercial dressings.

Healthy-eating guidelines abound and school catering services can all offer chapter and verse on how they are doing their bit in this regard. But these guidelines are applied within the limits of mass-catering processed foods; they rarely mean that children are given more fresh fruit and vegetables or more wholesome basic ingredients. On the contrary, the most tangible manifestation of healthy-eating guidelines is an increased presence of highly processed items in the form of 'low-fat', 'lite' and 'diet' foods and drinks.

There are different justifications offered for the 'healthiness' of these items depending on what they are. The first is that they use margarine or vegetable fat instead of butter or lard. Yet some scientists believe that the trans-fats in the former may be at least as unhealthy as the saturates in the latter. The second is the substitution of skimmed milk for whole milk. However, although it has less fat, experts do not agree over whether skimmed milk is better for children. The third is the substitution of artificial sweeteners for sugar. Sweeteners do contain fewer calories than sugar, but many scientists have reservations over the safety of the former and whether or not they actually result in lower sugar consumption.

So the jury is still out on all these issues. But the current net effect of well-intentioned 'healthy-eating' guidelines in schools is that children are eating more heavily processed, technologically altered foods than before, foods that have not been tried and tested over time and whose long-term effect on human health is not yet known.

Processed techno-foods fit in very well with the economics of modern school catering, which boils down to running a cheap, lowest-common-denominator service with as little waste as possible. There is absolutely no slack for experimenting with more natural and nourishing foods which might require more labour, some food education and scope for experimentation.

In fact the prevailing budget pressures on school caterers – whether they are privatised or public sector – mean that they cannot afford to take any risk at all and so instead it's now customary to major on the sure-fire 'children's foods' such as crisps, fizzy drinks and confectionery because these are guaranteed to sell. These items have a long shelf life too. No surprise, then, when the typical statutory school cafeteria fruit bowl – generally full of the dullest fruits around, such as mealy-textured, bruised apples, shrunken oranges, bright green or wizened black bananas – has few takers.

Children aren't always very good at describing school food. Here's a taste of some of the delightful dishes commonly on offer.

A menu of modern school meals classics

For main course:

TURKEY/CHICKEN KIEVS/NUGGETS, SPAGHETTI AND POTATO SHAPES

(Cheap, processed, intensively reared meat in fatty fried crumb coating; sweet, stodgy tinned spaghetti; reconstituted dried potato and additives in fatty coating)

HOT DOG ROLL/SAUSAGE ROLL, BEANS AND POTATO SHAPES

(More cheapest of the cheap meat full of additives and water, stuck in a pappy, over-refined white roll or coated with artery-clogging, fat-laden pastry, with sweet and salty beans, plus spuds as above for added stodge)

VEGETABLE CURRY, MIXED VEG AND RICE
(This more promising-sounding vegetarian alternative consists of frozen ready-cut vegetables defrosted in sweet, starch-thickened catering curry sauce with waterlogged frozen vegetable 'macedoine' and gluey white rice)

CHEESE AND BACON/BROCCOLI/SWEETCORN FLAN, TURNIP, POTATOES
(Rubbery Cheddar, miscellaneous 'savoury' ingredients and reconstituted dried egg in a greasy layer of under-cooked pastry, with boiled diced turnip – about the cheapest frozen vegetable that can be bought in and about the least likely to appeal to children – with a scoop of rehydrated 'mashed' potatoes)

SAVOURY PASTIE, PEAS, CHIPS
(An unidentifiable-by-ingredient mulch combining processed meat such as corned beef or starchy potatoes with industrial fillers and flavourings, encased in lardy pastry; watery peas and reheated chips)

MEAT CASSEROLE, CABBAGE, POTATO
(A small amount of meat, often sausage, in thickened starchy sauce with frozen vegetables; boiled-to-death cabbage and the regulation scoop of rehydrated mash)

ROAST MEAT AND POTATOES, SPROUTS
(Pre-cooked, thinly sliced meat reheated in catering brown sauce, ready-cooked roasted potatoes and sulphurous, over-cooked sprouts)

'HOME-MADE PIZZA'
(Thin slices of ready-made catering dough topped with watered-down tomato paste and rubbery Cheddar, then baked)

BATTERED FISH WITH TOMATO
(A small amount of desirable white fish dwarfed by its fatty batter, served with unadorned tinned tomatoes)

For pudding:

JELLY WHIP
(Shuddery synthetic dessert containing a litany of additives and no real anything else apart from generous amounts of sugar and gelatine)

DOUGHNUT AND CUSTARD
(Deep-fried, sugary stodge lubricated with extra sugar, colourings and flavourings, plus sugary, additive-laden 'custard', usually from a just–add–water mix)

CHOCOLATE CRISPIE/ICED SPONGE/CARAMEL FLAN/ FLAPJACK/GINGERBREAD AND CUSTARD
(As above, minus the frying)

SEMOLINA AND FRUIT
(Lumpy milk pudding which rarely appeals to children, even in its unlumpy form, served with sweetened tinned fruit)

'HOME BAKING'
(Cup cakes and tray bakes which are heavy on sugar, margarine and refined white flour)

To drink:

CARTONS OF FRUIT SQUASH AND 'DRINK'/ BLACKCURRANT DRINK/COLA/CARBONATED ORANGE
(A heavy-handed serving of sugar topped up with water and additives)

HOT CHOCOLATE/MILK SHAKE
(Sugar, milk powder, flavourings and thickeners mixed up with water)

It's no wonder that many children loathe school meals and abandon them at the first possible opportunity. But what about other school food?

School tuck shops have not served anything other than sweets, crisps and fizz since time immemorial. Nothing has changed in that department, except perhaps for the arrival of grain-based biscuits which purport to be healthy but whose heavy-handed sugar composition gives the lie to that.

What is new, however, is the arrival of snack and drink vending machines in schools. Filled exclusively with everything that is the antithesis of wholesome eating, these machines are becoming a common feature in many secondary and even some primary schools. Most teachers disapprove of them, but when a school is strapped for cash the income they offer can be tempting.

Looking at a secondary school in Merseyside in 1998, the *Guardian* reported that the profit to the school from its eight vending machines was forecast at £15,000 a year. Revenue on this scale can keep a music department in musical instruments or buy a much needed piece of equipment. But this system also handicaps the more wholesome alternative. In many schools nowadays, the only place a child can get a free and straightforward drink of tap water is in the washrooms!

School food has got so bad that it looks as if the government will reintroduce nutritional standards at least for school meals, if not for tuck shops. It remains to be seen how effective these will be in tackling the unhealthy monster that school meals have become.

But in the meantime, the current nature of school catering means that parents cannot assume that there is *anything* reasonably wholesome on offer on a regular basis.

How can we react to this? For solutions, turn to:

- School Food (pages 189–96)
- Twenty-five Good Snacks (pages 237–8)
- Ten Good Packed Lunches (pages 259–62)

CHILD (UN)FRIENDLY RESTAURANTS

Children in restaurants? Perish the thought! Our traditional 'serious' restaurant culture is not like that in other parts of the world, where children and restaurants are seen as two facets of normal life that can happily cohabit. British culture has always viewed restaurant-going as something special and unusual – an overwhelmingly sophisticated adult activity. As a nation we do not always find it 'chic' to have children around when we go out to eat. We tend to see them as philistines who ought to be fed separately in the privacy of their own homes until they attain civilised adulthood.

So we can't pop out to the accommodating French bistro, which will prop up children on cushions and serve them *moules marinière* and a massive napkin without flinching. Nor can we drop in to family-run Italian *ristorante*, where adults cluck with approval as your baby noisily sucks up linguine with tomato sauce splattering everywhere. Neither is it like India or China, where family groups meet in restaurants and feed prime mouthfuls of their food to the youngest members.

It's not unknown in the UK for some restaurants to have explicit 'No children' policies, while to take a child to others may entail pleading, negotiation and compromise: '*Yes, we will be finished by 8.45 pm (so as not to disturb your business clientele),*' or '*Yes, we will accept a freezing table more or less out in the lobby where no one else can see us.*' Many other establishments simply make it so expensive to bring children – by refusing to offer half-portions or make any concession to smaller appetites in their price structure – that they effectively prevent them from coming, without saying so in so many words.

The good news is that the climate is gradually changing – if only because some restaurants are enlightened enough to recognise that today's child diners could be tomorrow's clientele. Some fashionable and very 'grown-up' city establishments even become child-friendly zones at weekends, making positive efforts to attract families. Few restaurants fail to provide a high chair (especially if parents ask for one when booking) and many pubs that serve food no longer ban children.

But nevertheless, parents who would like to introduce their children to decent restaurant food from an early age still cannot count on a warm reception, and may fear a negative reaction based on past experience. However well behaved they think their child might be in a restaurant, few parents find it relaxing to be in an environment where they worry that staff eyebrows may be raised and fellow diners may 'tut' at the first sign of any restlessness or a querulous voice. So rather than run the risk of embarrassment and assume the stressful responsibility for seeing that the child behaves impeccably, many parents opt out and either don't eat in these establishments themselves or leave the children at home when they do, thus limiting their children's food experience.

But is this a problem? Aren't there plenty of less serious but perfectly acceptable 'child-friendly' restaurants at the cheaper end of the market which welcome children with open arms and cater for their every need until they matriculate in the world of adult dining?

You know the formula. They are cheap and approachable chain eateries. If they are out of town, there will be lots of free parking conveniently outside. If you are on foot, it can seem that there is one on every accessible high-street corner or in every food court. They are coming down with trolley parks, high chairs, feeder cups, bottle warmers, microwaves to reheat baby food, nappy-changing facilities . . . every conceivable bit of kit that adults with children might need. Bustling and noisy, they enable you to eat anonymously without feeling that the eyes of all staff and diners are on you.

And let's not forget that added incentive which any child will adore. Every day in these restaurants is like Christmas Day because you get a present to take away. We are not just talking about the usual giveaways, such as paper hats, balloons and badges which advertise the restaurant's existence and link it to cuddly characters designed to appeal to children. We are talking 'collectables', a covetable free toy which encourages loyalty (and repeat visits) in order to complete the set. That's a strong pull for young consumers.

It sounds so perfect for both child and parent . . . until you get to the food. The heart of the 'child-friendly' repertoire? Something fried with chips or something starchy. There's burger and chips, Kiev and chips, fishy shapes and chips and sausage and chips, all slathered with copious quantities of sweet and salty brown or tomato sauce.

Vegetarian leanings? Try a bean burger, fried veggie rissoles, mini-pizza or refined white baguette with garlic butter. Want to avoid chips? Try fried hash browns or deep-crumb crunchy croquettes for a change.

Feeling thirsty at the thought of that little lot? Why not try an attractively priced whole-meal package, with its 'free' fizzy or diluted 'contains-no-real-anything' drink thrown in for added value?

So what you get when you step across the threshold of your average 'child-friendly' restaurant is a depressingly limited range of the ubiquitous children's processed foods with a few stodgy snacks and fillers thrown in. It revolves around established 'kiddie favourites', formula food that children see all around them. Food that is predictable and ubiquitous. Food that does nothing to extend their horizons. Food that poses no new challenge whatsoever.

Most parents recognise that the food in such establishments is not that great – downright unhealthy even – but, under pressure to find a place that makes it easy to eat out with our children, we convince ourselves that it doesn't really matter.

After all, children don't live on restaurant food. Yes, we know that it is full of fat and sugar and heavily processed. As adults, we suspect that the raw materials are not exactly the finest around but, once in a while, what's the problem? The food is affordable and even though there may be little or nothing we ourselves want to eat, these restaurants are convenient and children seem to like them and see visiting them as a treat.

But are they really such a treat for children? They may say they like eating out in this sort of place, even plead to be taken there, but we need to meet this almost inevitable positive response with a large element of scepticism. For many children, such establishments cannot help being anything but a treat simply because they are the only restaurants to which they are ever taken. Eating out – wherever it is and in whatever circumstances – is always going to be more exciting for a child than just another meal at home.

If we examine what the children actually eat when they visit these restaurants, their enthusiasm for the food may be illusory. A significant part of the meal may end up uneaten because the *anticipation* is more fulfilling than the reality. The food element may often be ignored in favour of more rewarding diversions, such as playing with the free toy, making endless trips to the toilet, playing in the 'kiddie playpark' outside, or watching the toddler at the next booth who has got his head stuck under the table.

We need to address not just the limitations of children's experience in such restaurants but also the potential breadth of experience on which they are missing out. If this is the only kind of restaurant that children visit, they are getting no taste for the fascinating world of food that lies beyond their own homes. They are deprived of the opportunity of being seduced into trying something new just because it sounds, looks and smells fantastic – something different which extends their domestic food horizons.

When they are taken only to busy, fast-food outlets, they are also isolated from the stimulating sociability of sitting in a restaurant and the chance to enjoy the slower ritual which surrounds the delightful process of eating. Like keen readers stuck for ever on the same formula-book series, they are being denied the chance to discover something initially more demanding but ultimately much more fulfilling.

In fact, confining children only to formula 'child-friendly' restaurants is a huge missed opportunity. Handled well, most children can rise to the challenge of eating in a real restaurant serving real food. Even if a taste of real adult eating out is only a rare treat for a special occasion, it can nevertheless be one of the most effective ways of widening children's food horizons and combating the 'tunnel effect' described on pages 71–3.

In the right restaurant, under the right circumstances, even the most conservative child can learn to eat more adventurously than anyone might expect, and the more open-minded child will relish the opportunity. Turn to pages 226–31, The Fascinating World of Restaurant Food, for ideas about how to make the most of eating out and ensure that restaurant-going is a happy experience all round.

PART TWO

....

BREAKING THE MOULD AT HOME

THE REAL-FOOD APPROACH

When we decide that we aren't going to give in to the prevailing defeatism that says children will eat only junk, we make an important commitment to feeding them well. But in a world where children are under constant pressure to eat badly, how can we carve out a different path?

One common approach is to continue with the *structure* of modern children's food but try to change the *content* so that it is healthier and more acceptable. The idea is that children will think they are getting the undesirable things they want but, in reality, we are giving them something better.

The classic example here is the 'healthy lollipop'. These are marketed as better for children because they are flavoured with fruit juice, tinted with natural rather than artificial colours and use artificial sweeteners instead of sugar. But are they really such an improvement? The proportion of fruit juice in them may be very small indeed and, as discussed on pages 6–7, although they do not attack tooth enamel it is questionable whether artificial sweeteners are desirable in wider health terms. But all that is irrelevant because even if these lollipops did have undisputed plus points over their conventional sugary, synthetic counterparts, there is a problem. We are still encouraging children to think that it's all right to suck for long periods on something sweet and sticky. Do we really want to give them that message?

The same issue arises with popular foods that have had their original composition altered in line with modern 'healthy-eating' thinking. So now we have reduced-sugar baked beans, lower-fat crisps, 'healthy' sausages, oven chips, no-added-sugar yogurts, white bread with added fibre and so on. They purport to be better for children, though their merits are highly disputable. Although they might represent some improvement on the original junk food they still cannot measure up to the real thing (unadulterated yogurt, natural wholemeal bread etc.) in nutritional terms. The question remains, is this the kind of food we really want our children to eat or, at the end of the day, are we simply encouraging a slightly more acceptable face of the children's diet ghetto?

If you analyse this approach, it is basically a slippery slope which attempts to hold the line against out-and-out junk food by curbing its worst excesses. It could produce very small benefits but it remains a defensive strategy, where adults attempt to draw a distinction between what's not too bad and what's worse. Now that's a very difficult line to maintain.

What we need when we decide that we want our children to eat more nutritious food is a positive philosophy that challenges the assumptions on which children's ghetto-food thinking rests and breaks away from its structures. We want to reverse the existing situation where 'children's food' is shorthand for 'worst food'. How do we make this happen?

Let's begin by drawing up a profile of how we want our children to turn out eventually. We want them to:

- Enjoy food and delight in the pleasure of eating.

- Routinely eat a wide and varied range of foods from all food groups (excluding meat and fish if they are vegetarians).

- Select food that is good for them.

This is the opposite of the typical modern children's diet where children appear to view food as fuel and tend to select a narrow range that is so imbalanced it may even defy the laws of nutrition.

So how should we set about seeing that the children we feed don't go down this path? The single most important thing we'll ever do as concerned adults is to adopt a 'real-food' approach. This means that we feed our children from as early an age as possible on food that is as fresh, whole and unprocessed as possible.

Of course there can be very few households in the land who are able to avoid processed food altogether. Very few of us have the time, energy or inclination to make all our own jam or bake our own bread, for example. A real-food policy doesn't mean that we can never buy anything processed or take a short cut, just that the bulk of the food we eat is made up of fresh, unprocessed food that has been cooked at home – however quick and no-frills that cooking might be – and that we read the labels of any packaged foods we do buy to check that all the ingredients are wholesome, i.e. the sort we would use at home.

This doesn't mean we have to be fanatical. There's no need to feel a failure if you don't roll your own pasta, squeeze your own lemonade or stuff your own sausages. It just means that, time and energy allowing, we favour home-made food. This needn't be oppressively time-consuming. It takes very little more effort to bake potatoes from scratch than reheat oven chips, or to grill a piece of cod rather than a fish finger. It's actually quicker to serve a cut-up tomato than tinned tomato soup.

The first and most persuasive reason for adopting a real-food approach is that whole, natural, unprocessed food that has been cooked at home is just much more delicious than its equivalent bought ready-made in a box or tin. There is no better way to woo a child than the smell of good, freshly cooked food wafting through the house. Processed, ready-made foods just don't produce the same 'feel-good' effect. Once children become accustomed to eating fresh, unprocessed, home-cooked food they will enjoy it and develop a taste for it. This will give them real-food standards against which to taste other foods. By comparison, junky children's food will not taste so good and will be much less tempting to them. So the taste for real food will limit their consumption of junk.

The second reason is that whole, unprocessed foods in their

natural state that have been cooked at home tend to be much more nutritious than processed food. As the World Health Organisation has pointed out, 'It is widely perceived that obesity has increased in industrialised societies as families turn away from home-prepared meals and utilise more fast or takeaway foods.'

Unprocessed foods come as nature intended, without chemical additives. Nor have they had their formula adulterated to meet the high fat-sugar-salt requirements that make processed foods profitable and palatable – especially children's processed foods. Here are some examples of how processing changes the composition of food and makes it less healthy:

- 100 grams of baked cod contains 1·2 grams of fat. The same weight of cod fish finger contains 7·5 grams of fat before it is cooked and 12·7 grams of fat when fried.

- 100 grams of fresh raspberries contains 5·6 grams of sugar. The same weight of tinned raspberries contains 22·5 grams of sugar.

- 100 grams of raw lean beef contains 4·6 grams of fat and 61 milligrams of salt. The same weight of raw beefburger contains 20·5 grams of fat and 600 milligrams of salt.

- 100 grams of tomato purée contains 11·4 grams of sugar and 20 milligrams of salt. The same weight of tomato ketchup contains 22·9 grams of sugar and 1,120 milligrams of salt.

When children – or adults for that matter – eat a diet consisting of whole, unprocessed food cooked at home, it is quite difficult for them to eat a distorted, imbalanced diet. Of course it's theoretically possible. You could go mad consistently with the butter on your breakfast toast or lashings of cream on that favourite cooked pudding. But your diet is much more likely to go awry when it is composed of processed foods with their vast hidden presence of fat, sugar and salt. So when we base our shopping on whole, unprocessed food, without being self-consciously rigid about 'healthy eating', calorie counting or reading nutrition labels, we are giving children food that is much more nutritious and healthy.

The third reason for adopting a real-food approach is that real food can satisfy the tastes of adults and children alike, so the person who buys the food has one shopping list, not the ubiquitous two-household list that must cater for sophisticated adult tastes alongside children's junk-food palates. Obviously there are households where both adults and children live on processed food and there is no conflict. But where adults do have wider palates and hope that one day their children will share them, a real-food policy makes shopping much easier.

The fourth reason for a real-food policy is that it makes it harder for adults to cave in to demands for junk. How often do you hear adults admitting that they would never eat a certain food themselves but are just 'buying for the kids'. When you operate this policy, you won't be buying anything for the children that you wouldn't want to eat yourself.

Not everyone finds it easy to adopt a real-food approach. Although we all might like to, it can seem impossible given the time pressure we are under. The good news is that, despite food-industry propa-ganda which says that people have no time to cook any longer and portrays any 'real' cooking activity as laborious and time-consuming, a real-food approach doesn't have to mean endless hours of weary toil in the kitchen after work. It is perfectly possible to feed children on wholesome, fresh food without that. We just need to get into the habit of seeing that 'fast' doesn't always translate into 'junk'.

In our anxiety about fitting in cooking with all our other demands, it's easy to assume that a real-food approach would be too time-consuming and impractical. But if we stop to examine that assump-tion, we may be able to see that it isn't necessarily the case.

For example, it really doesn't take much longer to grill a chicken breast than grill or fry some turkey nuggets but it makes for a much better and more wholesome meal. We could slather it with bought pesto and stick it in a toasted pitta bread with some raw vegetables to make an instant meal that will probably appeal to children. A dip made with Greek yogurt and mint to be served with raw vegetable batons can be prepared in minutes and it's much healthier and ultimately more variable and interesting than chips with ketchup. See pages 239–51 for ideas for fast meals that appeal to both children and adults.

Other real-food meals need only a little forward planning. Once they're in the oven, you can forget baked potatoes. But they are a much healthier and more flexible option than instant oven chips and mini-pizzas because you can introduce more healthy and varied toppings and accompaniments. Sometimes, in our panic to serve food quickly we fall back on junk alternatives, forgetting that if we gave the children a more substantial snack we could buy the time to cook without pressure. See pages 237–8 for ideas for healthy snacks that will help children 'keep going' until the main meal is ready.

GETTING THE MESSAGE ACROSS

While our children are babies, it is relatively easy to keep them off the junk-food path. We control what they eat and they aren't aware of other ways of doing things. But as they become toddlers, then children, then adolescents, the way we communicate that message is going to make all the difference between sticking with our principled line and abandoning it at the first hurdle.

Parents are obviously not the only people who influence what children eat. Children can pick up food habits or ideas about food from many sources, such as other children, extended family, childcarers and teachers. They are also highly susceptible to tremendously powerful advertising, which exerts pressure on them to eat junky 'children's food'. So when we adopt the real-food approach, we must expect that children will hear conflicting messages about food – some positive and some negative – and see many models of people who eat quite differently from them.

The real-food strategy will work only if they are convinced enough of its merits to hold firm when they are under pressure to eat junk. We can't be with children at every moment of the day, standing there in the sweetie shop urging them not to buy those chewy gums or in the school cafeteria where the fruit bowl is hidden behind the chocolate crispies. Ultimately, we have to rely on them developing their own good judgement, so that, for example, when everyone else is eating crisps, they are happy with a satsuma. We want them to choose food that is good for them. We are asking them to eat well not out of a sense of duty but because they share our philosophy of food. The best way to achieve this is to make that philosophy explicit to children from as early an age as possible. There are different ways to get it across.

Enthuse about real food

The most important way to get our real-food message across is to 'talk up' the pleasure factor. We have to convey to children that real food is basically a lot nicer than processed junk and pick out high points to enthuse about. Once more, we have truth on our side. We might say, for example, *'Taste this mango. Have you ever tasted such a delicious thing in your life?'* or *'Wait till you taste how lovely this soda bread is when it's toasted,'* or *'I love these oatcakes, they're so crunchy,'* and so on. By sharing our legitimate enthusiasm for real, wholesome food with children we can help them to focus on the pleasure of eating it. Unless they experience that pleasure, all our efforts will fall on stony ground. It's still fine to say, *'You should eat that, it's so good for you,'* but we should remember to add, *'And it tastes good too.'*

Tell them what's wrong with junk

Explain to them why the standard children's junk foods they see around are bad for them. The sophistication of that message depends on the age of the child. For toddlers and younger children, one might keep it very simple. Statements like, *'Those will make you spotty, do you want that?'* or *'Your teeth will go all black and wobbly if you suck on that,'* are crude but do the trick.

A slightly more educational tactic for younger children is to use the concept of 'wrong-way-round foods' to explain what's wrong with junk. We can tell children that these are foods that are full of the things we should eat very little of and have almost none of the good things of which we need a lot.

Older children these days hear a certain amount about nutrition at school. With them, a more refined approach is simply to list off the ingredients on the label and ask what they make of them, heavily emphasising the excessive amounts of sugar, fat and chemical additives. We can share our cynicism with them about the sorts of foods that are hyped on television too, pointing out how some food manufacturers make billions out of selling rubbish to kids.

Bad-mouth junk

Miss no opportunity to sow seeds of doubt in children about the taste of these undesirable foods. The health disadvantages of junk food won't cut any ice with children if they still think they taste nice, because the instant desire to have them overrides the long-term bad consequences. So try to establish that not only is it bad for them but it tastes horrible too.

We can say things like, '*Yuck! That drink is so sweet it's disgusting*', '*How can you eat that, it smells like blackcurrant bath bubbles?*' or '*Those Kievs were so greasy I can't get the taste out of my mouth,*' or '*Those crisps have a really unnatural, chemical flavour – they make my mouth feel tingly.*' However we do it, we need to take every opportunity to bad-mouth the flavour and taste appeal of junk and unhealthy food – something that is not in itself a huge challenge because there are ample grounds.

If we keep this up over time we are encouraging children to think about what they put in their mouths, alerting them to issues like excessive sweetness, the thirsty aftermath of eating fatty-sugary-salty junk, dishonest chemical flavours and the 'feel-bad' effect that often follows the consumption of apparently attractive unhealthy foods.

It's often a particularly successful technique with young children. If you start young and keep it up they should just take it on board. Older children might delight in being contrary but as long as you don't preach at them, just state your objections in a take-it-or-leave-it way, there is a good chance of the message getting through eventually.

The point of expressing our objections is so that children will develop a more critical and questioning approach to the junk they come across and will have some ready-made conceptual categories to apply to it. In other words, they'll have more chance of seeing typical 'children's food' for what it is.

Cash in on concern about appearance

As well as telling children about the health benefits of eating good food, we can also point out that by eating this way they will both look and feel better. This works especially well with teenagers, who become increasingly preoccupied with how they look. They get fretful about being spotty, they wish their hair was shinier and their eyes brighter. Girls especially can get obsessed with their weight to such a dangerous degree that they adopt bizarre and deeply confused eating habits. Teen magazines reinforce an association between thinness and attractiveness but they also contain lots of advertising for unhealthy junk foods. No wonder teenagers get confused. It's a good time to remind them that eating well is one of the most important things they can do for their appearance. Stress that that doesn't mean calorie counting or adopting ruthless and unsustainable crash diets but eating a wide-ranging, nourishing diet, especially lots of fruit and vegetables.

You might say that using these mechanisms to get children to sign up for the 'real-food' approach amounts to brainwashing. But children are being brainwashed all the time from other quarters anyway. Nowadays they are under sustained commercial pressure to eat badly. Only a very strong mission statement from home can counteract that. With the exception of the relatively small amount of health education they may get at school, children hear no clear wholesome food message. So it's down to parents to redress the balance. It may seem an uphill struggle against the odds, but we have the potential to instil stronger values in our children than those they might pick up elsewhere, provided we stick to our guns and remain consistent.

You might also say that brainwashing is counterproductive in the long term. One popular theory is that it is pointless proselytising children to eat wholesome food because they will react against it and go the opposite way. Sometimes this is a sincere view; other times it is little more than a justification for doing nothing. There is some limited truth to it when it comes to directly banning or proscribing 'bad' foods. As discussed on page 91, bans don't work and aren't recommended. The emphasis instead should be on setting a framework within which children will choose food that is good for them. But if we don't try to win children over explicitly to a real-food philosophy, we are basically sitting back and accepting that they will probably end up eating badly.

We do, however, need to bear in mind that we might need some brainwashing ourselves. Without being aware of it, we may be giving mixed messages through our actions. One of the very irritating characteristics of children of all ages is that they are quick to notice contradictions and exploit these. That means we have to practise what we preach. Take the classic example of being with the children at a friend's house where they are automatically offered only a choice of fizzy lemonade or cola to drink because that's what the children in that household routinely drink. If we let it go, they will come away with the impression that it isn't really that important what you drink and that it's fine to accept the sugary drink. '*But you let us drink it at their house,*' is the predictable chant that will probably ensue. If, instead, we ask politely for a fruit juice or water (not every household has the former but they all have the latter), then we show them a precedent to follow.

Basically, any lapse we make will be jumped on by children and exploited. We might, under pressure, give in to demands for a confectionery bar or packet of sweets to buy peace so we can get on with whatever we need to do. Short-term, this may work. Long-term, it's a pact with the devil. Even the youngest kids can figure out that if it was okay to get sweets on Tuesday it ought to be okay to get them on Thursday, too. Why did we say 'yes' that day and 'no' today? So, tough though it may be, we need to establish a line and stick to it, unless we want them to confront us with our own inconsistencies. As far as sweets are concerned, it's easier just to state that they are not something we routinely buy.

Children also need to believe that we really mean what we say when we tell them that junk food is horrible and real, wholesome food is best. Many adults need to examine the language they use because often when we speak to children we betray the fact that we think junk is nice or, at least, that we expect they will like it.

One common example of this is saying to toddlers and young children something like, '*If you eat this up* ('this' being the healthy savoury option) *you can have that* (the sweet unhealthy option)' – a strategy that's deeply engrained in many adults. As discussed elsewhere, this simply says to children that good food is a penance that has to be endured so that you can get to that tempting junk – not what we really want to get across at all. We also need to make it apparent that we don't encourage or expect a conservative reaction from them. It's quite common to hear adults saying things like, '*I don't think you'll like that*', or '*I can't get her to eat that*', or '*Roisin won't want that*', and so on. As discussed on pages 71–3, The 'Tunnel Effect' and How to Prevent It, it's important that in every interaction we have with children over food we give the impression that we expect them to be adventurous and open-minded about what they eat – even if we aren't entirely convinced of that ourselves.

SPENDING PRIORITIES

Children's junk food has many faults but one of the things that make it attractive to adults, as opposed to children, is that it appears to be cheap. As with most heavily processed food, however, it is not actually great value for money. Any wholesome ingredients in it will have been bulked out with chemical additives and cheap fillers, so if you were to cost it out ingredient by ingredient you would most likely find that it doesn't represent a good deal. Weight for weight, for example, the fish in a fish finger costs at least twice as much as unprocessed white fish. The important point, though, is that the typical children's items of fish fingers, sausage rolls, mini Kievs and flavoured yogurt *seem* cheap.

That means that many adults have got into the habit of thinking that children's food should be at that price level. So if you consider making the transition towards the real-food approach outlined on pages 55–60, you might get a bit of a shock. A typical processed-food children's tea consisting of fish fingers, oven chips, ketchup and a flavoured yogurt dessert will cost less than the real-food equivalent of a small white fish fillet, green beans/fresh peas and home-made tomato sauce followed by, say, a Greek yogurt with honey.

So when you decide to adopt a real-food approach you cannot escape the fact that you are going to have to spend a bit more on your children's food. The real food is more nutritious and represents better value for money but, at face value, the processed alternative is cheaper.

Many households up and down the land are just so short of cash that they do not have that option. It is a sorry reflection on our food production system that it is becoming cheaper to buy over-processed junk than wholesome, unprocessed food, and a welfare scandal that so many people live in poverty and can't afford good food.

However, even for households that can afford to feed children on more natural, unprocessed food there is often a certain prejudice against doing so. It's quite common to hear relatively affluent adults saying, '*There's no point buying that for the kids because it would be wasted on them.*' This is voicing a deeply entrenched view that children are basically philistines who can never be made to appreciate good food.

Viewed charitably, this defeatism may have been born out of hard experience. Perhaps there are millions of children around the country who would routinely turn down the most delicious food if it was put in front of them. But viewed uncharitably it amounts to self-justificatory cynicism. We assume, quite wrongly, that real food is 'wasted' on children and censor in advance what we present them with.

Why? One reason is that it isn't just children who have been brainwashed by the food industry, adults have been too. The typical repertoire of children's processed food has been hyped to parents as food that caters specifically for children's palates, which gives them all they need in the way of nutrition and which guarantees a surefire 'yes' response from them and therefore no waste. By devising foods aimed specifically at young consumers, food manufacturers have fostered the expectation that it is only natural that children should want to eat a distinct range of foods. This effectively undermines our confidence in offering our children the same food as we eat. We anticipate difficulties when we might not, in fact, encounter any.

The next reason is that typical children's foods appear to offer an easy option because they can be stored for ages, come in handy single units and can be prepared almost instantly. As a result of the sustained commercial pressure on children to desire this sort of food, there is a strong likelihood that they will want to eat them and think they like them. So adults don't have to put much effort into shopping for them or seeing that they get eaten.

The final reason is that we will be quids in because processed children's food seems (quite falsely) so cheap. Even in affluent households, it takes a strong commitment to real food to buy that small pineapple for the same price as one bumper bag of attractively packaged 'mini' chocolate confectionery.

One of the irritating but nevertheless heartening characteristics of children, however, is that they do have expensive tastes and, when presented with good wholesome food composed of interesting and delicious ingredients, they will go for it. Consider the example of a fruit salad.

Getting the thumbs-up for a fruit salad

All nutritionists would agree that children should eat lots of fresh, unprocessed fruit. Serving up a fruit salad is one obvious way to do that because the fruit is chopped up and prepared, making it more approachable for children than 'fruit bowl' fruit.

However, the type of fruit used in that salad makes all the difference. A standard 'boring' fruit salad might contain apple, banana, orange, kiwi fruit and possibly a few grapes, covered in fresh fruit juice. Some children will like this but many more will find it dull in both colour and flavour and decide that they don't like one or more of its constituent fruits. In the long run, when offered this kind of fruit salad, many children won't see it as an attractive option and may decline it.

If, on the other hand, those basic fruits were combined with a larger proportion of grapes (two colours, preferably), some pineapple, some mango, strawberries or other berries, melon (two colours again, preferably), some stone fruit like nectarines or cherries, then only the most diehard junk-food children will be able to resist. It will look more colourful, taste better and the fruits will make a compulsive natural juice. In other words, the more money spent on that fruit salad, the more chance there is of children wanting to eat it.

Of course most people, adults included, can't afford to eat this ultimate-luxury fruit salad every day, even supposing this fruit selection was seasonally available. But it illustrates how spending money on prime raw ingredients can improve children's consumption of good food. Even a simple two-fruit salad such as melon and kiwi fruit or mango and strawberry will look good and taste more exciting than the standard apple/banana/orange combination.

It's true for many other foods too. It is not uncommon, for example, to hear of children who love smoked salmon and who would happily eat a packet if allowed. It's quite likely that a child (or an adult for that matter!) who refuses to eat unsweetened muesli will accept it if it has a few fresh strawberries sliced over the top. Many children turn up their noses at a standard tasteless large tomato but wolf down a carton of more expensive, but sweeter and tastier cherry tomatoes. Children aren't stupid – they do notice when food tastes better.

When we recognise that children's willingness to eat good food can be exploited by including prime raw ingredients, we then have a hard decision to make. Few people can afford to feed their offspring on smoked salmon and raspberries all year round, but we can examine our financial priorities and readjust the way we think about the children's-food element of it. Instead of going down the well-trodden path of effectively buying the cheapest and worst food for children and seeing that as normal, we can decide that the best food should be earmarked for them, at least as and when we can afford it.

That is not an easy choice to make financially. Present children with a really nice but expensive bunch of grapes and they can be consumed in a flash. For the same money, we could have had a biscuit tin brimming over with cheap 'snacks'. But we will have the satisfaction of knowing that those grapes will help our children grow into healthy adults with a discerning palate. If that is important to us, then we need to be prepared to pay for it.

THE 'TUNNEL EFFECT' AND HOW TO PREVENT IT

Many adults now believe that children can be expected to accept only a very limited number of foods and that resistance to more variety is normal. This assumption is usually based on both personal experience of a few failed attempts to get children to eat certain foods and that of other people we speak to. It's quite common to hear adults sitting around clucking in mutually consoling resignation over children's reluctance to eat certain foods – generally the healthy ones that we would like to see them enjoying.

It's true that even a couple of futile attempts to win a child over to 'new' or more adventurous foods can be really discouraging. Negative experiences like these reinforce the prevailing assumption that children are automatically difficult to feed.

Since few adults have the time, patience or persistence to bang their heads against a brick wall indefinitely, it's all too tempting to throw in the towel and simply present children with a very small repertoire of foods that are likely to be accepted. This is particularly the case for adults who are hard up and simply can't afford to waste food. But so begins the 'tunnel effect' – a downward spiral of narrowing food preferences which limits a child's palate and makes it doubly difficult to extend it thereafter.

Although in theory it may seem that the way to get children to eat is to present them with a fixed number of familiar, popular 'children's' dishes, usually of the anything-fried-with-tomato-ketchup-on-the-side followed by sweet yogurt variety, the reality is that they slowly but surely become intensely bored with these, although they may not be articulate enough, or have enough insight into their own feelings, to express their boredom. Almost inevitably, this results in a situation where children eat even *less* than before.

So we find that the child who used to eat those mini Kievs now refuses to do so unless the crispy crumb coating is scraped off. The same is true of the child who used to like pizza but now rejects it unless any evidence of tomato or cheese is obliterated, or the child who used to eat any pink fruit-flavoured yogurt but now will only consider the white chocolate, toffee-flavoured one.

If adults give in to the tunnel effect, it begins with children who eat a very restricted and constantly dwindling number of foods and ends up with children who eat almost nothing remotely wholesome whatsoever, to such a marked extent that it raises worries for both their short- and long-term health.

How can we prevent this situation happening? An alternative approach needs to be based on recognising two apparently contradictory characteristics of children. The first is that they are generally more conservative in their food preferences than adults. The second is that they love variety and change. By refusing to cave in to the first limitation and by manipulating the second, adults can be successful in widening children's food repertoire.

Start by realising that because children are usually less adventurous than adults it's to be expected that they will reject a significant proportion of what you offer them. But don't be disheartened by that. My totally unscientific observation is that a 50 per cent success rate is probably a realistic rule of thumb and you can work with that. But remember that if you present children with a range of only twenty foods you will be doing well if you get them to accept half of these, so they'll end up eating only ten. If, on the other hand, you offer them a much wider selection of foods – say a hundred – although the same conservative reaction will take place, they will end up eating around fifty. So the guiding principle is to make a conscious effort to offer children as wide a range of foods as possible, all the time supplementing tried and tested successful foods with new ones. Progressively, the children will end up eating from a much wider selection of foods and accepting new tastes and textures.

Obviously, this kind of approach will be onerous if you subscribe to the view that 'children's food' is substantially different from adults' and therefore shop differently for a distinctive larder of foods and dishes that are said to appeal to a child's palate. Food preferences are all about expectations. If you allow children to think that everything they eat must be dinosaur-shaped or packaged with TV cartoon characters, you'll end up buying heavily processed junk food that purports to make the task of feeding children easier but which, in the long term, becomes a stick with which to beat yourself. If, on the other hand, you adopt the philosophy that children should basically eat adaptations of the general food supply that the adults in their household consume, then extending the variety of foods on offer over a period of time is straightforward.

'Variety' in this context doesn't have to mean an infinite selection of weird and wonderful exotic foods – although if you want it to, there's no harm in that. It consists of an interesting rotation of meals and dishes where a reasonably wide range of ingredients from all food groups (excluding meat and fish if you are vegetarian) is offered to children, cooked and presented in different shapes and forms. In other words, if the adults in the household eat in this way, it's reasonable to accept that children can be accommodated in the same eating plan. Have a look at pages 96–101, Good Food That Children Like, if you are searching for inspiration.

EATING TOGETHER AND WHY IT MATTERS

Okay, so you have decided that you don't want your children to go down the junk-food path. You're committed to giving them real food like you yourself eat. You think that if you eat a good and varied diet, and offer this food to them, you'll produce children who approach food in the same way. So far so good. But then you hit on a big problem – they won't eat it.

So what's wrong? It's easy to assume that you have an infamous 'picky eater' on your hands. You offer red pepper, for example, on a couple of occasions and it is rejected. You assume that your child doesn't like it, won't eat it and that it's pointless to go on offering it. But it may well be that, in common with many other parents, you are fighting with one hand tied behind your back because you are attempting to feed children on their own, at a separate children's mealtime, not as part of a household meal.

We aren't talking about babies and small toddlers here. They simply can't be kept waiting for food and they need to be asleep early. But from age three to four onwards, children are still up in the early evening and the habit of separate eating makes feeding them much more difficult.

As adults we often forget that liking food isn't just a simple yes–no, accept or reject exercise. We lose sight of the fact that at this stage children have to *learn* to like good food – like finding out how to do up their shoelaces or wash their hands – and that learning isn't an instant event but a process.

In countries such as Italy and France the institution of the family meal is seen as an important cornerstone for socialising children into adult ways of eating. That doesn't mean just questions of etiquette, such as how to hold a knife and fork correctly. At communal meal-times children watch adults eat and the expectation is that they too, in time, will eat the same way. In other words, shared mealtimes can be a pleasant and effortless way to get children into the habit of enjoying good food and adopting relatively adventurous adult eating habits – much easier than a single adult trying to persuade a child to eat on his or her own.

When communal mealtimes are the norm, children end up eating better. The child who refuses red pepper at first soon loses his or her resolve when everyone else eats it regularly. The constant pres-sure to eat what everyone else eats is very strong. So the red–pepper refuser will eventually get bored picking the pepper out of the lasagne each time it's served, begin to eat it and decide it's not as bad as all that.

In the UK the modern habit of feeding children separately means that we don't take advantage of this potential ready-made learning situation and make life a lot harder for ourselves. In contrast to more food-loving European cultures, only half the children in the UK regularly eat an evening meal with the adults in their household and many British adults remain baffled by why they cannot get their children to eat what they eat, to like what they like – a strange state of affairs when most adults would agree that, even for themselves, eating alone is infinitely less preferable to eating with others. Food just isn't as much fun when there isn't anyone with whom to share it. Everyone, adults and children alike, eats better when there is a feeling of companionship and conviviality, of sitting down around a table and communicating while we eat, a natural opportunity to discuss the day, swap stories and share our reactions to the food on our plates.

What stops us eating together with children? Even parents who see the clear benefits of eating communally can find the practical mechanics of doing so very daunting. If busy, stressed-out adults arrive home late from work when young children are tired, cranky and hungry or older children are rushing out to everything from football practice to the Brownies, it can be difficult to see how a household can eat together. But it is still probably more straightforward than we might think. How can we hang on to some notion of communal eating and cope with all the complicated time commitments that affect both adults and children?

If we are starting with a blank canvas, we can begin as we mean to go on. This means establishing the principle of communal mealtimes as the norm. It doesn't mean that adults are *never* allowed to eat on their own, or separately with friends, just that more often than not there is a communal main meal of the day.

If this is at all possible in your circumstances, it will be an important way to socialise children into eating a broad and varied diet. It removes the pressure on the cook of having two meals to dream up and shop for. Because you know that you will end up eating the food yourself, you'll be motivated to concentrate your efforts on preparing it. It will reflect more sophisticated eating preferences and taste good, so it's likely to be more appealing to everyone – including the children.

If you are trapped by working hours that dictate that at least one adult can't be home until late, then there is a series of compromises to be made. The most obvious one is to give children a substantial snack when they get in from school which will stop them getting bad-tempered and tired and buy time until the main meal is ready. Twenty-five Good Snacks (see pages 237–8) will give you ideas.

If eating together is really not an option during the week, then at the very least it's worth trying to eat communally at weekends. Looking more closely at weekdays, though children may have to eat separately on certain nights, on other nights the adult who is cooking for them can opt to eat the main meal with them, leaving the late-coming adult to eat the same meal later. This is a neat reversal of the usual adult companionship/separate child mealtime pattern. It makes the important statement to children that they are the focal point of a meal and that efforts to please and tempt them have been made. It says that their mealtime is 'the main event', not merely a sideshow. The quid pro quo is the expectation that because they are being treated as important people they will behave as such, which means eating a good part of what is put in front of them. With time and commitment from participating adults, most children will feel inclined to conform to this.

If communal mealtimes are simply out of the question most of the time, there are two remaining positive strategies. The first is for the cook to prepare one meal for the adults to eat later on, at least parts of which can be served earlier to the children. Although the children may miss out on the socialising companionship of communal eating, they will at least be offered the food element of it, and that is likely to be a whole lot more varied, wholesome and appetising than the ubiquitous 'children's-food' alternatives.

The second is for the available adult to sit down at the table with the children at their mealtime even if she or he isn't eating at that point. The presence of an adult who can gently prompt the children into eating what's on offer can make a big difference to how much they'll actually eat. It also makes the children's meal much more of a formal 'sit-down' occasion and that is helpful because it slows down a tendency on the children's part to view the meal as just another quick snack to be consumed 'on the hoof'.

THE 'NEVER-SATISFIED' SNACKER

Children need to eat more often than adults; that's just a fact of life. Most adults can 'keep going' even if they are hungry and will expect to eat enough at one sitting to see them through a significant part of the day. Babies and children, on the other hand, tend to consume less when they do eat, and appear to burn it up quicker, so they need to eat more often than adults. Unlike adults, who can live without any snacks whatsoever, snacks represent a normal and predictable feature of any child's diet.

However, snacking can easily get out of hand. Many children get into an eating pattern where reliance on junk-food snacks blunts their appetite for real meals and proper food. When they sit down to eat a meal they cannot do justice to it. All too soon after, they start demanding food once more and insisting that they are hungry. Unreasonable and irritating though that demand might appear to adults, for the sake of peace another snack is usually offered, and so the process continues in chicken and egg fashion.

This sort of eating pattern produces children who are never really properly hungry for, nor totally satisfied by, the food they eat – the 'never-satisfied' snacker. They are always on the lookout for food, yet permanently resistant to eating it. They campaign vociferously for food at all sorts of inconvenient times but don't want to eat it when adults put it in front of them.

Managing snacks so that this syndrome is avoided is one of the biggest challenges adults face when feeding children. Left to eat this way, children can become inveterate snackers who will not make the transition to more conventional mealtimes and adult eating patterns.

Few child snackers compose their diets from good food; instead it's almost invariably junk. If they start this way they are likely to continue bad food habits into adult life, even though these give them little or no real pleasure in eating. In the worst scenarios, they end up as adults with a problematic relationship to food which may ultimately express itself in eating disorders and obesity.

How can the 'never-satisfied' snacking syndrome be prevented? The first thing to grasp is that adults need to be proactive, planning children's food to a certain extent, anticipating their likely demands and working out how to cater for them in a way that is consistent with a wholesome food policy.

Many adults simply react to children's food demands on a short-term, crisis-management basis. '*You're hungry? Well help yourself to the crisps or take some biscuits,*' becomes a standard response. Children's junk foods have lots of faults but they are extremely convenient for busy adults trying to buy time to get on with a string of tasks. It's very easy to fall into the trap of letting a 'snack' become synonymous with 'junk'.

A more proactive approach might be as follows: decide on a pattern of meals for most days which represents to children the food 'staging posts' throughout the day – and stick to it. Babies and toddlers generally eat a good breakfast but older children can drift away from this beneficial habit because they know they can graze on snacks throughout the morning. Many adults cave in to the demands of older children and teenagers who protest that 'they don't like breakfast' and 'can't eat it'. Pressure from friends often says that breakfast is 'uncool' and that a breaktime trip to the newsagents or tuck shop for junk has more street-cred. At this stage it's very important for adults to re-emphasise the need for breakfast and to promote the benefits of more stamina throughout the morning and the prospect of much nicer, ultimately more satisfying food.

Having established the principle that some kind of sensible breakfast is sacred, there needs to be some provision for a reasonable lunch, either at home or at the childminder's, or at school or nursery in the form of a canteen or packed lunch. These meals mark the food day until it's time for the main meal, usually in the evening, where children will eat communally with adults.

Now having established in children's minds that the basic food structure of their day is breakfast, light lunch and communal main meal, thought has to be given to filling the hunger gaps with acceptable snacks to keep them going.

The frequency of snacks depends on the age of the child. Toddlers and young children will need a mid-morning snack but this may become redundant for older children, especially if they do eat a good breakfast. For most children, the peak snack period is in the late afternoon. You cannot count on schoolchildren having eaten anything much at lunchtime. They may dislike the canteen meal, or have abandoned their packed lunch so they can play with friends. Whatever the circumstances, by late afternoon they are quite often famished. Babies and toddlers may reach a boredom and tiredness threshold by this point in the day which makes them want food as comfort.

The demand for a late-afternoon snack is entirely predictable and needs to be planned for by keeping a stock of foods that lend themselves to snacks but which are wholesome and give the child the slow release of energy needed to get through another couple of hours. Chocolate biscuits, crisps, sweets and other typical junk snacks can give a feeling of instant satisfaction but this quickly goes, leaving the child hungry and dissatisfied once more and making a repeat request for even more junk highly likely.

Instead, it might be good to offer a more substantial snack, which will satisfy the child properly and fill the gap before the main meal. Turn to Twenty-five Good Snacks (pages 237–8) for practical suggestions for wholesome, attractive snacks that can be substituted for junk.

DON'T KEEP FOOD YOU DON'T WANT CHILDREN TO EAT

How often do we hear adults complaining that they can't get children to eat certain foods and that, despite their best efforts, all they want is sweets and junk? Such statements betray a particular type of self-deception in which many adults specialise. The truth of the matter is that one of the reasons their children eat junk food and children's 'treats' is that adults routinely buy those for them and keep a supply in the house.

However much you believe in children's long-term potential to develop more sophisticated eating habits, it has to be recognised that there is overwhelming pressure on them to eat mass-produced junk. That means that if there is such food in the house, and unless the children in question have already developed a more discerning palate, they will want to seek it out and consume it.

One common adult view is that, like it or not, junk food is a fact of life, that children have always wanted to scoff sweets and guzzle fizzy drinks, therefore it is futile to try to fight against the system. So a stock of children's junk food in the house is rationalised as inevitable. Children are often told that they must eat the wholesome 'real' food first, and that if they eat enough of this they can have the junk as a treat – a sort of stick-and-carrot approach with two different tiers of food on the go simultaneously. But this logic is faulty. The coded message we give to children when we describe foods as 'treats' is that they are better fun and more pleasurable than non-treat food. Actually, we should be presenting things the other way round.

It's also important to realise right from the beginning that the very presence of junk in the kitchen actively undermines the chances of children eating the desirable food. If you give in to the idea of keeping junk in the house, slowly but surely you will be left trying to maintain a wholesome food front against a relentless campaign for junk. That's because children know that if they go on for long enough, most adults will give in to their demands eventually. So even the most sensible adults, committed to feeding their children well, find that against their better judgement the children are actually eating less good food and more rubbish. So the issue becomes how much junk and how often? Is one bag of crisps acceptable, or two, or half a dozen? Because adults' verdicts on this are basically arbitrary and inconsistent, children get no clear message about what quantity is acceptable and naturally go on demanding more and more, be that from a parent, a childminder or a grandparent, each of whom is probably applying different guidelines.

The more junk they succeed in wheedling or extracting, the less children eat the wholesome stuff and develop a taste for real food. So adults find themselves caught up in a vicious circle where, unless they want to say no endlessly, they can only surrender to demands for food that undermine their loftier objectives.

This situation very often escalates if children are looked after during the day by someone other than their parent. While parents may have bought those biscuits, ice creams or confectionery for very occasional consumption, the daytime carer gets worn down and gives them liberally to the children. While the parents fondly think that junk is being served judiciously, in fact it's becoming a mainstay of the children's diet.

Once the parent acknowledges the problem it can be very hard to broach the issue diplomatically with the daytime carer because he or she is relying on junk to get through the day and the children are expecting it. What's more, be it childminder, nanny or grand-parent, many parents will tolerate a carer who indulges children's taste for junk if that person is good with the children in other ways.

An alternative approach involves being consistent, sticking to your guns and adopting a 'no junk in the house' policy. In other words, don't keep food or drinks in the kitchen that you don't want your children to consume. (For advice about controlling what children eat when they are being looked after in someone else's home, see pages 169–75, What You Can Expect from Childcarers.)

If children are being looked after in their own home, we can start by recognising that although they are under pressure to want junk food, and will certainly demand it, at least while at home they are a captive audience. It is a fact of life that they will end up making a selection of what they eat from the household larder. So the child who arrives home from school famished will accept a piece of toast and peanut butter, a banana and some milk or water rather than half a packet of biscuits, a packet of crisps and a can of fizz. If there is only one main meal on the go, and no alternative 'children's' option as backup, the child will end up eating at least some of the main meal and, with time, make the progression to a good and varied diet.

The bonus for adults is that although initially a 'no junk' rule demands bravery, quite quickly it takes the pressure off them because children soon appreciate that there's no point campaigning for something that isn't there. Adults get respite from pestering demands and the children get into the habit of choosing their food from a better and wider selection. Quite quickly, they'll learn to see this as normal and enjoy eating good food.

Obviously, it's easiest to start from scratch with babies and toddlers who don't know any differently. But what can be done about children who have already become accustomed to that well-stocked biscuit tin and fizz collection and prefer it to the contents of the fruit bowl and the fruit juice in the fridge?

The good news is that even the most dedicated junior consumers of junk can be converted slowly with stealth and commitment. Adults who are alarmed about the amount of junk the children are eating may be tempted to impose a sudden and draconian 'no junk' policy, but that is counterproductive. It comes over as a penalty, and reinforces the undesirable message that eating real food is some sort of penance. But by slowly running down the amount of junk food that's bought, all the while upping the presence of wholesome but attractive alternatives, it is possible to wean children progressively into eating better food.

It's important that some creative thought is put into these alternatives, so that adults are seen to be trading something children like with something they may like even better. For example, most children like a small bunch of grapes or a plate of chopped and prepared fruit and nuts. Many children who will reject vegetables will still eat carrot sticks if there is a gooey dip to stick them in. Only the toughest junk-food kids can resist the seductive smell of warm home-baking – scones, bread, pancakes or muffins. Even buying ready-made baked food and reheating it in the oven can make it more appealing to children without spending time cooking.

The key to a gentle conversion, though, is working with children's stated preferences, accommodating them to a certain extent so as to appear reasonable, but all the time extending their horizons.

Take the example of children who have become accustomed to sweet 'fruit' squash and infinite supplies of biscuits. Because they are used to the artificial sweetness of squash, they will probably show resistance to water or milk. But they may well accept a diluted pasteurised real fruit juice from a carton if it contains sweeter 'tropical' flavours, such as mango and pineapple juice. Rather like drug addicts, having been weaned off totally synthetic squash on to natural but sweet juice, they may then make the progression on to more acidic juices, such as orange, and eventually on to water. On the biscuit front, a slice of bread and butter with jam might be an initial substitute because it is still sweet, but slowly, more savoury toppings such as peanut butter may be substituted for the butter and jam while wholemeal, more rustic bread can take the place of white and so on. For further examples of wholesome snack foods see pages 237–8.

The long-term goal of a 'no junk' policy is to get children to eat a wide selection of foods from the general household supply and to cut their dependency on undesirable rubbish. But it shouldn't be confused with a total moratorium on any food that doesn't meet rigid 'healthy eating' strictures. This means that there's no point trying to integrate children into the general household food supply if the larder reflects the shopping list of a crash-diet health farm. If children are being discouraged from eating those ruthlessly hyped sweets and crisps, it's only reasonable to offer them some attractive substitutes, which may indeed contain some of the ingredients that are widely condemned as dietary baddies, such as sugar and fat. But if they are presented in more wholesome versions and make up only a small part of the total diet, these should constitute no nutritional problem and still accommodate both children's and adults' predictable desire for something indulgent. Rather than ignoring that sweet tooth entirely, it needs to be catered for to some extent, but preferably in the context of wholesome, unprocessed food.

Two categories of food come into their own in this respect. The first is home-made puddings. From simple crumble to bread and butter pudding, few can resist and they satisfy a deep urge – especially on gloomy winter days – for toothsome comfort. The second category is home-baking, which can encompass everything from relatively savoury items such as bread and scones through to tray bakes and cookies. Even with their often hefty sugar and fat make-up, in home-made forms they are still preferable to mass-produced and additive-laden junk foods because they consist only of natural ingredients in a more unprocessed state and are basically much more satisfying. The supply is obviously more limited because they are home-made, and this restricts consumption, unlike biscuits and sweets which can be bought by the barrel-load. In moderation, home-baking can satisfy that universal craving for something indulgent. For those who just don't have the time to make something at home, then the occasional good-quality chocolate or 'premium' ice cream, made with only natural ingredients, will also stop any sense of deprivation setting in.

PRESENTATION, BOREDOM AND THE 'YUCK' REACTION

In the received wisdom about encouraging children to eat, it is traditional to stress all manner of presentation devices to hoodwink them into eating food they might otherwise reject. The classic example is toast 'soldiers' – thin slices of toasted bread to dip into egg or cover with spread. The basic assumption underlying this approach is that there are some foods children won't want to eat and that changing the manner in which we present them is the way to get around that. Thus a large slice of toast, with crust intact, is seen as unwieldy for an infant or toddler. But if the crust is removed and the bread neatly squared or cubed, we expect a more enthusiastic uptake.

This traditional approach has in recent years mushroomed into a sort of presentation mania. If our children won't eat a certain food, we are exhorted to get out the pastry cutters and re-form it into any shape we can lay our hands on, from shooting star, through zoo animal to gingerbread boy. Now toast doesn't just have to be a 'soldier', it has to have lovable stick-out ears. Any sponge cake must be topped with sugary glacé icing and a lurid red glacé cherry or sprinkled with multi-coloured hundreds and thousands.

The same thinking has gathered a head of steam in food manufacturing. Nowadays a rectangular fish finger is considered dull and less appealing than fishy marine 'shapes'. Fried poultry meat rissoles have been reincarnated in various prehistoric 'fun' forms. And to be truly commercial, fruit juice in cartons has to carry the image of a popular cartoon or familiar children's 'fun' character.

There is a school of thought which says that any device that helps children find food more attractive is welcome. A child who might decline an ordinary plate of pasta might instead be wooed by a bowl of alphabet pasta shapes, especially if a funny face traced in tomato ketchup has first been squirted on it. Sooner or later, so the logic goes, little Sam or Ayesha will graduate on to pappardelle with roasted peppers and chilli.

But is this the case? Is it not just as, or even more, likely that he or she will become an adult who lives on attractively packaged ready meals and shuns natural, unprocessed food served in a 'real' form?

And do children really eat *more* of foods served in gimmicky ways or do they just like the idea of them? Every child is intoxicated by the vision of a tall glass brimming with five flavours of ice cream, whipped cream, melba sauce, day-glo hundreds and thousands, chocolate flake and a paper parasol, but very few can even begin to finish it. Most children can finish and digest a simple slice of banana cake or a straightforward scone. Few can lick their way through a slick of white icing or a bar of toffee without leaving bits and complaining of nausea.

The flaw in this way of thinking about presentation is the assumption, so familiar in our attitude to children's food in general, that children do not go for the look of real food and need to be served a special range of distinctive foods. But this is a fundamentally conservative self-fulfilling prophecy. Obviously if we think that children won't like the look of real food, we won't serve it to them. If we don't serve it to them, they won't get used to it and learn to like it. Instead, they will be on the lookout for the latest kiddie gimmick. Such gimmicks are passing and fashionable. They do not build loyalty to a wider repertoire of ingredients or widen the scope of what a child will consider. Instead they provoke a predictable boredom reaction, a permanent quest for novelty. The consequence of this is a tendency to eliminate any real food in favour of child-targeted junk. Once in a while, it's a good idea to let children try the gimmicky foods they crave, such as the sundae with the sparklers in, otherwise they may appear to be tantalising 'forbidden fruit'. And when they do taste them, they often discover for themselves that the idea was preferable to the reality. But a better overall approach is to get children accustomed to eating as wide a range of foods as possible, in as many different forms as possible, and to discover what fun this can be.

All we have to do is offer them attractive adult food in a naturally appetising state. And that is less work for us. While it may test any adult's ingenuity to make six turkey nuggets and a stack of oven chips look appealing, most 'real' food just cannot help looking good anyway.

A simple golden-roasted chicken with crisp-skinned potatoes is so much more tantalising than deep-fried, re-formed bits – and that's even before you smell it. No special presentation (or even alphabet shapes) is required to make children want to eat a plate of spaghetti, topped with a bolognese *ragù*, except perhaps for a dusting of Parmesan! Nearly any salad looks good when it blends colourful salad leaves and vegetables. Children, just like adults, will lick their lips at the prospect of getting stuck into an almond and pear tart with oozing caramelised edges without setting a sparkler atop it. And most can learn that a plate of Greek yogurt topped with a few strawberries is actually much nicer than the strawberry-flavoured gloop in the lovable cartoon container.

When we decide to abandon presentation gimmicks, it's good nevertheless to think about ways of making things look easier to eat. Certain foods are somewhat daunting and it is tempting not to serve them, but most challenging foods are easily to be made more accessible and appealing to children. For example:

MEAT ON THE BONE

Rather than always serving boneless fillets, we can either scrape the meat off the bone (for younger children) or simply tell them that it's fine to use their teeth and fingers.

FISH WITH BONES AND SKIN

Instead of giving them only fillets or fish fingers, we can serve the cooked fish whole but take out the backbone and minor bones at the table. We can scrape off the skin, or even ask them to try a bit if it is crisp and tasty.

UNPEELED CITRUS FRUIT

An orange can be tough going for children, but rather than give them only easy-to-peel satsumas we can simply peel the orange for them or, if they are older, show them how to do it themselves.

FRUIT WITH PIPS

Don't assume that children will be put off. As soon as they have grown out of the small-baby-who-could-choke stage, get them used to eating grapes with pips. If the pips bother them, tell them it's okay to swallow them or spit them out – whatever they prefer. Rather than thinking you have to stone every cherry before you offer one, show the child how to eat one whole and spit out the stone.

'REAL' BREAD WITH A PROPER CRUST

Don't insist they tackle it in neat slices or automatically remove the crust. Show them how to attack it with their hands and break off small, manageable mouthfuls with their fingers.

The point of these ideas is to get children used to eating food in all its varied and interesting forms. We often forget that when we were children we disliked certain foods because they were served only in one form. We think we dislike fish in general, but in fact we just didn't enjoy the fact that fish was always cod, fried in a crumb coating and served every Wednesday night! When served fish cooked in a more diverse and stimulating way, surprise, surprise, we find it's quite good.

That is why we have to accustom children to the idea that real food comes in a multiplicity of states. Some of these require more effort than others but this is compensated for by the taste. Yes, many children do like baby cherry tomatoes. But we need to give them large tomatoes sliced or cut into segments, too. If we can show them yellow tomatoes, plum tomatoes, fat stripy tomatoes, tart green tomatoes for chutney, then all the better.

It is also very easy to give in to the 'yuck factor', a reaction that handicaps children when presented with any food that looks too close to its natural form and therefore demands hands-on treatment. Often it is parents and carers who predict a 'yuck' reaction when otherwise there would not be one, and unilaterally de-list that item from the menu. We might assume, for example, that children would not eat mussels because they would be put off by the appearance of the flesh and the shells. Yet by showing children how to use an empty shell as a pincer we can enable them to set about tackling mussels with gusto. What's more, it can be much more fun than mixing the contents of one yogurt compartment into another.

Obviously, babies need their food specially adapted (see Part Four, Getting It Right with Babies and Toddlers), but go too far down that route with older children and you end up serving them something that closely resembles invalid food. It will be samey, homogeneous, undemanding and ultimately unrewarding. Under these circumstances, they will end up eating not more but less.

SWEETS, TREATS AND BANS

If you want children to develop good food habits, sweets are a true challenge. They are bad for their health, damage their teeth and corrupt their palates with heavy-handed servings of sugar and fat. If they eat a lot of them, the true flavours of real food may become unappealing to them. But wherever children turn, they are surrounded by sweets. Friends are eating them, the corner shop is selling them, children in T V ads are munching them, the tuck shop sells them, adults distribute them. They are ubiquitous. So how can we handle the vexed issue of sweets?

One extreme way is to go for an outright ban. This can work to a certain extent with younger children if the parents have very strong food opinions of their own and still control what their children eat. Basically, the children just don't know any other way of doing things. But as they grow up and inevitably find themselves in situations where there are sweets to buy and they have money of their own, it is likely to break down. Bans make sweets feel like forbidden fruit and therefore all the more desirable to children. A total ban on sweets can encourage children to be sneaky and dishonest about what they are eating. Most parents see that bans are counter-productive and feel that it's futile to try to go against the tide. They accept, reluctantly, that daily consumption of chocolate confectionery and sticky sweets is just an inevitable fact of life.

So the most common approach amongst concerned adults is to restrict quantity, on the comforting assumption that if sweets are kept in check they do no harm. Familiar mechanisms for imposing this include 'sweetie money' – a fixed allowance per week – and a 'sweetie day' – one day a week when children are allowed that coveted sweet 'treat' or a daily sweetie quota.

But as many people who have tried these mechanisms testify, they are extremely problematic. The first difficulty is with younger children, especially toddlers. They basically do not see why they should be allowed a 'treat' one day and not the next. This spawns those all-too-familiar scenes at the till where the child has a screaming, bawling tantrum over an apparently arbitrary refusal to buy that sweet that day, while the adult attempts to justify it with, '*You've had your sweets for today*', or words to that effect. The distinction between a 'yes' occasion and a 'no' occasion is inexplicable for such young children.

The second difficulty is with older children. Although they may seem to go along with the idea of limits in theory, that doesn't stop them testing those limits in practice. They are less likely than toddlers to make a fuss when you say enough is enough, but that won't stop them keeping up a long campaign of attrition to have those limits interpreted liberally. Common tactics include pleading for more, casting up the example of friends who get sackloads every day, sulking because their sweetie allowance is already consumed although it is only Monday, and demanding an increase in their allowance. Children are dirty fighters and they'll play on everything from guilt to pester-power to wear adults down on this one. Adults can easily find themselves with their backs to the wall, trying to defend holes in their own logic about why it is okay to have a packet of X but not a tube of Y and so on.

The third problem with the idea of restricting sweets is that adults are effectively collaborating with the idea that sweets are nice and building up their profile as a special 'treat'. This makes them even more desirable from a child's point of view.

To sum up, the idea of restricting sweet consumption is hard to stick to on both sides. Children are inevitably going to demand more and more, and adults are equally likely to get ground down by these demands. Slowly but surely, you end up with the hypocritical situation where, though in theory sweets are restricted, they are actually being permitted quite liberally. In all but name, children have a constant and free supply of sweets.

So what's the way out? If we are talking about toddlers and young children who do not yet have their own pocket money, then two skills are required. The first is predicting and avoiding situations where you will be trapped into buying sweets – such as exploitative food hall and supermarket checkouts which play to pester-power with sweets aimed at children both in their line of vision and within touchable distance. Clearly, if you get stuck in this 'sugar trap' with a crotchety toddler, there's either going to be a scene or you are going to have to give in.

The second skill is anticipating when children will get fed up and start demanding sweets so you can make sure that you have some more acceptable alternative to offer them. This means that when you set out on any significant expedition, from the local shops to the doctor's clinic, you need to remember to take food (and often drink) backup, or at least know where to stop off to buy it. Even cranky and unreasonable toddlers can be diverted away from sweets if they are promptly given something they quite like instead.

Fresh fruit is the first category of alternative to go for, closely followed by chewy bread such as a French stick, croissant or Italian panini, or breadsticks and rice crackers. Compromise possibilities include a few small squares of good-quality chocolate, a cereal bar or 'fruit leather' (from a wholefood shop) or a better biscuit made from just a few natural ingredients such as butter shortbread. See pages 237–8, Twenty-five Good Snacks, and pages 114–20, Healthier Look-alike Alternatives to Common 'Children's Foods', for ideas.

Whatever you offer them, remember that toddlers and small children, though unreasonable, are easily conned. You are a lot cleverer than they are and can outwit them. Most of the time when they are campaigning for sweets they are just tired, grizzly or bored. Offer them an alternative quickly before they have the chance to work themselves into a frenzy, present it as a treat and they will most likely accept it.

Older children are more of a problem. They aren't always under our supervision, have firmer desires of their own (often fostered by junk-food advertising) and mainly have their own spending money. Since we aren't always with them, we have to encourage them to think that they do not really want sweets that much anyway.

How can we achieve this?

Let's go back to one of the key principles discussed earlier: we want children to choose a wide range of food that is nutritious and good for them. That means motivating them to make a good choice, even when we aren't looking over their shoulders. The single most effective way to achieve this is to substitute something other than sweets as the 'treat'.

Here's the scenario.

CAROLINE WANTS SOMETHING AT THE SHOPS

Like all children, Caroline is fascinated by the idea of buying sweets at the shop. She has been given her own money (a weekly allowance), which she is allowed to spend as she pleases. She knows that there are no sweets in the house and that her parents think they taste horrible and are unhealthy, but if she still wants to spend her money on them, they will not stop her because it is her money.

But they have also pointed out that the shop has other things that she likes which aren't sweets. She could choose her treat from the selection of magazines, notepads, scissors, glue, postcards, jotters, tubs of blowing bubbles, stickers, folders, playing cards and other small toys that the typical corner shop stocks. If she spends her money on sweets, she will be using her precious allowance up and won't be able to buy these.

So by substituting general pocket money for 'sweetie' money, Caroline's parents have set up a conflict in her spending priorities which means that sweets have strong competition from the other bits and pieces she likes. Her parents haven't banned sweets, so she doesn't see them as forbidden fruit, but if she buys them she is going to have to take responsibility for the fact that she'll have less of that other category of goods she likes.

This forces her to examine how much she really wants those sweets in the first place. If Caroline eats real food at home, and her parents have brought her up to be suspicious of children's junk food, she may well decide that she'd rather have that magazine instead.

Caroline's case is an illustration of how you can set up a choice for children which means that the knee-jerk urge to eat sweets doesn't always win out in their priorities. It can work in many different settings – for example, in the supermarket, where children can be offered the alternative choice of a book or other stationery items like pens and paints. Setting up this conflict between sweets and other desirable items is also a useful strategy for older children who have pocket money to spend each day. In 1998, when the caterer Gardner Merchant surveyed children's eating habits, it found that the average child spent nearly £1 a day on what have come to be known as 'The 3 Cs': confectionery, crisps and canned drinks. It also found that 45 per cent of children bought sweets on their way home from school. If children see money spent on sweets as less to spend on something else – be that nail varnish or collectable stickers – then sweets have tougher competition.

The tactic of offering an attractive substitute for sweets, or setting up conflicting demands for spending priorities, obviously needs to be backed up at home, using the many other strategies covered in this section, such as routinely talking up the delights of real food, bad-mouthing junk food and feeding children the same food as adults.

If parents can stick to this, over time they have a very good chance of producing children who have no problem controlling sweets and who may even actively choose the carrot or clementine over the cola chew.

GOOD FOOD THAT CHILDREN LIKE

Every child is an individual with taste preferences. At one end of the spectrum there are the notorious 'picky eaters' who adopt a 'no' policy to any vaguely wholesome foods as a point of principle. They may be very conservative by nature, or have developed a junk-food palate so early that any real food tastes odd to them. At the other extreme, there is a significantly smaller group of children whose adventurousness with food surprises even adults, as they consume with relish testing items like squid or olive paste.

The vast majority of children clock in somewhere in between. However, it is possible to map out some middle ground and establish the kinds of real food that are most likely to appeal to this huge middle grouping. Of course, there are always exceptions, but we can start by recognising the seven broad categories of food that many children appear to have difficulty liking. Here they are.

Thumbs-down foods

'MIXTURES'

Dishes such as chop suey, mixed-vegetable combinations, 'layered' dishes like moussaka, hotpots, fish pies, quiche. The problem seems to be a suspicion about what exactly the 'bits' are, especially if they are lurking under a sauce, gravy or pastry.

MULTIPLE-INGREDIENT DISHES

The longer the list of visible ingredients, the less likely they are to eat it. The presence of ingredients children think they don't like – mushrooms, for example, or a sprinkling of a green herb – may put them off eating others in the dish that they do like, such as carrots.

MORE ELABORATE 'TRANSFORMED' FOOD

Children like to be able to identify the ingredients in a dish. They may be prepared to eat a piece of smoked fish in its raw or simply cooked state but refuse it when it has been made into a mousse. Fancy and elaborate 'chef-type' food, where many ingredients are worked on and presented in an altogether different form, may get the thumbs-down. Basically children don't like too much happening on their plates.

VERY RICH FOOD

Items such as rich chicken liver pâté, intense chocolate puddings, heavy creamy-buttery sauces, recipes with a large number of egg yolks, very 'cheesy' dishes are all problematic. Children may be tempted by the sweet versions but often cannot finish them.

UNCOMPROMISINGLY FIERY FOOD

Although many children enjoy food spiced with flavours like cumin or ginger, very few can take any significant amount of hot chilli or cayenne. Those who grow to like it usually come to it by degrees in adulthood.

SPONGY OR SLIPPERY 'WET' TEXTURES

Foods such as aubergine, mushrooms and oysters, savoury foods that 'wobble', such as omelette, over-cooked courgette, mushy cabbage, anything 'shuddery' that isn't sweet, such as uncrisped fat on meat, these can all be challenging to children (and many adults too!).

VERY ACIDIC OR BITTER TASTES

Few children go for the acid taste of rhubarb, tart plums or gooseberries, though many more will eat it substantially sweetened – for example, in a crumble. Bitter flavours such as grapefruit or chicory don't usually appeal to children.

So those are the 'no-go' categories. But what broad categories of food do a lot for children tend to like? The good news is that actually they like quite a lot. But they do clearly favour simple, relatively uncomplicated, quite 'plain' food. The less that has been done to it in the way of cooking or culinary elaboration, the more they will want to eat it. So they are likely to give the thumbs-up to foods which fit the following bill.

Thumbs-up foods

FOODS WITH DISTINCT AND SEPARATE INGREDIENTS

The opposite of 'mixtures' and food with 'bits' in, they can see exactly what they are. If they are not touching on the plate or mingling, all the better. Younger children are much more likely to eat simple mashed potatoes than they are to eat them with added ingredients such as cabbage, even though they may eat the cabbage alongside the mash. Older children get better about mixtures, so it's worthwhile trying them out again as they grow up.

FOODS WITH A REASONABLY SMALL NUMBER OF PERCEPTIBLE INGREDIENTS

Even if some ingredients are 'hidden' in sauces or foods, such as onions and garlic in a bolognese sauce, the effect is more approachable. This is why smooth puréed soups are often more popular than thin broths with tangible 'bits' floating in them. There aren't any obvious 'suspect' ingredients, so children can let their guard down and eat it. The inclusion of more challenging ingredients doesn't put them off the ones they already like and accept.

SIMPLE AND LIMITED COOKING

Many children who won't countenance a particular food when cooked will happily consume it when it is raw. This is especially the case with vegetables. Half an avocado served in slices, or with a spoon to scoop out the flesh, will go down better than guacamole. A child who eats plain boiled rice may veto a seafood risotto. Although some older children may really appreciate flavoursome sauces, many smaller ones regard them as suspicious cover for disliked ingredients. Rich sauces may just be too much for a child's palate, too.

FIRM AND CRUNCHY TEXTURES

The texture of food seems to be almost more important than taste to many children. They seem to favour actively foods that have a reasonably firm texture and offer some body and pleasantly slight resistance before yielding in the mouth. Meat and fish fit the bill and so does pasta, as long as it hasn't been overcooked. Once they have proper teeth to eat with, many of them really go for crunch in a big way. They will consume items like carrot sticks in some quantity if presented in this form.

Here are some menu guidelines for the broad categories of dishes that could be served at a communal mealtime, taking into account common likes and dislikes amongst children. Although they set out to accommodate children's preferences, these suggestions should be more than acceptable to most adults. You can give them an Italian, Thai, Chinese, Indian or British slant by varying the optional sauce or relish on the side or the style of presentation. But in whatever national guise, they should still be greeted enthusiastically by many children.

The 'popular but good' menu

FISH

Peeled Prawns (with a light dipping sauce, mayonnaise or relish on the side)
Baked or Grilled White or Oily Fish
Thai-style Crab Cakes or Fish Cakes
Smoked Salmon

MEAT AND POULTRY

Stews and Casseroles (where the vegetables are small and almost imperceptible in the sauce)
Traditional 'Roast Dinner'
Meat- or Poultry-only Stir-fry
Home-made Meat Balls, Burgers and Kofta
Bolognese Sauce (*Ragù*)
Grilled or Roasted Meat, Served Hot or Cold
Good-quality Sausages

VEGETABLES

Salads and Crudités (raw and unaltered vegetables on their own or with dips or vinaigrette on the side)
Lightly Cooked, Still Crunchy Vegetables (seasoned perhaps with oil or lemon)

Simple One- or Two-vegetable Purées
Baked Vegetables (such as squash, sweet potato, potato)
Liquidised Soups

CARBOHYDRATES
Rice, Couscous, Cracked Wheat, Barley or Other Grain (steamed or
    lightly boiled)
Baked, Mashed and 'Gratin' Potatoes
Pasta and Noodles (in simple, one-flavour sauces, such as smooth
    tomato, pesto or mild cheese)
Savoury Pancakes and Crêpes
Bread and Toast
Pizza

FRUIT AND DESSERTS
Prepared and Cut-up Fresh Fruit
Baked or Poached Fruit (such as purées, compotes or fools)
Fruit Pies and Crumbles
Sponge and Baked Puddings
Thick Natural Yogurt (fruit, honey or purée on the side)

In the long term, these suggestions involve compromises that some
adults may find boring. You may yearn to slip some beansprouts
and pepper into that chicken stir-fry or spinach in with that lamb
curry. Gradually, you can try that out. Spinach could be so smooth
in the sauce that it doesn't worry the children. The pepper can be
left in large enough chunks to be fished out if it's causing problems.
Over time, the children may come to like these adult deviations from
their more conservative horizons.

    From the time they are weaned, babies can get into the habit of
eating well from this list. As they become toddlers, then children,
try out more sophisticated variations on it. Don't go too fast, though,
and always give in to opposition. Even if children eat only from this
relatively restricted menu, they will be eating well.

WHAT CHILDREN SHOULD DRINK

A few decades ago water was the standard children's drink. Now it has been sidelined by a proliferation of more expensive drinks, all of which pander to the relatively modern notion that children will not accept the plain, neutral taste of good old water and must have it flavoured with something.

From the minute they are weaned from the bottle or breast, even tiny babies are now commonly offered drinks which purport to be 'specially formulated' for their tiny palates. This is nothing more than dishonest food industry doublespeak for 'sweet'. And that is the nub of the matter. Children are now routinely encouraged from the earliest age to seek a sweet flavour in every drop of fluid they drink.

Given the sheer amount of liquid that most children consume in one form or another, this means that, even setting aside entirely what they may be eating, many children are developing from a very early age a palate that is on a permanent quest for a sweet flavour.

Once children have developed the expectation that drinks must taste sweet, it can be very difficult to break the habit. Naturally if children are given a routine fix of sweet flavour (such as squash or 'baby juice') in every drink, ordinary water will taste odd by comparison because they will have become accustomed to that familiar background level of sweetness.

Effectively, their palates are corrupted – not only for water but for food too. Natural levels of sweetness in unprocessed foods may seem unpleasant to them and get the thumbs-down, basically because they drop below the sweetness threshold that children have come to expect.

All of this means that for parents who want their children to eat along the real-food lines explained in The Real-food Approach (pages 55–60) the issue of drinks calls for a fairly radical stance as early as possible. We have to decide that we are not going down the path of routinely quenching the children's thirst with sweet liquid. But what should we offer instead?

Establish water as the standard drink

There is only one liquid that children really *need* to drink: water. It is cheap, freely available and our bodies need it in substantial quantity to stay healthy. Some 70 per cent of our body weight is made up of water and this gets used up throughout the day, so drinking water plays a vital role in replenishing our reserves. Water is essential for a wide range of body functions. It rehydrates our bodies, flushes out waste products through the kidneys, supports digestion of food and absorption of nutrients, as well as regulating body temperature.

Besides being vital for the proper functioning of our systems, water, unlike sweet drinks, contains no calories and is beneficial for tooth health because it rinses away sugars and acids that might attack it. So it is the perfect liquid accompaniment to a healthy, real-food diet.

The easiest time to start children drinking straight water is from the time they are weaned. Small babies have no other point of comparison apart from milk. If they become accustomed to drinking plain water (boiled and cooled) at this stage, they will just grow up taking it for granted.

Making that transition isn't always easy. When we first try to wean them, many babies resist at first any liquid other than the milk to which they have become accustomed. They may seem to reject water when they first try it and we, in turn, may assume that straight water isn't a success and feel tempted to add a slug of 'baby juice' or diluted fruit juice to make it more palatable. When we do this, we are simply anticipating a resistance that may not really be there, often because we too have been inculcated with the idea that children need to be given sweet liquid.

Instead, if we stick to our guns and keep on offering them straight water, we will usually find that they do come to accept it. And if we can achieve that, we will be making a really important contribution towards helping them to develop a good, natural, real-food palate.

Obviously, the earlier you start with water as a child's main drink, the easier and the better. But children of any age can be converted slowly by gradually diluting further and further the amount of 'squash' or 'drink' in every glass of water you give them.

In the longer run, if you progressively stop keeping drinks in the house such as canned fizzy drinks that you really don't want children to have, as described on pages 81–5, they will slowly but surely end up drinking more straight water. One of the great things about water is that when children are really thirsty, they will drink substantial amounts without questioning it. What we need to do is work on them to see water not just as a one-off thirst quencher but as their regular 'default' drink.

There are, however, some issues to think about if we do succeed in establishing water as the standard drink. The first is what type of water. The obvious candidate for most people is **tap water**. However, there are some concerns about its quality. In theory it is tested by the local water authority or company. Official sources say that 99 per cent of UK tap water meets European standards, but according to some environmentalists water purity statistics are massaged by averaging out test results. These cover up the fact that in a certain area, at a certain time, water may not be up to standard. Substandard water could, for example, be carrying agricultural and industrial pollution from pesticides or heavy metals, or could be contaminated by food poisoning bacteria.

For people who are particularly concerned about the quality of water they give their children, one obvious solution is to invest in a **water filter**. Filters vary enormously in price and you basically get what you pay for. Cheap, simple filters that are not installed into the water supply may be effective in removing only some contaminants and not others and their filters need to be changed regularly or they can cause contamination themselves. More sophisticated filter systems cost a lot more and need to be installed and maintained by a specialist company. However, they are capable of purifying tap water in a more comprehensive way.

Whatever reservations there may be about the quality of tap water, this is not a reason for offering children a typical children's drink such as squash instead. All of these drinks contain tap water as a main constituent anyway, so there's no avoiding it. What's more, there is no reason to think that the quality of tap water in drinks would be any better than what comes out of your tap. In addition they contain a lot of sugar, sweeteners and additives which need to be avoided. (For more information about these see pages 3–9, The Modern 'Children's Diet'.)

For people who are concerned about the quality of tap water, **bottled natural mineral water** is one alternative. Unlike tap water, which needs to be purified before it conforms to drinking-water standards, natural mineral water must by law be 'free of all traces of pollution' without undergoing any purification whatsoever. One other attractive point of mineral water is that it can be bought in sparkling form, which can appeal to children as an alternative to a sweet fizzy drink. (For the potential of sparkling mineral water in children's drinks see pages 251–8, Ten Good Drinks.)

But there are two large objections to natural mineral water as a standard children's drink. The first is cost. It has been calculated that bottled water costs 700 times more than tap. Even allowing for paying back the one-off cost of installing the most high-tech, elaborate water-filter system in your home, bottled water is vastly more expensive than straight tap or purified tap water. The second is inconvenience. Bottled water is heavy and cumbersome to buy in any quantity and the bottles are a drag to dispose of.

The biggest waste of money on the bottled-water front is **spring water**. Unlike natural mineral water, which matches the purity of tap water without any purification, the title 'spring water' can refer to any water that bubbles up out of the ground which conforms to minimum bacteriological standards. So bottled spring water is no solution for water-quality-conscious households.

Nowadays flavoured bottled waters are being heavily marketed and may appeal to parents as a 'healthy' alternative to cola and other fizzy drinks. This impression is totally misleading because these bottled waters are loaded with either sugar in one form or another or artificial sweeteners, chemical flavourings and preservatives. (For more detail, see pages 3–9, The Modern 'Children's Diet'.)

Many parents who are concerned about what their children eat and drink see **fruit juice** as a healthy alternative to cola, lemonade and other fizzy drinks. Unlike the typical children's fizzy drink, which ought to be labelled as 'containing no real or beneficial anything', fruit juice can be a good way to pass on to children some of the nutritional benefits of fruit: namely vitamins and associated micro-nutrients which are essential for good health.

However, there are some problems associated with fruit juice of all types which mean that they are not good substitutes for water as a standard children's drink. The first is that fruit juice contains sugars which, although they are naturally occurring, are of the kind that erode the surface enamel of teeth. The second is that they also contain natural fruit acids (citric and phosphoric acid), which have the same effect.

So the benefits of fruit juice need to weighed up carefully against the disadvantages. Fruit juice can provide useful vitamins but it is also bad for the teeth. How can we interpret this?

The common-sense approach is to see fruit juice as a useful source of vitamins but not to allow it to become a child's standard drink as an alternative to water. In other words, a fruit juice once a day might be a good way of improving a child's intake of nutrients from plant sources, but because of its high sugar/high acid properties, it is not a good idea to let a child consume it in bulk, as we might encourage water.

The tooth-rotting characteristics of fruit juices are particularly relevant to babies and infants, who may be sucking on drinks in bottles or feeder cups for long periods throughout the day. This means that their still-developing teeth may be coated for hours at a time in fruit acid and sugar. So for these younger children fruit juice is not recommended and, if it is given, should be heavily watered down to dilute the sugar and acid.

For older children, who generally consume a drink quickly and quite often eat something along with it which would neutralise the sugar and acid, fruit juice is less of a problem. It provides vitamins and represents an infinitely healthier alternative to a typical children's fizzy drink such as cola. However, the general point remains that, for children of any age, fruit juice is not a good alternative to water.

For parents who do want to give their children fruit juice because of the vitamin content, it is important to bear in mind that the term 'fruit juice' is used very loosely to cover a huge range of drinks that vary massively. Drinks manufacturers often use the health-giving connotations of fruit to endow their products with a positive image that is not really deserved. The table that follows shows the best and the worst in the fruit-juice category.

Fruit juice from best to worst

DRINK	GOOD POINTS	BAD POINTS	VERDICT
Home-squeezed or pressed fruit juice which contains most of the pith and pulp of the fruit and is drunk right away.	Contains all the useful vitamins and the micro-nutrients found in fruit, especially vitamin C. No additives of any kind.	Natural sugars and acids attack tooth enamel.	A very good source of vitamins for older children on a once-a-day basis but it is a good idea to rinse the mouth with water or eat a neutral food after. Dilute for younger children.
Freshly squeezed or pressed juice bought outside home, sold refrigerated with a long shelf life.	As above, but some of the vitamins will have been destroyed in storage and more of the nutritious pith and pulp removed in juicing.	As above.	As above but not quite such a good source of vitamins.

DRINK	GOOD POINTS	BAD POINTS	VERDICT
100% un-sweetened fruit juice.	Contains some vitamins. No chemical additives.	Natural sugars and acids attack tooth enamel. Has been pasteur-ised, which destroys some vitamins. May legally have up to 15 grams of sugar per litre added, even though this is not stated on the label.	A reasonable source of vitamins.
Sweetened fruit juice.	Contains some vitamins. No chemical additives.	As above except that 50–100 grams of sugar per litre can be added.	Heavy pre-sence of natu-ral and added sugar makes this a bad choice.

DRINK	GOOD POINTS	BAD POINTS	VERDICT
Fruit nectars.	Contain a minimum of 25% fruit pulp, which does provide some useful vitamins.	Natural sugars and acids attack tooth enamel. Has been pasteurised, which destroys some vitamins. Heavy on fruits that are very sweet naturally, such as mango. May contain up to 20% added sugar.	Small amount of fruit pulp plus a heavy presence of natural and added sugar makes this a bad choice.
Fruit drinks.	Contain a minimum 5% fruit juice, which does provide a limited amount of vitamins.	Full of added sugar and/or sweeteners, colourings, preservatives and other chemical additives.	Any benefits from inclusion of 5% juice are dwarfed by disadvantages of other ingredients. Prominent 'added vitamins' do not make this a healthy drink.

DRINK	GOOD POINTS	BAD POINTS	VERDICT
Fruit-flavour drink.	None.	Contains no fruit juice. Full of added sugar and/or sweeteners, colourings, preservatives and flavourings.	No good points whatsoever. Prominent 'added vitamins' do not make this a healthy drink.

Milk of any type – cow's, goat's, sheep's, soya – has its place in children's diets as a good source of protein, vitamins and minerals – especially calcium, which is essential for healthy teeth and bones. But because of the nutrients it offers and the calories they represent, we need to think of milk not as a drink but as a food. In other words, milk is not a suitable substitute for water, so it is a bad idea to allow children to get into the habit of quenching their thirst with milk or seeing milk as their regular drink. The same applies to milk shakes, cocoa, hot chocolate and malted drinks.

Government nutritional advice recommends that children under two are given full-fat milk. After the age of two, it is felt that, provided they get enough calcium from other foods, semi-skimmed milk is better because although it has fewer vitamins than full-fat milk it also has less fat. It is questionable, however, whether we should get too concerned about avoiding fat in natural foods such as milk, when we are talking about children and teenagers. Teenage girls in particular often boycott milk, thinking it is bad for them because it contains fat, and they end up not getting enough calcium for good health. Rather than run the risk of confusing healthy food with diet food in children's minds, an alternative common-sense approach is to concentrate on feeding children natural, unprocessed food. If our children aren't eating routine fatty junk foods such as crisps, chips and breaded nuggets, then we don't need to get too worried about the fat in whole unprocessed foods, such as milk.

When parents do manage to establish the fundamental principle that water is the standard children's drink it is reasonable to expect that children, especially older ones, will crave some sophistication and variation from straight, unadorned water. One useful area to explore, however unlikely it may seem, is **herbal and fruit teas**. These are quite commonly drunk by babies and children on the Continent though they are still largely seen as adult drinks in the UK. Not to be confused with herbal 'drinks' aimed at babies, which generally contain large amounts of sugar or other disguised sweetener, herbal and fruit teas are straight infusions, usually in teabag form but sometimes loose.

From a parent's point of view, they represent a good way of getting a child to drink more water, since they contain no calories and no sugars or sweeteners of any kind. If children get the chance to taste them, they often appeal because of the sheer variety of flavours and tastes on offer, the exotic names (Tranquillity, Orange Dazzler, Winter Warmer), the pronounced flavours and, last but not least, the eye-catching packaging. Although some fruit-flavour teas do contain rather aggressive synthetic flavourings (which must be declared on the packet as 'flavouring'), most teas in the herbal range contain only natural ingredients.

There is also considerable scope for interesting children in regular teas too, with obvious candidates including fragrant Chinese teas such as jasmine and oolong, refreshing Japanese green tea and other weak infusions of non-tannic black tea such as Earl Grey. As they become teenagers, straight tea becomes more attractive.

From the time that a child can hold a cup of warm liquid safely without spilling it, parents can offer lukewarm teas of most kinds. Older children can be encouraged to experiment with them at will as soon as they are able to boil a kettle and pour out the water safely.

There will be occasions when children expect more flavourful, less everyday drinks than water or even a herbal tea. Turn to pages 251–8, Ten Good Drinks, for ideas about healthier occasional drinks that are attractive to children and can be served as an alternative to a junky fizzy drink such as cola.

HEALTHIER LOOK-ALIKE ALTERNATIVES TO COMMON 'CHILDREN'S FOODS'

If we want our children to learn to like real food, then we have to get them used to it, using the strategies outlined earlier in this section. But it would be unrealistic not to recognise that children love the look of common children's foods – most of which are either heavily processed versions of otherwise good food (such as yogurt) or just out-and-out junk (such as colas). Reluctantly, we have to accept too that they often like the instant 'feel-good' taste of foods containing that familiar fat-sugar-salt trio.

Obviously, our long-term tactic is to help them develop a palate that prefers natural, good food to the limited modern 'children's food' repertoire. But our problem is that if we never let them have any of the much-hyped junk they think they want, then it comes over as tantalising forbidden fruit. They may resent never having it like their friends do and end up feeling deprived. How can we make concessions to their point of view without appearing inconsistent or giving them mixed messages?

A practical and workable solution is sometimes to give them foods that have the *look* of the foods they want but are actually a lot better. This way, we don't appear too rigid and can make concessions without undermining our principles in any significant way.

Here are ideas for better look-alike alternatives to the foods children commonly eat. Though some that meet that bill can be found in supermarkets, don't overlook smaller wholefood shops, which these days carry a surprisingly big range of attractively packaged foods that can appeal to children.

Savoury food look-alikes

CRISPS, EXTRUDED SNACKS AND CRUNCHY THINGS

Be sceptical about anything in this category that purports to be low or lower fat. These claims are not set by law and one brand's low fat can be higher in fat than another brand's regular crisps/snacks. Concentrate instead on finding ones that contain a very short list of ingredients (potatoes or corn, vegetable oil, salt) and only natural (as opposed to chemical) seasonings. Avoid those that contain chemical preservatives and artificial or other sweeteners.

There are several variations on this theme for which to look out. Wholefood shops and some delicatessens sell crisps where the skin has been left on the potato, making them more nutritious. They also stock some less fatty brands of tortilla and blue corn chips, puffy snacks that contain only ground corn, peanut butter, oil and salt, chickpea snacks (chickpea flour, oil, spices) and Bombay mix.

Italian grissini (breadsticks) keep many children happy and the classic two-in-a-pack wrapping appeals to them. For a more nutritious version, go for those containing sesame or poppy seeds.

Another category of crunchy to try out is the rice cracker in its many proliferating forms. The basic puffed-rice cracker can be quite good for babies and toddlers who don't know anything else, but older children may find it boring. These days you can buy them in every form from mini-snacks to crackers and crispbreads. Some offer the sweet-salt appeal of conventional crisps and snacks but in a healthier form, using seasoning and flavouring ingredients such as brown rice syrup, plum paste, rice wine, sea salt and soy sauce. They also often contain discreet amounts of positively beneficial ingredients such as sesame seeds or seaweed flakes. Worth trying out, these often go down surprisingly well.

RECONSTITUTED MEAT OR FISH PRODUCTS (BURGERS, KIEVS, SAUSAGES, FISH FINGERS)

Boycott any versions that are specially targeted at children – these are likely to be the poorest quality around and the most over-processed.

Making a home-made beefburger is dead simple (just mix together lean minced beef and seasoning) and you will control what is in it. Buy the most expensive sausages you can afford – in this category, you get what you pay for, and they will have a higher meat content and fewer, if any, additives. Instead of buying Kievs or fish fingers, try children out on whole chicken breast or fish fillet. Thread it on to sticks for additional appeal. Alternatively dip fillets in flour, egg and home-made breadcrumbs or serve fillets in crumbed ready-made form.

CHIPS

Rather than routinely serving oven chips or other pre-cut, pre-cooked chips, make fat home-made chips from floury potatoes once in a while as a big treat (or try the recipe for potato wedges in a paper bag on pages 273–4).

YEAST EXTRACT

A very salty spread so, if they must have it, go for versions that have no chemical additives such as caramel. Ready-made teriyaki sauce (from Chinese supermarkets or wholefood shops) can be spread thinly on bread. Try out black or green olive paste and pestos of various types, thinned down with extra oil.

PIZZA

Home-made pizza is blissful and you can use the best ingredients, but if you have to rely on bought versions, read the label very closely – they do differ. Buy only those that list ingredients you would use at home, not items like soya flour, fatty acids, modified starch, lemon juice concentrate and citric acid: these are signs of over-processing. Add your own topping ingredients (better cheese, roasted vegetables, good-quality air-dried ham or bacon) to the basic boring bought pizza to make it more interesting and add some useful nutrients to the carbohydrate stodge.

Sweet food look-alikes

SWEET BREAKFAST CEREALS

Root around in your local wholefood shop for healthier versions of traditional puffed-rice and cornflake-type cereals. These days there is a big choice, often featuring more unusual, nutritious grains (such as spelt, flax, amaranth, buckwheat, quinoa, kamut) alongside the more familiar ones like rice and corn. These are often in gimmicky packaging of the kind that appeals to children. Such cereals are less refined and therefore more nutritious than their conventional look-alikes. They also tend to use sweeteners such as unrefined cane sugar, honey or maple syrup, which are by and large preferable because they have some slight nutritional advantages over straight white sugar. Don't assume, though, that because they are in a wholefood shop they are healthy. Taste them to see for yourself how sweet they actually are.

If children are tempted by crunchy, granola-type cereals, which are usually high in fat and sugar, try them on an unsweetened muesli with sweet fresh fruits added. Wholefood shops generally carry a wide range. Rather than buying ready-made muesli, whose particular composition and ratio of fruit to nuts, grains to seeds and so on may not appeal, try out the easy recipe for home-made muesli on pages 280–81 and vary it according to individual preferences.

If you are shopping in a more limited supermarket with the usual standard cereal range, boycott 'frosted' or chocolate cereals that are fairly obviously stuck together with sugar and those with sweet ingredients such as chocolate polka dots or sugared nuts. As a compromise, go for the more old-fashioned, traditional cereals, which are generally less sugary and fatty, such as Weetabix and cornflakes, or for Shredded Wheat, which is sugar-free.

CHOCOLATE-BASED SWEETS

Give them a few squares or a small bar of good-quality chocolate. A straight chocolate bar with no additions should contain only cocoa solids and cocoa butter, sugar, milk solids (milk and white chocolate only), lecithin (an emulsifier) and natural vanill*a*, not chemical vanill*in*. Children usually prefer milk or white chocolate. Good-quality milk chocolate contains around 30 per cent cocoa solids, while white chocolate should contain only cocoa butter, not the less healthy and less delicious vegetable fat. Once in a while, buy more expensive fresh cream ranges of chocolates and give everyone one as pudding.

If your children won't accept any substitute for the standard chocolate confectionery, get them used to eating it in bite-sized mini versions.

CHEWY FRUIT-FLAVOURED SWEETS

Wholefood shops stock fruit leathers – chewy strips of concentrated apple and berry pulp with no added sugar. They also have sweets similar to fruit gums, consisting of fruit purée made firm with pectin and cornstarch. These are preferable to the sugar, gelatine and additive mix of their standard counterparts.

Another variation on the chewy theme is bars that are a combination of fruit purée or concentrate and cereals. These are more nutritious and less sweet than fruit leather.

BISCUITS AND CAKES

Before you hand out biscuits or cake, think of offering instead a slightly sweet bread, such as a croissant, scone, pancake or brioche. These contain less sugar.

If you are choosing from conventional biscuits, select those that contain only the ingredients you would expect in a home-made version, such as a straightforward butter shortbread. Favour makes that show some awareness of ingredient quality – for example, ones that contain butter, oil or non-hydrogenated or fractionated vegetable fat or margarine, rather than hydrogenated vegetable fat or margarine. Hydrogenated fat is chemically hardened and is not healthy or natural. Go for raw cane sugar or honey instead of sucrose, and sea salt instead of ordinary chemical salt.

Explore all the possibilities within the cereal bar category. Some are extremely fatty and sugary and contain artificial flavourings and unnecessary chemical preservatives. Others are quite low-sugar, low- or virtually no-fat combinations on the dried fruit, nut, cereal theme. Because ingredients need only be listed by order of the quantity used, not in percentage terms, it can be hard to tell from the labels which are healthier. Try them out yourself before you give them to children and trust your own palate as to whether they seem excessively sweet or fatty.

When or if you have time, make a simple home-made cake but don't bother icing it. Encourage children to get used to plainer cakes made with good, natural ingredients. Use a little organic wholemeal flour if you can in recipes calling for refined white flour. Err towards cakes such as carrot cake, banana bread, apple cake, teabreads or fresh fruit muffins, which include ingredients such as fruit or nuts that improve the nutritional value of the basic carbohydrate-fat-sugar-protein mix.

YOGURTS AND FROMAGE FRAIS

Most of the brands that are targeted at children tend to be highly adulterated, so read the labels carefully. They are usually extremely sweet, containing sugar in various forms and often also artificial sweeteners, thickeners (gelatine, modified starch, carob and guar gum, pectin, carrageenan), preservatives, artificial flavours and colours.

Go for varieties flavoured with fruit purée, sugar and natural flavouring only. If children are used to very sweet yogurts or fromage frais, choose ones that contain more naturally sweet ingredients such as mango juice.

Try them out on creamy Greek yogurt and allow them to add their own sweet additions such as maple syrup, honey, grated chocolate or unrefined raw cane sugar. Even with these add-ons, they will probably be less sweet than the standard children's equivalents and will have a much truer, more natural taste.

ICE CREAM

Ice creams targeted at children are generally extremely synthetic combinations of milk powder, chemically hardened vegetable fat, sugars and sweeteners, emulsifiers, colourings, flavourings, acidity regulators, all whipped up with lots of air. They tend to contain very little of anything that is beneficial.

Go for less fatty frozen yogurt or 'premium' ice creams, which contain only natural ingredients – cream, milk, sugar – plus natural flavouring, fruits and nuts.

LOLLIPOPS

These are generally high in sugar and additives. You can buy wooden sticks and lolly moulds and freeze fruit juice or fruit purée in them at home for a much more nutritious alternative.

PART THREE

....

THE GENTLE ART OF PERSUASION

DEALING WITH CHILDREN WHO SAY NO

Suppose we try to follow the approach described in Part Two, 'Breaking the Mould at Home'. This outlines the fundamentals of feeding children well, which are:

- Feeding them from the same supply of food as adults – one household food supply, not two

- Trying to eat together as much as possible

- Not keeping food in the house that you don't want children to eat

- Presenting children with as wide a range of food as possible

- Anticipating and catering for food demands by getting children into a rhythm of eating which revolves around regular mealtimes and food 'staging posts' throughout the day.

This common-sense approach revolves around placing a series of expectations on children that they will eat well and, when adults are consistent in this approach, most children will go along with it most of the time.

That's all very well, but there will still be times when children say no and there are some children who tend to do that quite a lot. We, in turn, may feel like blowing a fuse. At the very least it will be disheartening and it can seem that we have lost any good-food battle with them. So we give up reluctantly and accept that they are just going to eat the same restricted repertoire of junk on which so many other children seem to survive.

But such pessimism isn't justified. Because we live in a culture where the stereotype of the 'picky eater' looms large, we hear many negative stories about children with iron wills and devastatingly limited palates. So much so that many adults are inclined to believe that feeding children is bound to be dispiriting and difficult. The truth is that, over time and with a little bit of commitment, most children can end up eating well if the adults who look after them are so minded.

The way to achieve this is to try to develop a relaxed approach which operates to a clear set of goals but is not rigid. In other words, we need to expect setbacks. It can be disappointing and frustrating when children reject a dish we really hope that they will eat. It is toughest when they are still at the weaning stage, when that dish is not just what everyone else is eating but something we have prepared especially for them. But the art is not to be disheartened and plunged into gloomy fatalism – the next day we may have a victory. We don't need to get worried about the odd setback as long as we can see that, over time, we are moving broadly in the right direction. That means emphasising our successes and not getting hung up on the failures. So we go out of our way to avoid fights over food and accommodate children's preferences as long as these aren't totally counter to our general real-food policy.

However intransigent children can appear, their objections to a particular food or category of food are not always as all-embracing as they may seem. So when we meet with opposition, we don't need to interpret this as evidence of our failure and give in to 'picky eater' fatalism, but should see it as a predictable response, one that needn't defeat our long-term real-food objectives.

Provided, that is, we can take a deep breath and try to deal with these potential conflicts of will in an effective and constructive way. Where do we begin? The chapters that follow explain how to go about it.

AVOIDING THE SAME OLD MISTAKES

Remember the panic and horror of being made to swallow food that you disliked as a child, often at school but sometimes at home? If so, you'll instantly appreciate that forcing children to eat is pointless, because as well as making the business of eating unpleasant, it establishes food as a territory for fights between adults and children. Stand-offs that revolve round, *'You're not leaving the table until you eat . . .'* and so on are a total waste of time as well as being dangerous. It's all likely to end in tears and uncontrolled eruptions of rage and frustration which achieve nothing. This underlines one cardinal principle: it is entirely wrong and totally counterproductive ever to force children to eat something they don't like.

Fair enough, but what else does that leave us with? Classic bribery techniques of the *'If you don't eat that, you won't get to watch that programme you love/play on your bike'* type are equally ineffective. These give children the message that eating good food is a drag while the other activities are fun – the stick-and-carrot approach. That's a deeply confusing message to transmit, because in the long run we want children to equate food with pleasure, not penance.

That old scam of trading off the nasty food (for nasty, read savoury, real and healthy) against the nice food (for nice, read sweet and junky) is even wider of the mark. Think of the subtext children pick up when we say things like, *'If you want the ice cream, you must eat up the carrots.'* Yet again, we are effectively telling children that some food is horrible and is to be tolerated only in order to get the pleasurable stuff. Yet somehow we expect them to turn into adults who realise spontaneously that the food they have been made to eat is actually nice. But why should they, when it conjures up only images of eating under sufferance?

By adopting any of these tactics, adults hand children a weapon to do battle with them and, once they realise it works, the children won't hesitate to use it.

Head-on rows and confrontation are a total waste of time too. Many children know that if they refuse to eat for some time, adults will eventually give in. That is not a great precedent to set because they get the idea that adults don't really mean what they say and so a lot of it can be ignored.

Toddlers especially can exhibit spectacular obstinacy and simply won't give in. What's more, they will use any melodramatic tactic, from deliberately falling off their chairs and bursting into tears to pretending to throw up at the table, to wriggle off the hook. Adults almost invariably lose their cool in these circumstances and display a fit of rage which they regret afterwards. In the highly unlikely event that we do succeed in making children eat, we have turned mealtimes into volatile, adversarial occasions where children see themselves as being forced to eat things they hate. That is the opposite of the cooperative relationship we need to foster in them.

If we want to encourage children to eat well, we need to avoid that confrontational battle of wills and take the heat out of mealtimes. The next chapter explains how to achieve that.

SETTING UP A COOPERATIVE FOOD RELATIONSHIP

Okay, so we want to motivate children to eat in a positive way. But how do we do this? We can start by accepting that children, just like adults, have the right to express *reasonable* food preferences. That doesn't mean that they can veto every food that is placed before them, however, just that there exists a cooperative relationship between themselves and adults when it comes to food.

This cooperative relationship works on the shared understanding that the adults will generally offer children appetising and tempting food so that it is reasonable to expect them to eat it. Because the children see that adults respect and accommodate their tastes most of the time, they want to participate in that relationship by eating most of what's on offer.

However, if a cooperative food relationship is going to be more than adult wishful thinking, it is obvious that children must be given an opportunity to define their side of the contract initially. They must feel that their views have been respected. We can demonstrate this respect, hopefully enough to satisfy them, by agreeing with them that there are certain foods they are allowed not to like – and therefore not to eat – no matter how galling this may be for us.

One simple way to start is by drawing up a jointly agreed list of foods that are off-limits. A child might be allowed to nominate, say, half a dozen 'hated' foods. It may depress us to see foods on that list that we think the children should like, but there will always be viable alternatives to offer, so all is not lost. A child's hate list might be tomatoes, peppers, poached egg, chickpeas, herring, marmalade. These then become the foods that the child will not be expected to eat, at least for the time being.

Most children, of course, will have a much greater number of foods they don't fancy and view with extreme suspicion. But by establishing that hate list, this larger list by contrast represents foods about which, implicitly at least, children have agreed to keep an open mind. Already, that's a progression from a giant, ill-defined mass of disliked foods.

The hate list is, of course, just a fraudulent adult device to convince children that they have been consulted about their preferences and that these have been taken on board, but it can work. However, the list has to contain specific items, not entire categories of food. So while it is reasonable for children to put an item like tomatoes on the hate list, they cannot put *all* vegetables there. With the exception of meat and fish for children who are vegetarians, no whole category of food should appear on the list.

REFINING OBJECTIONS TO FOOD

Many children present huge blanket objections to food. Adults react in two main ways. First, with an equally blanket insistence that children must eat the food in question, leading to unproductive fights. Second, by giving in and collaborating in the process of allowing children to restrict drastically what they eat.

If adults really want to encourage children to eat better and more widely, the challenge when presented with food objections is to compromise by refining that objection into a more acceptable, less comprehensive form. This means restricting its scope.

Here are some practical examples of how to do this:

CHILD	ADULT
'I can't eat tomatoes.'	*'But you like them when they are cooked/raw and you liked the baby cherry ones, didn't you?'*
'I can't eat broccoli, it's chewy.'	*'All right, leave the stem and eat the "tree" bit.'*
'Don't like green bits.'	*'That's coriander but you liked parsley last week.'*
'I hate cheese.'	*'But you like Parmesan, don't you?'*
'It's got peppers in it.'	*'I'll pick them out for you.'*
'I can't cut it.'	*'Then eat it with your fingers.'*
'This crust is too scratchy.'	*'Then soften it in your soup/sauce.'*

The point of these adult 'spins' on children's objections is to try to salvage a little bit of something positive out of every 'don't like/ won't eat' statement.

The following example shows how even a blanket refusal can be turned into a limited success.

JAMIE WON'T EAT SOUP

It's a drag if Jamie won't eat soup because, apart from being too wide a category of food to dislike, soup is a good way to get him to eat vegetables. So let's establish what it is about the soup that causes displeasure. Perhaps it's the fact that he has to eat it with a spoon and that is more difficult than fingers. So let him drink it from the bowl. Table etiquette is less important than encouraging eating.

Maybe he doesn't like soup with bits in it (broths, minestrone and so on). Don't let this be a problem. Let him eat the liquid part and leave the bits. Next time, liquidise the soup and give it a different 'non-soup' name, vichyssoise for example. He might love it.

Experiment with other flavours of soup. Jamie may hate spinach soup because it's green but love tomato because it's red. If he gets hooked on liquidised tomato soup and won't consider anything else, surreptitiously blend in some herbs to introduce the idea of different flavours in his favourite red soup. Then gradually purée it less thoroughly to leave more texture, eventually reintroducing the dreaded 'bits' now he likes the idea of that soup.

The short-term goal is to get Jamie eating soup of some description, however limited, and to weaken the 'no soup' veto. The long-term aim is to broaden out the range of soups he will consider.

SERVING UP PRAISE BY THE BUCKETLOAD

Sometimes we're so uptight about what our children will or won't eat that we brace ourselves for rejections and forget about motivating them by using simple praise and encouragement. But even children with very limited, highly conservative eating habits can end up eating better if we employ these tactics.

'Well done, you ate all your scrambled egg.'

'That's brilliant, you tried cheese and that's the first time you ever tried it.'

'Now you know you like pineapple after all, clever you.'

'You ate both your tuna sandwiches today, what a good girl.'

'You remembered your apple, well done.'

These are all ways of heaping on the praise and stressing the positive, and children adore that. All children have some food they like to eat that is actually quite wholesome and reasonably healthy. So pick this out and milk it for all it's worth, because it's important that even the most limited eaters don't see themselves as such. Even if, in reality, the repertoire of food some children eat is far too small, it's essential to focus on the good things they do eat.

Above all, it's important never to let children get the idea that adults view them as difficult or 'picky' eaters. Even if, in reality, their food horizons are worryingly restricted, it doesn't make our job any easier if we let them see themselves that way. In exasperation, often in earshot of children, adults let off steam by saying things like:

'He never eats anything. That child's impossible. He won't eat any-thing I give him.'

'She's so choosy. She's a really picky eater.'

This only reinforces food-rejecting instincts in children. They take it on board to such an extent that they may even go around saying quite proudly, '*I don't eat that, I'm a picky eater.*' The irony is that the adults' negative verdict on their eating preferences actually becomes a way of justifying them.

Instead, when tempted to come out with a negative comment we can bite it back, try hard not to be downhearted, pick out one positive liking or preference to stress and heap on the praise. Ignore that much bigger list of dislikes for the time being.

It is vital to focus on the positive, even if it is just a glimmer of hope in what seems like an overwhelmingly futile landscape. We adults can get understandably very anxious about feeding children, and often we can fall into the trap of seeing their tastes as impossibly restrictive. But in fact, if we stopped to think, we might see that they actually eat a lot more that's good and healthy than we realise.

It is not uncommon, for example, for children to be generally anti-vegetables but simultaneously quite keen on several fruits. Although long-term we will want to break down that opposition to vegetables, we can make ourselves feel better by thinking about that good fruit.

One way to keep thinking positively is to draw up a list of all the real, good foods that a child seems to like. It is often longer than we imagined, even if it is shorter than we would have hoped for. Rather than getting hung up on what they won't eat, we need to focus on what they will.

MAKING MEALTIMES WORK

As discussed in 'Eating Together and Why It Matters' (pages 74–7), an important first step towards getting children to develop more varied eating habits is to include them in communal eating, not to cater for them separately from a different repertoire of 'children's food'. But when we take this step, it is important that children find the experience positive. They need to know from experience that they will usually find something on the menu that they like to eat.

This may mean that we adults have to make a few acceptable compromises. Although ultimately we want to produce children who enjoy real food and have reasonably sophisticated tastes, it will take even the most adventurous children some time to achieve that, depending on their individual temperament and age.

Although tales of the enterprising 'gourmet child' who loved black olives while still in nappies are almost as ubiquitous as those of the infamous 'picky eater', few children appreciate straight off being served uncompromisingly adult food with no concessions made to their tastebuds. Extremely spicy or rich food, elaborate food where ingredients have been transformed out of their natural state, dishes where lots of different ingredients have been combined – these are all categories of food that adults routinely eat but are problematic for children. (They are discussed more in Good Food That Children Like, on pages 96–101).

Put this uncompromisingly 'adult' food in front of children and it can all too easily seem to the child that there is nothing that they can eat or want to eat. This is totally counterproductive, because children will just refuse to cooperate at mealtimes.

So when we think about what we are going to cook, as well as building in interest for the adults, it's important to look at what's on offer from the children's point of view. There should always be one element of the meal that has sure-fire appeal, alongside the less familiar, more challenging elements. Here's an example.

A WEEKDAY COUSCOUS SUPPER

Tonight's menu is a mildly spicy tomato, vegetable and chickpea stew, served with couscous and harissa (hot chilli paste) followed by natural yogurt and fresh fruit. Couscous is a food that most children like when they've been given the chance to taste it. It's likely to be a safe bet. The vegetable stew is likely to thrill them less, especially if it contains a mixture of more unusual vegetables such as aubergine and courgette.

But we can offer the stew anyway and, if there is resistance, agree to pick out the more acceptable vegetables, say carrots. At least they are eating some vegetables. Other children may boycott the vegetables and eat the chickpeas; that's fine too. Next line of retreat is to agree to no vegetables or chickpeas and offer just the saucy liquid on the couscous – or on the side for children who don't like ingredients to mingle. In extremis, let them eat just couscous.

The harissa is going to appeal to the adults but don't assume that the children won't eat it. A few may actually like it, so much the better, but most will certainly enjoy the bravado of deliberating over whether or not they should test out this fiery food. Warn them that it's hot, of course!

For dessert, we can take the easy option of serving a mild and creamy natural yogurt rather than acidic ones or skimmed-milk versions with a more watery consistency. (This is a relatively minor concession if the alternative is a sweetened commercial yogurt.) And since natural yogurt, however creamy, is probably a less attractive proposition for children who may be used to sweet and flavoured versions, we can make it more appealing by serving small, seedless grapes to mix in or some other cut-up fresh fruit. Cut-up, ready-prepared fruit is much more user-friendly for children than untouched whole fruit.

For the relatively small number of children who don't like fresh fruit, a good compromise might be a small teaspoon of runny honey or maple syrup. These are sweet additions but in small quantities aren't a problem if they encourage children to eat the yogurt.

The knack with this meal, as with every other communal meal we might consider, is choosing a menu that has something in it for everyone. Of course, this isn't always straightforward. All adults who cook regularly have fallow periods when it comes to thinking about what everyone is going to eat that night. The additional complication of children with preferences to be accommodated can seem like the last straw. We end up not being able to think of anything at all.

If you need to be reminded of the surprisingly wide categories of food that large numbers of both adults and children might like, turn to Good Food That Children Like (pages 96–101). For specific ideas for main courses that might prove popular with everyone in your house, irrespective of age, turn to Ten Main Courses That Both Adults and Children Like (pages 239–50).

THE SCOPE FOR INSISTENCE

While it is wrong to force a child to eat or to let food become a battle of wills, with all but the most obdurate children it is usually worth trying a little insistence, provided that you have already attempted to accommodate and refine their objections as described in the previous few chapters.

The success of insisting depends on just how deeply entrenched the objection is. Some children may positively dislike what's before them and have decided actively that they don't want to eat it. Others are just not that interested, not concentrating or in a bad mood. This latter category can be coaxed and encouraged into eating with a little judicious insistence from adults. There are two quite effective ways to do that. First, we can ask children to 'try' food. 'Trying' food is different from agreeing to eat it and so children know that they aren't giving in so much when they agree only to 'try' something. Adults can establish that 'trying' means, say, three mouthfuls. Some children may actually find they like the food in question and eat it, but most will probably insist that they still hate it. But at least they have tried it. Three mouthfuls is better than no mouthfuls.

The second approach is to insist that the child can't leave everything on the plate and must at least eat some of it, as follows:

'You don't like the fish? Then eat the green beans. Don't like the green beans? Well, you need to eat three of them if you are going to leave the fish.' 'Eat two more spoonfuls of yogurt and then you're finished.'

These are all ways of insisting which build in a compromise and seem reasonable to children. When their objection is not that strong, tactics of this type can work well. They also let the child see that blanket 'don't like/won't eat' statements won't necessarily be accepted and that some concession on their part might be called for.

Gentle insistence is fine and can get good results but there are limits. We need to back down when positions seem to be hardening and it looks like turning into an unwinnable stand-off.

Another useful tactic is the pragmatic approach of simply not offering any alternative. It is important for children to realise quite early on that if they don't eat what everyone else is eating, there are no substitutes. Basically what's on the menu is it – that's your lot.

Some adults anticipate that children won't like something and keep backups on hand on a 'better-they-eat-something-rather-than nothing basis'. However, relatively few Western children are living at the threshold of starvation or food deficiency and it is rarely vital that they must eat at any given point in a particular day. The bigger worry is that once children realise that if they reject the main household meal they will be offered 'children's' alternatives, then adults will be fighting a losing battle. It's highly likely that children will continue to refuse the main meal and expect to be catered for separately all the time. So once in a while, if children refuse to eat their meal then it doesn't really matter. You may worry that they are going to starve but, of course, they won't.

While children should never be forced to eat something they don't like, they need to learn that if they don't eat what's on offer, there won't be anything else, except perhaps a piece of bread or some fruit from the fruit bowl. They will soon see that if they don't go with the flow, no one is going to put any energy into catering for them separately. It's amazing how that realisation makes them more generally amenable to eating whatever is on offer.

GIVING IN GRACEFULLY BUT . . .

There are times when, despite all our best efforts, we find that children just won't be brought around to what we would like them to eat. Quite often these 'brick wall' experiences happen on days when we later recognise that the child was not on form, tired, coming down with some illness, or just in a bad mood.

Rather than being discouraged, we need to learn to give in gracefully, which means, above all, not pressing the food or making a big issue out of it. On another occasion, when the child is in good form, we might get a much more positive reaction. It's the old motto of 'If at first you don't succeed, try, try and try again.'

One way to retreat from a potential stand-off over food rejection is to accept the child's wishes, all the time leaving open the door to restarting that particular debate in the future: *'You didn't like that today but you might like it next week, mightn't you?'* or *'You don't like it now but you will do when you're a big girl, won't you?'* or *'Next time we'll leave out the lemon, won't we?'* These are all statements that indicate to children that today's objection, although respected, is just temporary, and that they are expected to keep an open mind about the food in question. In other words, as fast as children try to close down food options, we can do our best to keep them open – at least theoretically. This way we don't compound children's objections to a specific food on one occasion by letting this food become a huge no-go category, set down in tablets of stone. Children's stated food preferences change all the time so, apart from the agreed 'hate list', we don't want to collaborate in writing off any foods in perpetuity.

Here's one example of how children can surprise us.

LIAM AND CHEESE

Liam's parents like to eat real farmhouse cheese which is full-flavoured and characterful. Thinking that the mature flavours and pungent smells might be too much for Liam, his mother has selected a medium farmhouse Cheddar for his packed-lunch sandwiches, assuming that this is the one most likely to please him. Liam, however, brings back the sandwiches uneaten, saying that he doesn't like the Cheddar. He wants his parents to buy some processed cheese that he has seen advertised on television or a rubbery plastic cheese that he tasted outside the house. They are disappointed that they can't get Liam to eat 'proper' cheese but agree to buy the cheese he asks for as they don't see any alternative. One day, his mother runs out of the cheese he likes and has no choice but to fill his sandwiches with a full-flavoured and smelly Irish farmhouse cheese that he has never tasted. Surprise, surprise, he eats it and reports that, although he doesn't like this sort of cheese usually, this one made a change and it had a nice flavour.

When Liam first rejected the real farmhouse Cheddar, Liam's parents assumed that this meant he didn't like all 'real' cheese. In fact, Liam just didn't like the particular Cheddar they had selected, and preferred a cheese that was *more* demanding and adventurous.

Two points are worth noting here. First, although smaller children may never seem to tire of a few foods they especially like, many older children get progressively bored with eating the same ingredients. This makes them more open to new or reintroduced familiar ingredients than many adults might assume. Second, adults have a tendency to exaggerate and generalise children's food dislikes. Just because children refuse a food once, we don't have to stop offering it to them on subsequent occasions. We need to remember that children have to *learn* to like foods and will gradually learn to like what they are given. They won't be able to do that, though, if we stop offering it. We may want to give some thought to presenting that ingredient in a different form the next time, but a rejection, or even several rejections, doesn't mean that we have to give up on that food entirely.

PART FOUR
....
GETTING IT RIGHT WITH BABIES AND TODDLERS

YOU KNOW BEST

Me, know best? It doesn't always feel like that, especially when you are a first-time parent trying not to get into an acute state of anxiety about feeding your baby. We lack confidence in our ability to get it right. When a first food is proffered and rejected, we can feel bad and lose faith in our ability to cope. We can become immersed in a whole clutch of 'difficulties', such as establishing which foods are healthy, what should be given at what stage in what form and, last but not least, getting the baby to accept what seems appropriate. The whole business of feeding them can leave us nothing short of desperate, dashing out on last-minute errands to stock up on the latest food or item of equipment suggested by the health visitor or the baby magazine that might help solve the problem. We can easily lose any sense of perspective and faith that we will ever get feeding right before the child becomes ill with some serious nutritional imbalance.

Baby-food manufacturers make a profitable industry out of exploiting these anxieties and our desire to feed our babies the best way we can. In 1998 the UK baby-food market was worth almost £164,000 million and growing. Manufacturers nod sagely and reassure us that sadly, yes, feeding babies is a difficult business. As described in The Rot Begins With Those Little Jars (pages 18–22), they offer their hand-holding solution: products 'specially formulated' by 'expert nutritionists'. Through devices like 'helpful' checklists, they appear to give babies something special – better, even, than we could make at home. It's easy to become dependent on these 'special products', which seem to do all the thinking about feeding babies for us, as well as the preparation.

But while most manufacturers would insist that their proprietary baby foods were simply there to help out the 'busy Mum', not to undermine home-made food, they are keen to foster this psychological dependency. When shelves are stacked high with products that claim to be perfect for small babies, the effect is often to cause parents to question their own judgement about what their baby needs. When parents are anxious and unconfident anyway, the existence of these products doesn't help. That little jar says '*First* carrots'. Does that mean our ordinary household carrots puréed aren't as good, we wonder?

With dilemmas like this, it's tempting to throw in the towel and put our baby's nutrition into the omnipresent and ever-helpful hands of food manufacturers who say with total confidence and assurance that they know exactly what they are doing.

But if we want our babies to grow into adults who enjoy a wide variety of good, natural foods, then, from weaning on, we need to get them accustomed to eating real, unprocessed food – not the commercial gloop that comes in packets and jars, however 'specially formulated' it appears to be. That means that we need to make as early a break as possible from the baby-food industry's 'advice' and believe instead that we know best.

And knowing best isn't that difficult. There are just two guiding principles:

1. We need to feed our babies on fresh food, prepared from good-quality raw materials which have been only as minimally processed as is necessary before we cook them.
2. We need to accustom them gradually to eating the same food as we ourselves eat, just in a more baby-friendly form.

Following these two principles, it is clear that the food we prepare at home will be the best food. Why?

- We can select the best-quality raw materials. (With the exception of some organic brands, most raw ingredients for baby food are sourced from the standard bulk manufacturing supply. We can do better than this.)

- It will retain more natural nutritional goodness. (Commercial brands are so highly processed that they lose much of their goodness. This is one reason synthetic vitamins are added.)

- Our baby won't be eating the cheap industrial fillers (maltodextrin, whey, emulsifiers), hidden sugars (words with 'ose' on the end such as fructose, maltose or glucose), disguised salt flavourings such as yeast extract and generous amounts of added water that characterise many baby foods, especially second-stage ones. (Why feed these when they have no nutritional benefit whatsoever?)

- The food the baby eats will taste better because it is just mushed-up real food. (Most commercial foods are made to special 'baby' recipes with a limited repertoire of bland and samey flavours.)

- Our baby will get used to the wide variety of flavours found in real unprocessed food. (This will make it easier to get them to like these when they are toddlers. Most ready-made baby foods prepare babies for the over-processed flavours of commercial 'children's food'.)

- We can vary the textures and reflect the differences that occur naturally in unprocessed food. (Ready-made baby foods in jars all have the same smooth, manufactured texture. If babies get used to this they may almost have to be weaned a second time off this homogeneous texture on to different ones.)

- It will save money. (Jars and packets of baby food are surprisingly expensive.)

- We can start off feeding them the same food we ourselves eat, only in a different form. (This saves us having to think about baby food as a separate consideration and allows us to integrate the baby's food needs into our own from almost the first months of life.)

For many anxious first-time parents especially, the application of these principles can feel like a heavy responsibility which demands a huge leap of faith. It seems easier just to buy custom-made baby foods as lots of other parents do. But as many more experienced parents can testify, the leap is worth it – babies can surprise us with the diversity of tastes and textures they enjoy. And for these babies, the transition to a wider real-food diet will be infinitely more effortless.

There are, however, just a few things you need to appreciate to help you through any potentially sticky moments when you might begin to doubt yourself:

- Weaning doesn't go on for very long; in fact it's only a matter of months which you will soon forget as your baby turns into a toddler. However horrible and fraught it may seem at the time, it won't go on for ever; feeding does get easier. Remind yourself of this when the going gets tough.

- Be cynical about feeding 'advice'. There's a lot of it about. Although some may prove useful, a lot is either beside the point, downright misleading (even from sources that ought to know) or comes from commercial sources with a product to sell. Don't be afraid to throw away other people's rule books. Just stick to the guiding principles of what foods to introduce when (see pages 151–62) and trust your judgement.

- Unless you have a baby who is premature or has some special health problems, there is nothing intrinsically complicated about feeding. It mostly boils down to common sense from the parents on the spot.

- Try to cultivate some of the confidence of typical second-time parents who have the benefit of hindsight. While their first baby was constantly under their nutritional spotlight, the next one most likely thrived on a large measure of neglect! Relax, and try to programme yourself into thinking that it will all come right in the not too distant future.

THE ESSENTIAL BLENDER

When we decide to wean our babies on food we make ourselves, there is one item we cannot live without – a blender. It will allow us to turn most foods, either singly or in combination, into an infinite variety of smooth purées which babies will eat from weaning onwards (around four months) until they progress gradually on to food in more normal forms (from about nine months). This basic item of equipment is standard kit in many homes anyway, but when a baby arrives some are more useful than others.

Food processors may be fine but unless they have a mini-bowl you may have to put more food in than you really want. Obviously you can make a lot and freeze it in yogurt pots or ice-cube trays. But babies are unpredictable and they can become bored with too much of the same thing, just like adults. Also, food processors aren't ideal for making the very smooth purées needed for first foods.

Conventional **liquidisers** are often better on smaller quantities but they still may produce more food than you want and, like food processors, add significantly to the washing up. Old-fashioned mechanical mouli-légumes can cope with small amounts but require more cleaning afterwards too.

Both food processors and blenders have one shortcoming: they turn potatoes into glue unless they are accompanied by a large amount of liquid.

Perhaps most useful is the relatively inexpensive, portable, **electric hand-held blender**, which can be used to purée almost any food, however small the quantity and whatever receptacle it is in. It allows you, for example, to take a ladleful of unseasoned soup out of the communal pot and mush it up in the baby's bowl. It is blissfully easy to clean, too.

The science of making a purée of a consistency that a baby will eat is inexact. There are no rules. All babies are different. Some actually like quite textured purées from weaning. Others still like things as smooth as possible by toddlerhood. You just have to try out various combinations and expect to win some and lose some.

The general idea is to purée some solids with just enough liquid – milk, stock, fruit juice, water – to make it palatable without losing the flavour of the solid ingredients. As a working rule of thumb, the younger the baby, the more smooth and liquid the purée should be; the older the baby, the stiffer and more bitty or textured (like normal, unliquidised food).

If you are reserving just a serving of the communal household meal for liquidising, then even minus any excessive seasoning it will still tend to taste good. But if you are making food to be liquidised into purée just for the baby, it's a good idea to taste it yourself. The recipe might sound really promising but when you sample it you might appreciate why a baby could have difficulty liking it! It's worthwhile remembering that if you don't find that baby mixture too appetising, there's a good chance your baby won't either.

All babies have individual likes and dislikes. Babycare books often promote the myth that there are certain sure-fire hits that all babies like – for example, apple purée. But there are lots of babies who don't like apple purée and won't eat it. Rather than falling back on received wisdom, just experiment until you find a few combinations that your baby seems to like.

Here are some ideas for purées to try. Vegetables and hard fruits should be streamed or boiled until soft before puréeing.

- Butternut squash

- Broccoli

- Parsley, spring onion and potato

- Spinach and pear

- Banana and finely grated fresh apple (for babies over six months)

- Carrot and leek

- Peas, courgette and mint

- Apple and plum

- Sweet potato and parsnip

- Apple and rehydrated dried apricot

- Spinach and soft-cooked rice

- Pear and blackcurrant

- Roasted red pepper, carrot and potato

- Broccoli, soft-cooked pasta and Cheddar cheese (for babies over six months)

- Turnip or swede, soft-cooked millet and onion (for babies over six months)

- Pumpkin and carrot

- Rehydrated dried apricots or prunes and soft-cooked rice or semolina (for babies over six months)

- Nectarine or peach

INTRODUCING THE WORLD OF FOOD

Okay, we decide that we can probably make quite a good job of feeding our babies without relying on commercial baby foods. And because we want our babies to grow up to like a wide variety of wholesome, unprocessed foods, we want to introduce them to as wide a range of flavours and textures from as early a stage as possible.

This approach turns conventional baby nutrition advice on its head. We won't be thinking in terms of 'foods that are suitable for babies' as a separate special category divorced from 'normal' food. That all too easily becomes the precursor to the ubiquitous separate 'children's diet' that we want to avoid. Instead, we will be looking on nearly all wholesome, unprocessed foods as suitable for babies, with just a limited number of exceptions.

There are two categories of exceptions:

- Foods served in a form with which babies cannot cope – causing them to choke.

- Foods that can cause allergies and digestive upsets when babies are given them too young, or when they are given to babies with a family history of allergies or food intolerance.

How can we get this right? We want to introduce our baby to as many flavours as possible as soon as we can, but we can't just rush in and hope for the best. How do we balance commitment to opening their food horizons with a sensible precautionary approach to their health? Actually, it isn't that complicated.

Below are the essentials you need to know about what broad categories of food can safely be given and at what stage. Also A Few Potential Problem Foods (pages 160–61) flags up the foods that most commonly provoke adverse reactions in babies, while Foods and Drinks to Avoid (pages 161–2) describes various additives that all babies are best without on health grounds. The Modern 'Children's Diet' (pages 3–9) describes the type of food that all babies, toddlers and children are much better off without. The point where we stop thinking 'baby' and start thinking 'child' may seem like a long time off. But junk-food manufacturers are knocking at infants' doors from a surprisingly early age and would be only too delighted if our baby's first finger food was a potato hoop rather than a carrot baton! So it is good to appreciate the limitations of this repertoire quite early.

Apart from these guidelines, we need to trust our common sense and good judgement. Obviously, we shouldn't introduce too many new foods too fast in the early weaning stage. But that doesn't mean going along with the traditional model which characterises babies as inherently conservative and fit only for a few bland, limited flavours. It just means that we shouldn't overdo the introduction of the new tastes and flavours and should give our baby only one new food at a time. This way, we have a better chance of both identifying any culprit food that might be causing allergy or digestive problems and picking out their food preferences.

The early weaning stage (four to six months)

At this age the baby's usual milk (i.e. breast or bottle) should still be the mainstay of their diet and it's important that their milk intake is not reduced. It's fine to try them out with a smooth purée of most sweetish fruits (not citrus) and any vegetable as long as it isn't too starchy because this is harder to digest. Starchier vegetables like corn or potatoes can be given in combination with more watery vegetables such as carrots, squash or green beans. Any vegetable-based 'adult' soup can just be liquidised, provided it hasn't been salted and was not made with salted stock or cubes.

Vegetable purées can have any spice or herb added, with the exception of chilli, cayenne and pepper. Stronger-flavoured herbs and spices, such as rosemary, sage or ginger, are best left until seven months on, or used only in the tiniest quantities as a flavouring.

The liquid element of weaning purées can be made up of:

- cooled, boiled tap water or freshly opened still, bottled mineral (not spring) water (but check that it contains no more than 20 milligrams of sodium per litre)
- vegetable or meat stock with no added salt
- expressed breast milk or formula milk
- vegetable or fruit juices (easy on the citrus).

Purées of fruit and vegetables, without any added salt or sugar, should be the backbone weaning foods.

We can also try smooth cereals. Commercial first-stage baby cereals are fine as long as they contain only cereal and, say, an added fruit – no added sugar or processing additives are acceptable.

Wholefood shops sell very finely milled cereals, such as fine oatmeal, which aren't always labelled 'for babies' but are perfectly suitable for this purpose. The classic safe offering of baby rice is entirely tasteless and many babies think so too! More flavoursome oats, finely milled, may be a more successful cereal candidate for most babies, especially when mixed with fruit, but babies with a family history of coeliac disease should avoid oats at this stage. Wheat-, rye- and barley-based cereals can cause allergies (see A Few Potential Problem Foods, pages 160–61) and aren't a good idea at this stage. These solid foods can be fed using a plastic baby spoon.

The scope for drinks other than breast or formula milk is limited.

But it is a good idea to offer cooled, boiled tap water or freshly opened still mineral (not spring) water in a plastic feeder cup. Many adults feel that water has to be flavoured with something more interesting if a baby is to accept it, and want to add some commercial 'baby drink' granules, 'fruit' squash or sweet juices such as apple. For all the reasons described in What Children Should Drink (pages 102–13), none of these is a good idea in either the short or the long term. We need to accustom children to the taste of plain unsweetened water from weaning on. In terms of forming their future palate to accept real flavours, this will probably be one of the most effective things we ever do.

Cooled herbal tea offers many possibilities for babies. Although this may sound a bit outlandish in the UK they are quite commonly given to babies on the Continent in countries like Germany. But avoid commercial baby herbal drinks which, despite their healthy-sounding herbal names, generally include sweeteners and other additives. Instead, make your own herbal tea, with boiled water in a pot, and allow it to cool. There is a wide range of straight herbal teas in most wholefood shops. Go for ones that contain only herbs and nothing else – such as artificial fruit flavourings. Since some herbs have medicinal effects, read the label carefully and avoid any that say 'not suitable for children', such as those containing valerian. Many common herbal teas such as camomile, fennel and peppermint are fine for babies.

From seven to twelve months

To the backbone fruit purées we can add tarter fruits such as citrus and red fruits like strawberries and cherries (minus the stones). To the standard vegetable purées we can add small amounts of protein such as unsalted fish (from eight months), poultry and red meat. Salty bacon or ham is out except in minute quantities as a flavouring. A small serving of an 'adult' meat casserole or stew is fine, provided more vegetables than meat are selected, and the portion is taken out before salt is added.

We can try out foods containing wheat, rye and barley (both wholemeal and refined versions), such as soft pasta (the smaller shapes to avoid choking) and bread. We can also experiment with boiled egg cooked firm (from eight months). But wheat, rye and barley foods and eggs do need watching. We need to be alert to any symptoms of allergy (see pages 160–61).

We can start preparing purées with more texture, gradually making the transition to mashed food.

A small amount of any pulse can be given, but for reasons of palatability and texture it's better to mix these in with slacker ingredients such as tomatoes or squash. (Some 'adult' lentil and mixed vegetable soup or dhal would be perfect, provided it is not salted or 'hot' spicy or peppery.) Of course the flatulent effect of pulses is notorious and babies are no different from adults in this respect.

We can experiment with larger dried fruits (apricots, prunes, dried fruit salad mixes) added in small quantities to other ingredients. Don't go too fast, though, as they may come out more speedily than they went in. Buy only unsulphured or organic fruits (i.e. ones that have not been treated with the preservative sulphur dioxide, which can provoke allergic reactions).

We can try out a little cow's milk in cooking (though not as a drink). But because this can cause allergies (see pages 160–61, A Few Possible Problem Foods), it should be introduced very gingerly. Goat's, sheep's and soya milk can be used in the same way and seem to cause fewer adverse reactions.

A small amount of yogurt can be offered too. Rather than choosing sweetened ones, we can start as we mean to go on and accustom our baby to natural and plain versions, even if we do mix in a little of a sweeter ingredient such as mashed banana or fruit purée. Soft curd cheeses, such as ricotta, fromage frais or cream cheese, are worth considering, provided they are ultra-fresh. Versions with added salt and sugar are best avoided – babies don't need these additives. More mature cheeses with higher acidity levels such as Cheddar or Parmesan can be used, but because of their high salt content they are best treated as a seasoning or flavouring rather than a main ingredient.

Babies should be given whole-milk rather than low-fat versions of dairy produce such as yogurt. However, they don't need any added fats over and above those they pick up from other food sources, such as fatty fish, eggs, dairy produce or plant sources such as avocado. If we feel, however, that a particular dish or food needs some anointing, extra virgin olive oil in small amounts is a sensible and healthy choice.

Every food a baby eats at this stage can have more texture. For example, an avocado or ripe mango can simply be coarsely mashed. Apple can be finely grated, not cooked and puréed. Fish can be grilled, then broken into flakes, and chopped-up meat can be served. The classic 'finger foods' – small bits of bread, clementine segments (pips removed) and whole strawberries – can all be given in soft versions. Items like carrot batons and cucumber are still a bit too hard at this stage. A basic unsweetened muesli is good if it is whizzed briefly in the food processor to eliminate any coarse nuts, seeds or dried fruit which would be difficult to swallow.

The plastic spoon should gradually give way to fingers. While a very few babies like being fed with a spoon, most get quite frustrated and are much more likely to eat more if they can participate themselves, using their fingers. Atrocious as the mess may be, if we want to encourage our babies to be happy participants in the business of eating long-term, then we have to accept the mess and clear up afterwards. This stage doesn't last for too long, and eventually they will cause less uproar and graduate naturally on to more civilised eating habits.

For babies who are teething, or as an alternative to a dummy, fingers of bread, slowly dried out in the oven, make a simple, healthy alternative to commercial baby rusks and if they chuck them away it is less of a waste.

Babies at this stage are thirstier and will be looking for more drinks, as opposed to feeds. Yet again, we can establish that water is the usual 'default' drink and keep sweet additions restricted to very small amounts of unsweetened fresh fruit juice.

One year on

This is when we can extend the range of foods we give our baby to include nearly everything we as adults eat, as long as it is good quality, fresh, wholesome and not heavily processed to start with. It's all down to common sense. Cows's milk can now be given freely (full-fat, not skimmed). The blender will be redundant and babies can be given almost anything as long as it is in a form they can manage without choking. Some babies produce teeth from an early age, others are slower. But as the ability to chew harder foods develops, we can gradually accustom them to real food served in adult forms, with just a few obvious concessions: removal of small bones or excessively hard and scratchy crusts and some helpful cutting up of otherwise hard-to-tackle foods.

When they begin to be able to chew and swallow most foods, we can teach them how to eat unsalted nuts and seeds (pumpkin and sunflower) and nut butters. These are good nibbles and provide excellent nutrition in the way of essential fatty acids and vitamins. (Watch out, however, for any potential nut allergy; see page 160.) Smaller dried fruits such as raisins or cherries (not glacé ones) are also a good choice, provided they have not been treated with the preservative sulphur dioxide.

Some shellfish can be introduced, such as carefully shelled crab meat or small amounts of peeled prawns (these are salty, so only two or three should be given). Bivalve shellfish (those in two shells such as mussels) are best avoided because they are more likely to carry food poisoning bacteria.

As babyhood gives way to toddlerhood, our aim is to integrate our children into communal household eating and away from special baby food, either bought or home-made. The mechanics of doing this have been described in detail in Part Two, Breaking the Mould at Home.

Summary of what foods and liquids can be given and when

* = *be aware of allergy potential*
\# = *be aware of caveats in text above*

FROM WEANING
Expressed breast milk or formula milk
Non-acidic fruits
All vegetables
Mild herbs
Mild spices
* Finely milled oats and rice
Cooled, boiled tap water or fresh bottled still mineral water (with a
    sodium content of no more than 20 milligrams per litre)
Home-made unsalted vegetable or meat stock
Very dilute unsalted vegetable juice
Very dilute unsweetened, non-acidic fruit juice

FROM SEVEN MONTHS
More acidic fruits, such as oranges
Unsalted fish (after eight months)
Unsalted white or red meat
* Wholemeal and refined wheat, rye and barley foods (pasta, cous-
    cous, bread)
* Firmly boiled egg (after eight months)
Pulses
Larger unsulphured dried fruits (prunes, apricots)
* Soft curd cheeses

* Natural yogurt
*# Hard cheese
* Cow's milk (in cooking)
Goat's, sheep's and soya milk (in cooking)
Cooled, boiled herbal teas

FROM ONE YEAR
* Unsalted nuts and seeds, unsalted nut butters
Small unsulphured dried fruits
Seafood
Lightly salted vegetable or meat stock

Better ready-made baby foods

Even if you prefer to give your baby home-made food, there are
bound to be occasions when it suits you to buy ready-prepared baby
foods – while travelling, perhaps, or as a backup when you haven't
got any food on the go that's suitable for a baby. In this event, the
challenge is to select commercial baby foods that are better than
most.

The quickest route to quality is to go for the organic brands. Not
only are the ingredients produced without the use of pesticides and
with concern for animals and the environment but they also tend to
be the most like home-made, containing little or none of the typical
processing aids you find in conventional brands. Many parents
already recognise this. In the UK, organic baby foods are the most
rapidly growing sector in the whole baby-food market.

But organic or otherwise, if you have to buy ready-made baby
food it pays to take a close look at ingredients. Go for ones with a
very short list of natural ingredients which you recognise and would
use in a home-made version – for example, carrots, oats, chicken.
Avoid any ingredients you wouldn't use at home, such as maltodextrin, vegetable extract, cornflour, flavouring or wheat starch, sugar

in any form (any ingredient with -ose on the end, such as lactose) or obviously sweet ingredients such as apple juice concentrate or salty ingredients such as yeast extract. Good-quality baby food should not need ingredients like these to make it palatable. Don't buy those that have water high up the list of ingredients either. Water should appear low down the list, and preferably not at all.

A few potential problem foods

Here is a list of the most common allergy-causing foods that some babies cannot tolerate:

- Cow's milk (This is why it isn't recommended as a drink for children under twelve months, although it can be used gradually from seven months as one ingredient in a composite dish if there are no signs of an adverse reaction.)

- Eggs (Some babies react badly to both yolk and white, but the yolk seems to cause fewer problems than the white.)

- Nuts (Peanuts seem to be the biggest problem and can provoke life-threatening reactions in some sensitive people, but other nuts can cause allergies too.)

- Wheat, rye, oats, barley and their derivatives (Pasta, flour, bread, breakfast cereals.) (These contain gluten, which some babies have difficulty absorbing and so develop an allergic reaction to it.)

- Orange

- Chocolate

- Sugar

Foods on this list can cause a variety of symptoms – everything from breathing problems to digestive upsets and hyperactivity. The onset of symptoms may happen very quickly, or manifest itself more gradually.

Obviously, other environmental factors such as house dust and pets can cause similar symptoms. But when a food reaction is suspected, contact your doctor for advice initially. If the reactions continue, ask to be referred to a specialist.

Foods and drinks to avoid

These make no useful contribution to any baby's health and may actively undermine it:

- Sugar (Offers no useful nutrients; contributes to excessive weight gain and tooth decay. Adding it to baby food or drink encourages in unhelpful 'sweet tooth' for the future. Sugar may appear on the label as sucrose, glucose, fructose, lactose, maltose, dextrose, honey, maple syrup, malt or fruit juice.)

- Artificial sweeteners (See pages 6–7 for more detailed reservations.)

- Sweet fizzy drinks (These have been linked with allergic reactions. It is not yet established which ingredients cause these but chemical preservatives and flavourings are heavily implicated.)

- Salt (Humans need very little salt in any form. Babies up to twelve months can't cope with salt because their kidneys cannot process it. It's a good idea not to add salt to food before this stage and to avoid salty ingredients such as yeast extract or stock cubes.)

- Additives and 'E' numbers (Though a small number of these contribute to making some food safe to eat, the majority have no benefit to health whatsoever, while a significant number are linked with adverse reactions in sensitive people. Until the age of twelve months, these have no place in the food or drink given to babies. Thereafter, they need to be scrutinised carefully. See pages 282–5 for a list of particularly suspect additives which it is wise to avoid.)

- Unfamiliar technical-sounding ingredients (In commercial baby foods these will be items like maltodextrin, whey 'and extracts' of meat or vegetables. The inclusion of these indicates over-processed, poor-quality food.)

PESTICIDE RESIDUE RISKS AND THE ORGANIC ALTERNATIVE

There is now a substantial body of research which suggests that babies, toddlers and children are more vulnerable to pesticide residues in food and drink than adults and more heavily exposed to them too: a sort of double whammy.

The first special weakness of babies and children is that their systems are immature and in the process of development. This makes them more vulnerable to any toxic substance in general, including those they might consume in the form of pesticide residues. Exposure to pesticides in early life has been linked to a greater risk in later life of cancer, neurological impairment and disfunction of the immune, endocrine and nervous system.

The second vulnerability is that their exposure to toxic pesticide residues has been underestimated. This is because they consume more of fewer foods than adults. So a baby's consumption of apples or apple juice, for example, is typically much higher in relation to his or her body weight than an adult's. Yet in the UK the 'safe dose' levels deemed acceptable for pesticide residues do not take account of this. This means that babies' and infants' exposure to such residues is being underestimated substantially – according to some experts by a factor of up to forty.

Disconcerting news for parents, and the latest US research into infants' and children's pesticide exposure confirms these worries. For example, in 1998 the US Environmental Working Group (EWG) reported that:

- One child in every twenty consumes unsafe levels of organophosphate chemicals every day.

- A child has a one in seven chance of eating an apple with an unsafe dose of pesticides.

More work had been done on children and pesticide residues in the US but there is no reason to think that UK results would be any better. Back in 1995 the government announced that a small percentage of UK carrots contained residues of highly toxic organophosphates up to three times over the 'Acceptable Daily Intake'. This was based on the average acceptable intake, which does not take account of children who may eat far more carrots in relation to their body weight than adults.

The debate over the presence of pesticide residues in babies' and children's food – and the potentially adverse health effects they might cause – is vast and complicated. Old assumptions about what constitutes 'safe levels' of exposure to pesticides are being called into question and the particular physiological vulnerability of babies and children to such toxic assaults is only beginning to be researched.

How should we react to this underestimated and, as yet, ill-understood risk?

Very sensibly, many parents are taking their own pre-emptive action and feeding their babies and children with as much organic food as possible. In recent years, even commercial baby-food companies have had to introduce organic ranges to cater for the greatly increased demand. Nowadays in the UK, some 10 per cent of baby food sold is organic and this sector of the baby-food market is growing by 50 per cent each year – much faster than sales of non-organic brands. It may not be too long before this country is like Germany, where already some 90 per cent of commercial baby food sold is organic.

For people who want to feed their babies on home-made food, then organic food – grown without the use of pesticides – is a very attractive proposition, particularly in the first year. This is the time before babies generally eat a more diverse range of foods and characteristically consume larger amounts of a few key foods such as apples, pears, carrots, fruit juices and bananas, which may make them move vulnerable to pesticide residues. For parents who want to have the convenience of ready-made food, at least as backup for home-made or for special situations such as travelling, ready-prepared organic baby foods are an attractive proposition.

If we are concerned about our children's exposure to pesticides, then by seeing that these mainstay foods are organic we can limit that exposure significantly.

Moving away from the issue of pesticide avoidance, there are other good reasons for favouring organic food for babies and children:

- It represents a strictly policed food production system which generates the most natural, uncompromised raw ingredients you can get.

- No ingredient will have been genetically manipulated in any way.

- Only a very restricted number of chemical additives are permitted in processed foods. All of these are widely thought to be safe.

- Meat, poultry and dairy produce come from systems with high animal welfare standards where animals are not routinely fed antibiotics and growth promoters. This makes for naturally healthier animals, much less prone to diseases such as salmonella which flourish in intensive systems.

For all these reasons, food from organic sources is likely to be better and safer for everyone – babies and children included.

PART FIVE

....

INFLUENCING WHAT CHILDREN EAT WHEN YOU'RE NOT THERE

WHAT YOU CAN EXPECT FROM CHILDCARERS

Selecting somebody to look after our cherished offspring is one of the heaviest and most momentous decisions that many of us ever have to make. It is not easy to relinquish care of our children to other people, no matter how competent they might be.

By the time we have satisfied ourselves that the candidate is not a cunning psychopath whose forged references hide persistent cruelty and child abuse but a warm, patient and caring person, we relax a bit. Then we work through a tick list of attitudes for compatibility with our own views. Do they expect to go out each day with our children and what activities would this involve? How much television do they think is appropriate? If they believe in disciplining children, how do they believe this should be done? Do they expect to tidy up after the children or do they see their role just as playing and caring?

For most parents, even those who consciously want their children to eat healthily, attitudes towards food come pretty low down the hierarchy of criteria against which we judge candidates. Most people feel relieved just to find someone who appears trustworthy and kind, with a bit of get up and go. Having got this far, it can seem petty, even obsessive, to quiz them on their attitude towards sweets, snacks and treats. The bolder amongst us may go as far as saying that we care about what the children eat and don't want them to eat too much junk. Most candidates will endorse this general attitude anyway, but the detail of how they propose to go about achieving that usually goes unspoken.

Once we have hired a childcarer, however, food generally comes back up the list of issues we need to negotiate with them. The carer is, after all, spending a significant amount of time with the children during the day at a pre-school age when many food habits are being formed. Parents might have a real-food approach when they are around but if the carer is operating differently then they will be undermined and it will be harder to get the children to eat well.

So what can we do about this? Much depends on whether your carer is looking after the children in her own home or in yours.

In her home

When the carer is in her own home, the scope for controlling what your child eats is limited and becomes more so as the child grows older. The carer decides what food is in her house and probably has children of her own. When you agree to let her look after yours, you are effectively giving a vote of confidence to her style of parenting. Although you haven't given her carte blanche to do whatever she likes with your child, by hiring her you have implicitly said that her way of doing things is, by and large, fine with you.

With babies, eating is not such an issue. Many parents prefer to send the baby along with a packed lunch and snacks as appropriate. But as the baby becomes a toddler who sees that there are other food options in the house, she or he may want to share what everyone else – especially older children – is eating. If these are attractive junky foods that are prominently advertised on TV during children's programming, then that pressure is even more intense.

At this stage, there is little room for negotiating over children's food. On a practical basis, you are not there to see what the eating arrangements are and you aren't stocking the larder. If you have misgivings about how the children eat while they are with the carer, it is a very delicate issue to raise and one that calls for excellent diplomacy. If you say something like, *'I'm worried that the children are getting into the habit of eating too many biscuits during the day,'* this can come over both as interference and as an implied criticism of her approach to feeding her own children. You may get it wrong too, because you aren't in a position to know exactly what your child is eating at the carer's.

You might notice, for example, that your child is asking for biscuits all the time at home or rejecting fruit juice as 'too sour' and asking for squash like she gets at the carer's house, all of which might make you think that she's getting into bad habits. But even if you have the nerve to raise a query about food, you aren't there to police whether or not it has been responded to. You could go as far as saying, for example, '*I'd like Lucy to eat fewer sweets and biscuits during the day.*' This could offend your carer, or elicit a reassurance to the contrary. Either way, you still won't really know what's going on.

So what practical things can you do to try to influence the way your child eats in a carer's home?

If you have not yet chosen a particular carer, in the course of interviewing people you can consciously build in more queries about food than you might otherwise consider polite. Don't be embarrassed to ask, in a neutral way, what their own children have as snacks after school or as lunch on half-days. Responses are often really illuminating and highlight a potential candidate's food awareness. When you have hired a carer whose attitude towards food seems to be reasonably compatible with your own, then it's time to establish the ground rules of eating in more detail. Start by agreeing whether or not the carer is going to supply lunch/tea or whether you are going to send the child with a packed lunch/tea. If you go for the former, this is a gesture of faith in the carer and, having initially agreed on the sort of food you think suitable, you must then trust her judgement and leave her to get on with it.

If you go for the latter, you need to obtain her agreement that she will try her best to encourage the child to eat the food you send and not undermine it by offering alternatives. However, she must have the right to tell you when your child doesn't like it so that you can alter what you are providing. She must also have the right to offer a substitute when a child still seems hungry. The following sort of situation can be tricky to negotiate.

ALEX AND VEGETABLE SOUP

Alex's mother, Laura, has cooked and frozen a supply of meals for his lunch, something she has done ever since he started on solid food. Now that she is back at work and he is a toddler, he goes to his carer Susan's house three days a week. His current favourite is puréed vegetable soup but Susan reports that she can't get him to eat it. In desperation, and because Alex still seemed hungry, she gave him a fruit yogurt instead, which he wolfed down. Laura is puzzled because Alex usually, though not always, eats the soup when she is at home.

Laura wonders if Susan is patient enough to encourage him to keep on eating as she herself does. She is also aware that the existence of alternative foods eaten by Susan's children may be undermining those that she is sending. Susan, on the other hand, feels annoyed that Laura expects her to get Alex to eat food that he doesn't really like, and thinks that she fails to see that his tastes are changing. Susan cannot hide the food her family eats and it seems mean not to let Alex taste it. She is tempted just to pour the troublesome vegetable soup down the drain and give Alex something else, without telling Laura.

There may well be right and wrong in both sides of this interaction, with reality lying somewhere between each woman's view. What can be done to resolve this difference? Short of the Doomsday option of sacking Susan and going back to square one with a new carer, Laura has two realistic options, depending on the degree of faith she has in Susan's overall suitability for the job:

- She can go along with Susan, allowing her to provide the food for Alex, resigning herself to the fact that, although it may not be what she would choose for him, it's still good enough, easier and a lot less fuss. After all, Alex is at Susan's for only part of the week and she herself controls what he eats for the rest of it.

- Alternatively she can hold firm and insist that she wants to send Alex's food, but without making it explicit that she is worried about 'slippage' from her own tighter food standards to Susan's more relaxed, junk-tolerant ones. In this scenario, she has to concede that the vegetable soup isn't doing the trick and come up with some other alternatives for Susan to try. This makes the point to Susan that Laura takes account of what she says but that the principle of getting Alex to eat Laura's home-prepared food still holds.

RECONCILING HOME FOOD WITH THE CARER'S FOOD

If you are lucky enough to find a carer whose attitude towards feeding children is consistent with your own – great. But when there is a difference in approach between carer and parent, it is important to be quite clear about how you handle things. Being philosophical about it, parents just have to accept that when they hire a carer in her own home, they are not going to be able to control totally what their children eat. The chances are that even with the most food-aware carer, there will be differences in approach.

But if you have a carer who is more tolerant of junk than you, and your children seem to be picking up habits at the childcarer's that you don't like, what should you do?

Begin by realising that even from a very young age, children can differentiate between what is acceptable in one situation and not in another. So it's important not to fall in with expectations they have learned with their carer, but instead to establish that, while at home, you do things differently. How does this work?

NO SQUASH AND BISCUITS AT HOME

Caroline had got used to having fruit squash and biscuits for a snack while she is at Vicky's, her carer. Now when she is at home she is beginning to reject the healthier alternatives her parents give her — fruit, water, milk — and ask for snacks like she gets at Vicky's house. Her parents, Dave and Rachel, are beginning to get downhearted, and reluctantly reach the conclusion that they too will need to provide squash and biscuits. If they do this, then they will have lost the battle. Squash and biscuits will become the norm and a precedent will have been created which tells Caroline that if she campaigns enough, her parents will give her what she gets at her carer's. Good intentions of bringing Caroline up on a more wholesome, natural diet may give way to a slippery slope, ending in a junk-food diet.

On the other hand, Caroline's parents can make it clear to her that while she gets squash and biscuits at her carer's, this is the exception, not the rule. They can explain that Vicky does things differently from them but that, because she is a nice person and it is her house, she can decide what everyone eats. However, when Caroline is at home, the old rules of more wholesome, real food still apply.

This underlines to Caroline that no matter what food she may eat outside her home, her parents are consistent in offering only food that they consider to be good for her, and much more delicious than junk.

Provided that Dave and Rachel explain to Caroline why they are holding firm, using the strategies outlined in Getting the Message Across (pages 61–6), and continue to offer her delicious and varied alternatives, Caroline will increasingly see home food as the status quo and her carer's food as a deviation from that. She will take what's on offer at Vicky's, without hoping that she will get the same thing at home.

In your home

When a carer is looking after children in her own home, you have to fit in with her way of doing things. But when someone is coming into your home to look after the children the situation is reversed, and it's reasonable to expect her to slot in with your thinking. So you can expect her to feed your children as you would like them to be fed.

You can largely control what she gives them when you are not there simply by the way you stock the larder. If you make sure that it contains a reasonably varied supply of good food, then this is what the children will end up eating. Unless the carer is prepared to buy consistently different food with her own money – a highly unlikely scenario – then she will feed them from what's in the house.

In this situation, if there is a divergence between your own and your carer's attitude towards food, it usually boils down to the frequency with which she offers certain foods to the children. For example, you may keep some foods in the house for limited consumption, such as good-quality ice cream, which you find are being eaten up rather more quickly than you had anticipated, while others are lying untouched. In this situation you can gently and diplomatically raise the issue with your carer and restate the balance you consider appropriate. If this doesn't work, then simply run out of those foods so that they aren't an option any longer. Keep them for weekends so that you can control exactly when, and how often, they are eaten.

If you have an arrangement that you sometimes leave money for your carer to buy food when you run out, make sure that this doesn't become a junk-food budget. Check what the money is being spent on and, when you can, stipulate what foods you want restocking. So, rather than leaving a blanket note which says something like, *'Here's £10, can you buy something for lunch?'* you can say, *'Here's £10, can you buy pitta bread, some fruit and eggs for scrambled egg?'*

NEGOTIATING WITH
NURSERIES AND PLAYGROUPS

When children start at nursery or playgroup, parents get their first taste of the power of peer group pressure. This is most children's first opportunity to watch other children consistently – especially the older members of the group – and learn from them. Inevitably, the desire to be like them can be quite strong.

This can be the first tough challenge to a real-food approach to eating. Children who may have been quite happy drinking water and eating fruit and crackers as their mainstay snack see that other children come to nursery with cartons of blackcurrant drink and chocolate bars. If a communal snack is provided by staff, fruit squash, packets of crisps and biscuits may loom large. On day trips out, chewy 'fruity' sweets or sugary boiled sweets may be routinely doled out to break the boredom or ward off travel sickness. A state of affairs that is quite predictable really, when you consider that a monthly visit to the Cash and Carry to stock up on juice and crisps is certainly going to be cheaper and less effort than a weekly shop at the local greengrocer's.

How should parents who want their children to eat well react to all this?

The first thing to realise is that no matter how children eat at nursery or playgroup a strong, consistent real-food message from home will still be the dominant one they hear. So before we become discouraged about the pointlessness of sticking to wholesome food when it seems that everyone else is eating junk, it's worth reminding ourselves that we still have the whip hand.

However, that doesn't mean that the challenge of junk at nursery is one we can afford to ignore. When our children see other children eating junk – and when this is being sanctioned by authority figures whom they have been told to respect – it's confusing and contradictory. This is the first time that toddlers are likely to start putting pressure on parents and 'arguing back' about the food and drink they are offering. Unless we want to go through tantrums and battles, we have to find a positive way of dealing with it.

But how can we argue that the food on offer should be changed without coming over as fussy, obsessive, uptight parents who don't quite live in the real world?

The scope for parents to influence what their children eat varies according to the nature of the establishment the children attend. There are four main types:

- The free local-authority nursery, where children have got a place fairly late after waiting their turn in a queue.

- The private paying nursery (there are two sub-types here: the most expensive 'You're lucky to get a place here, we're doing you a favour' establishment or the more straightforward 'There's a place if you can afford it' one).

- The primarily parent-run playgroup which parents organise themselves to meet their own childcare needs.

- The subsidised or free workplace nursery or crèche.

Local-authority nursery

If you want to raise issues about food in this context, you have certain things going for you. The first is that your child is *entitled* to a place which you have paid for indirectly through tax. This is just a straightforward question of your child receiving a statutory public service. If you aren't happy about that service, you have a right to complain or try to change it. In theory anyway, it is democratic, open and responsive to comments.

The second is that your child is being cared for by well-trained professionals with a reasonable degree of experience who can be expected to take in their stride parents' requests and demands without taking it personally or feeling threatened. It is reasonable to assume that they have some notion of wholesome, healthy eating through their training and should be prepared to build this awareness into the service they provide.

The third is that because the nursery caters for a wide range of children from various classes and ethnic backgrounds, it cannot impose any rigid eating policy, such as 'children must bring a carton of drink and a bag of crisps for snack'. So if all attempts to influence the food that's offered fails, children always have the right to bring their own snack or lunch.

The difficulty you might encounter is that such nurseries may be short of cash and this restricts their ability to provide wholesome food such as fruit regularly. Also, a wide range of children will attend, many of whom come from less affluent backgrounds where they are used to an overwhelmingly processed-food diet and items like fresh fruit are seen as an expensive luxury. Any notion of laying down rigid 'healthy-eating' thinking can be portrayed as divisive and insensitive. In the worst scenario, this argument can be used by staff who are more rigid and set in their ways to block any change or improvement in the food, even though many other parents would welcome it. The staff may be more conservative than many of the parents.

Scope for action: *Good in theory but you will have to marshal your arguments well first and approach staff supportively, being sensitive to the constraints within which they are operating.*

Private paying nursery

In theory, private nurseries ought to be more responsive than local-authority ones because parents are paying directly for the service and can simply find somewhere else if they aren't happy with any aspect of it – food included. What's more, because the relationship between parent and nursery is more businesslike than in a local-authority context, one might reasonably expect to get a positive reaction to complaints or comments.

In practice, however, many private nurseries can be more dictatorial and set in their ways than local-authority ones. This is largely because there is generally more demand than supply, with parents desperately seeking places, especially for infants and toddlers who are too young to qualify for a local-authority place. Having got a place at all can seem like an achievement for a parent. Rock the boat too much and you may be met with a response of 'That's our way of doing things and if you don't like it, then take your child elsewhere.'

Unlike local-authority nurseries, which are run within educational and social guidelines agreed at a higher level, private nurseries – albeit with well-trained professional staff – are run primarily as small businesses, although they may also have a secondary educational or pedagogic philosophy underpinning them. When parents enrol their children it may be assumed that they are buying into the values on offer, with no opting out of parts of the total package. And by querying the way things are done, parents can be seen as 'difficult' and challenging those values.

This pressure is at its strongest in the most select nurseries, which promise early educational advantage. There is strong demand for places and a long waiting list. Any critical feedback can be met with a smug 'we know best' attitude and pressure from any parent to change things can simply be ignored.

This is often where food policy is at its most despotic, with notes shuttling back and forth from home to nursery stipulating what is 'suitable' for a snack and even a compulsory lunch which everyone must share. Occasionally, such strictures are used to shore up wholesome real-food initiatives: 'No sweets for snacks' and so on. But more often than not, they institutionalise junk. This is mainly because children's junk food is cheap to buy and easy to store and prepare. All this helps towards a healthy bottom line on the annual accounts.

Scope for action: *Limited, unless you are lucky enough to find a nursery with a forward-looking and explicitly healthy food policy.*

Parent-run playgroups

In food terms, playgroups are less all-embracing than nurseries because most children attend for only a couple of sessions a week. Very few serve lunch and most children will simply eat a snack when they attend. Although the bigger, more established playgroups employ some paid staff, the emphasis is on shared care by parents, so there is no hierarchical bureaucracy to get through if you want to raise questions about the nature of the snacks offered to children. In theory, if you want to get that snack changed, you just need to attend the organising committee meeting and raise the question.

If parents are like-minded, playgroup food can be healthy and wholesome. But the problem is that, unlike any other type of pre-school care, the group is not run by professionals who can be expected to deal coolly and calmly with feedback and suggestions. So if one parent suggests altering the snack on offer, this can stir up defensive attitudes amongst other parents whose children are accustomed to junk. One parent may suggest something innocuous – such as substituting half fresh fruit juice and water for squash – and find that this is surprisingly controversial, provoking others to come up with all sorts of arguments against it: *'My children wouldn't drink that'*, *'It's too expensive'*, *'It's too bossy'* are just some common counters. Such arguments often cover up feelings of guilt in parents who don't like having to face the fact that they have gone down the junk-food path with their children and may resent the other parent for making them realise it.

Scope for action: *Could be extensive but extremely skilful diplomacy is called for.*

Workplace nurseries

In theory at least, workplace nurseries combine some of the best characteristics of local-authority and private nurseries. Like the former, there is the notion of entitlement to the service and no precious exclusiveness. As with the best private equivalents, workplace nurseries are generally well resourced. Their driving ethos is providing a service to a specific group of employees that meets their requirements, not just carrying out some obligatory statutory service. And since the nursery is founded on pragmatic rather than commercial principles – a number of employees needing childcare in the same place at the same time – they tend not to have a set of values to which parents are expected to subscribe.

Most workplace nurseries are set up by large public-sector bodies or companies with a reasonably go-ahead and progressive attitude, so it's reasonable to assume that they will be open to at least hearing about a more wholesome food approach.

Scope for action: *Good.*

A strategy for tackling nursery and playgroup food

In a fantasy world the ideal nursery would serve children a wide variety of delicious and wholesome snacks, lunches and drinks, and parents wouldn't have to bother about the food at all. In the real world, many nurseries are about as far away from this as it's possible to be. So if you want to try and change things, it is generally best to start with limited demands and gradually improve on these. Attempts to proscribe undesirable foods are a waste of time, except in situations where there is widespread agreement amongst parents. It is usually best to avoid a head-on confrontation (for example, by demanding a 'no sweets' rule) and instead to limit the circumstances in which undesirable foods are offered by increasing the presence of more wholesome alternatives.

Whatever kind of nursery or playgroup you choose, the bottom line for any parent concerned about food is that over the course of a week there is some *choice* in what the children are offered. So unless they have an explicit healthy-eating ethos, any nursery that won't allow children to bring their own choice of snacks and packed lunch needs to be discounted straight off – unless, that is, you consider that other good points make up for food limitations.

Having established the principle of choice, the next step is to make this a *qualitative* choice. The issue isn't whether to serve blackcurrant drink or orange squash, or digestives instead of custard creams. This wider choice needs to represent an improvement.

On the drinks front, a reasonable starting point would be to ask that plain water is always offered. 'Offered' means poured out in a jug, not available from the tap if a child asks! The next step would be to see that squash is replaced by real fruit juice (no added sugar) in cartons and similarly diluted with a generous amount of water.

A final outcome on the drinks front might be to get the nursery to tell parents that children should not bring carbonated soft drinks (cola, orange drink) with them to nursery and that water, diluted fruit juice (and the occasional hot chocolate in winter) are the standard nursery drinks.

When it comes to food, the bottom line is to ask that each day, as well as the ubiquitous crisps and biscuits, some *fresh* food is prepared and offered. Obvious candidates include peeled, chopped or sliced fruit and vegetables, bread, scones, oatcakes or crackers with something like butter, jam or cubes of ham or cheese.

Some healthy storecupboard staples could also be suggested, such as bowls of sunflower and pumpkin seeds, dried fruits and variations on that theme. Many more ideas can be found in Twenty-five Good Snacks (pages 237–8).

When a cooked nursery lunch is made on the premises (standards vary but the worst are bought in from other mass catering institutions, are dire and beyond reform), you can reasonably ask that the emphasis is on freshly prepared foods rather than convenience foods from the freezer. Baked potatoes could be baked that day, not reheated, salads and fruit cut up freshly. Sandwiches could be made on the spot, not bought in ready-made.

Long-term, and if there is widespread agreement, parents can push the nursery not to offer sweets and crisps routinely and to write to all parents explaining that these are being discouraged.

ANSWERING THE OPPOSITION

Make suggestions about changing nursery food and you are likely to meet with some predictable excuses/rationalisations about why things should stay the same. Here are some common ones:

- 'No one else is bothered apart from you' (the implication being that you are just a fusspot).

  A typical 'blocking' device used by people who can't be bothered or don't want to start thinking about the issues. Often, it just isn't true. Even in the smallest group, there is likely to be at least a few other parents with similar concerns. Try to identify them and raise the matter jointly or on a group basis. Even if no one else is bothered, you can ask for a meeting or volunteer to send out your own questionnaire/survey into parents' feelings on the matter ('Are you happy with nursery snacks? Would you like to see fresh fruit as a snack? What do you think could make the food more healthy? What foods would you like to see more/less of? Would you be prepared to pay 50 pence more a week for fresher food? etc.).

  Even suggesting such a questionaire will stir up the powers that be. You will probably find that, when approached, many other parents want changes too but they may have just become resigned to the status quo. Others simply haven't thought about it, but when they do may well think that improvements should be made. Using the responses in your survey, you will be on stronger ground to press for changes.

- 'What you are suggesting would cost too much. We can't afford it.'

  This isn't necessarily the case. Water, for example, is free; sugary squash isn't. But most of the time there is some truth in this. However, the marginal cost may be much less significant in real terms than is being made out. It's worth pointing out that even if they are providing a snack for, say, twenty children, this represents quite a minor total amount of food or drink. Small children eat small amounts of food. For example, you could give twenty children each a snack consisting of a quarter of an apple (five apples for the class), a cracker/oakcake (a packet of crackers/ oatcakes); a teaspoon of sunflower seeds (a small bag of seeds); and fruit juice diluted with water (half-litre carton of juice). Yes, this snack will cost more than squash and biscuits but is it really that significant in the nursery's total budget? It clearly won't break the bank but it will give the children a substantially better, healthier and more varied snack.

- 'Many of the children here wouldn't eat that kind of food because they are not used to it.'

  The implication here is that you are an insensitive middle-class meddler trying to force healthy food on poorer kids who are accustomed to eating over-processed junk and can't be weaned off it. This is more often than not a fairly cynical excuse for doing nothing and rarely genuinely based in fact. Many 'good-food' initiatives (for example, taking a fresh fruit van round schools in deprived areas) have shown that poor children like fresh food and will eat it when it is offered. Openness to food has very little to do with social class and much more to do with an individual child's temperament. Some children are just more adventurous than others.

  You can also point out that you are not asking for a total change of all food, just that some more wholesome, fresh and varied options are offered on some days. (This argument is so reasonable that it is hard to oppose.) There is also an educational argument to be made that if some children have very restricted food horizons it is precisely the job of the nursery to widen these by offering foods that children might not otherwise encounter.

- 'The food would not be eaten and it would just get thrown out, which is a waste.'
  This is simply not the case. An interesting wholesome snack of the kind mentioned above will appeal to many children. If no alternative is on offer, most children will happily eat it, or at least part of it.

THE FRIEND'S HOUSE

Many children have a special 'best friend' and end up spending quite a lot of time at their house. It's possible that the friend's parents have the same approach to food as you, but if they don't, then you potentially have a problem on your hands. If the best friend routinely gets sweets, crisps and fizzy drinks, your children will be eating them too. They might even decide that they don't like what you are giving them and campaign for the same snacks as their friend: the 'Rory gets it so why can't I?' problem. And if your children are increasingly finding themselves in situations at school or nursery where other children also seem to eat what the best friend gets, they may feel less inclined to stick with the more wholesome real-food approach to which they have become accustomed.

Unlike nursery or school where, as described on pages 177–85, 189–93, there is scope at an official level to push for more varied, high-quality food, you have no direct room for manoeuvre with the best friend. You may be actively friendly, or at least have an affable passing relationship, with the parents and there is no way you can let them know that you think their children live on junk and that you don't want yours to do the same. To do so would be effectively to criticise their style of parenting and you could expect to be met with very touchy defensive reactions which often cover feelings of guilt and failure. Many parents don't feel good about the fact that their children will eat only a very limited repertoire of junk. One of the ways we justify this to ourselves is by saying that this is normal and inevitable in the modern world. Parents who don't subscribe to this philosophy and have children who are accustomed to more wholesome real food can be a major pain in the neck and prick the conscience in an irritating way.

So do we just have to ignore what children eat when they are with friends or is there something we can do about it?

The first thing to realise is that the problem is actually quite short-term. In the pre-school years and the first couple of sessions at primary school, many toddlers and small children yearn to be the same as everyone else and that means being like their friend: having the same clothes, playing with the same toys and eating the same food. But quite early on they start diverging again, as various ways of doing things begin to emerge. Children soon find out, for example, that everyone in their class does not go to bed at the same time each night, or watch the same amount of television, or have the same amount of pocket money. The same applies to food. Children realise that different parents operate in different ways.

Children, of course, will always tend to report different ways of doing things selectively in order to bolster up their demands. You won't hear about the girl who gets £1 pocket money each week, for example, just the one who gets £10. So the first thing to establish with children is that just because the best friend seems to live on cola and crisps, this doesn't mean that you will let them do the same. As children become older, they will accept these differences quite pragmatically. So if you are trying not to cave in to demands for junk, your task will become progressively easier.

Using some of the approaches described in Getting the Message Across on pages 61–6 (bad-mouthing junk, cashing in on concern about appearance), we can explain to our children that we think that the best friend doesn't have such nice food as they do and that it is not that healthy for them. We can tell them that we don't want the friend or their parents to know that this is our opinion, just that this is our private understanding.

The next thing we have to do is make sure that our children don't get the idea that they are being deprived of 'goodies'. If they see that the best friend is getting, for example, the latest fizzy drink being hyped mercilessly during the adverts on children's TV, we need to fight back with something that seems better and more indulgent, such as a really mouthwatering home-made milk shake made with their favourite fruit, say, strawberries. It's important that children get the idea that they have treats in their house too and that what's on offer isn't consistently less attractive than at their friend's. And although it may be dirty tactics, it's not a bad idea either to try consciously to seduce the friend into better snacking habits by wooing them with a few irresistible but wholesome snacks. It helps if the friend thinks that your child's food can be pretty nice and doesn't visit your house with an 'I don't like any of the food or drink they have here' attitude.

Then we have to give our children some guidance about what they should eat and drink at their friend's. There is no way that we can, or ought, to say, *'You aren't allowed to have that.'* Realistically we must accept that they will snack on whatever is being offered and see that in the relatively small amounts involved, it's not something about which to get hot under the collar.

Nevertheless we can point out that they can, quite politely, pass up on some things and ask for others without causing offence. If, for example, squash is automatically being put in drinks, a child can ask just to have plain water. It's worthwhile remembering that even when the ubiquitous children's snacks are the first line of food and drink on offer, many households have other foods around that children can ask for. When the friend says, *'I'm having a bag of crisps, do you want one?'* another child can simply say, *'Can I have a banana instead?'* or even, *'What else is there to eat?'*

SCHOOL FOOD

For all the reasons discussed in Goodbye Dinner Lady, Hello Cash Cafeteria (see pages 40–47), in all but the most exceptional schools, parents can't assume that there is any decent food on offer. How should we react to this depressing situation? This depends on what the other options are and these in turn depend on whether the children are at primary or secondary school.

Primary school

The line of least resistance is simply to accept that the food is pretty bad but send children for school lunch anyway. The chances are that they won't like the food for various reasons. They will probably eat just enough of it to stop them feeling hungry and keep them going until they come home, where they will hopefully get a reasonable snack followed by a good evening meal.

If we send them off with something healthy and fresh for snack, such as a piece of fruit, then we may feel we can afford to turn a blind eye to what's on offer in the cash cafeteria. What's more, because most children think that school food is horrible anyway, there is less chance of this influencing them to demand similar foods at home.

There is a danger, however, particularly if they attend a school that puts pressure on them to eat up, that they get into a defensive 'no' attitude to food and decide that they don't like eating in general. This makes feeding them at home a lot more difficult. Other low-effort options are giving children lunch at home (rarely possible except for non-working parents who live next to the school) or giving children money to go out of school at lunchtime and buy their own lunch. For very legitimate security reasons, many primary schools discourage this practice, except for older children who are about to go on to secondary school. And given the limited range of junk-food options in most corner shops, combined with most young children's inability to make a wholesome food decision in a busy retail situation, it's very likely that the food they end up eating will be bad or even worse than that in the cash cafeteria.

The high-effort approach is packed lunch. The downside of this is that all through termtime we must remember, week in, week out, to see that there is a store of food from which packed lunches can be produced. And although older primary children can be shown how to make their own packed lunch, realistically it will nearly always be parents or childcarers who end up preparing them. If we want to relax in the evenings, or ease the rush to get everyone up and out in the mornings, then making packed lunches is one commitment we might feel we can live without.

The upside is that, as a general rule, most children prefer packed lunch and will feel more inclined to eat it. So we can fill the box with wholesome food and have much more control over what they are eating. And although the prospect of coming up with a daily packed lunch can seem quite daunting, once we get into the rhythm of it and settle on a limited number of combinations that the children seem to like, the actual preparation can become almost automatic. See Ten Good Packed Lunches (pages 259–62) for ideas and inspiration.

For those parents who think that school meals ought to be better than they are, and do not see packed lunch as an option, there remains the demanding possibility of trying to reform the school food on offer to make it more wholesome and healthy. This approach is probably only for dedicated battlers who are prepared to spend a lot of time working through the various school structures – head teacher, school board, parents' association and catering service – to bring about changes. And for the mixture of reasons already outlined in pages 40–47, radical changes are very difficult to achieve.

However, if you want to get involved without making this your life's work, there is potential if you think of it in terms of significant minor changes rather than wholesale ones. For example:

- Many primary schools find themselves being offered vending machines with sweet fizzy drinks which can generate substantial revenue for the school. These often put the head teacher on the spot because, although she or he may disapprove of them, the money will come in useful. Representations from parents against these can strengthen the head teacher's resolve not to have one.

- Some cash cafeterias no longer offer just plain water to children but always automatically add 'fruit' squash. You can ask for plain water to be reinstated. This extremely reasonable request costs nothing to implement and is difficult to refuse.

- Most tuck shops don't sell fresh fruit or nut/seed combinations, yet these have proved to be popular with children in schools that offer them. You can ask the school to stock some fresh seasonal fruit and trail mix routinely.

If you think the cash cafeteria in your children's school is just so bad that something radical needs to be done about it, you'll need to set about it in a systematic way.

The first thing is to go along to the cafeteria and see for yourself exactly what's on offer. Small children do report things selectively and may exaggerate the shortcomings, so make sure you know your stuff before approaching anyone in authority. A child might say, for example, that there is no fruit in the cafeteria. You might find that in fact there is fruit on offer but that it looks old and unappetising and is hidden behind the chocolate crispies!

So instead of going to the head teacher and asking for fruit to be provided, you can make suggestions as to how it could be presented more obviously and attractively. It's very important that you make your representations positively, and in a supportive way which acknowledges the constraints within which staff are operating.

If you sense that there will be bureaucratic lethargy or even downright opposition to changes, you'll need to be able to show that you have a lot of other parents behind you. One way to demonstrate this is to offer to survey parents' feelings using a questionnaire. This is best done under the auspices of the school board or another institution so no one can accuse you of being just an individual stroppy parent. Such a survey needs to allow people to express dissatisfaction but also probe their reactions about possible solutions. The questions can address general shortcomings and allow people to pinpoint their discontent. You might ask:

- How happy with the cash cafeteria are you? (Very, moderately, not at all?)

- If you aren't happy, what do you object to? (Cold food, rushed service, unhealthy food, too much processed food, etc.?)

- Are there any foods that you think are served too often? (Chips, custard, fried crispy crumb products, tinned spaghetti and beans, instant mashed potato?)

- Are there any foods or drinks you think should be dropped from the cafeteria? (Sweets, fizzy drinks, burgers, crisps, flavoured milk shakes?)

Having established dissatisfaction, the questions then need to offer solutions.

- What different foods would you like to see on offer? (Raw vegetables with dip, fresh fruit, wholemeal bread, more salads, more hot food, better vegetarian food?)

- Can you think of wholesome foods your children like that are not currently on the menu? (Pasta with tomato sauce, tuna salad, fresh fruit salad, baked potatoes, natural Greek yogurt, oatcakes?)

- Can you think of anything else that would make the cafeteria environment better? (More time for children to eat, smaller/ larger table groups, a lower counter so children can actually see the food?)

Once the survey responses are in, you will be in a strong position to press for changes, at least on the points on which there is a wide consensus. You can meet with the school cook/catering company, the head teacher and (in state schools) the local-authority official responsible for catering.

If requests get blocked at this level, the next step is to raise the matter with the chair of the local education committee (state schools) or the chairperson of the board of governors (private schools).

If you have a lot of energy and care about getting changes made, with the ammunition of a survey behind you, you might see results. But this is a long-term exercise.

Secondary schools

Once children start attending secondary school and become teen-agers, the prospects for school food are both worse and better.

The negative side is that cash cafeterias in secondary schools now operate on the basis that pupils must be treated as 'young consumers'. Though this sounds promising, it is widely interpreted as offering them ubiquitous, widely hyped, processed junk foods at prices that are competitive with those outside school.

When put on the spot as to why they offer teenagers so much junk in school, caterers will often defend themselves by saying that, while primary children are to a great extent a captive audience, secondary pupils can simply go out of school and buy their own food. If they don't supply 'popular' (for which read junk) foods, so the argument goes, kids will simply vote with their feet and eat out.

So in secondary schools, any lingering protectionist, anti-junk-food attitudes that insulate primary-school children are abandoned in favour of an approach that is philosophical about young people eating a poor diet. Thus secondary schools are much more likely to have vending machines for sweet, fizzy drinks and a repertoire of food that apes fast-food chains but consists of the lowest common denominator of catering junk. What's more, no one (apart from the odd concerned and diligent teacher) will be checking what the kids eat for lunch. If a pupil chooses a white roll filled with crisps, a portion of chips and a bowl of custard each day (and many do!) then nobody will intervene.

The positive side is that your children will be old enough either to make their own packed lunch or to find better possibilities outside the school. They aren't stuck with school food any longer and you needn't assume that you must take on the burden of the daily packed lunch either.

Parents who feel strongly about the food in the secondary-school cash cafeteria can try to change it, using the strategy described for primary schools on pages 191–3. But a better and more instant approach is just to boycott it and concentrate on helping your children to find better outside alternatives.

It's important to realise that if teenagers are to find something better and more wholesome outside the school, this won't be a cheap alternative. Cash-cafeteria food may be horrible and deeply unhealthy but it is cheap! Unfortunately, your teenager's lunch expenses are going to be no different from your own, and this is something that parents who still have the expectation of subsidised or low-cost school meals may have difficulty coming to terms with.

Of course, the streets around large secondary schools are lined with small shops offering cheap food for kids. Classics of this ilk include:

- half a deep-fried pizza, chips and fizzy drink (from the chip shop)

- burger in a white roll and fizzy drink (from the takeaway)

- miserable white-bread sandwiches (from the petrol station/ newsagent)

- pie/pastie/sausage roll with chips (from the cheap chain bakery).

Most of these can be had for under £1.

By contrast, all the outlets serving better and more varied food are servicing adults with money. It will cost at least twice as much to buy lunch there. A small bottle of mineral water can cost a teenager more than an entire composite 'pupil's special' from the local chippie. What can parents of teenagers do without spending a fortune on lunch?

The first thing is to investigate the options near the school. If you don't already know the area, go at a weekend with your teenager (to do so during the week would wreck his or her street cred!) and assess the possibilities for yourself.

It's important to remember that younger secondary pupils especially tend to stick with the herd and frequent the shops that are popular with school kids. They may not see some better alternatives because they view them as adult establishments which are a bit scary. They may feel unsure about going in, thinking that teenagers aren't welcome, or may find it too difficult to choose from the wider range.

By taking them in for lunch, or just going through the food on offer, you can open their horizons and show them some affordable but better options they hadn't realised were there. You can allay their fears by demonstrating that as long as they don't go in as part of a cheeky, noisy rabble who look as if they are on a collective shoplifting spree, the assistants will be quite nice to them – nicer, probably, than the cynical outlets servicing the teenage market. And, particularly for teenagers who are concerned about their looks and know that diet has some bearing on them, you can point them in

the direction of the healthier alternatives and they may be surprisingly receptive.

When you've jointly identified the best place or places to buy
lunch, it's a good idea to look at how the daily spend could be kept
down without compromising on quality. The best way to do this is
to supplement what's bought with food and drink from home. For
example, buy a small bottle of mineral water one day, then fill it for
a week or so after with tap water. A couple of pieces of fruit from
home can always be taken to school each day, leaving the teenager
to find only a main savoury element for their lunch.

PART SIX

....

TESTING SITUATIONS

SHOPPING TRIPS

No scenario for a modern supermarket would be complete without a background din prominently featuring children crying. We have all witnessed, either at first or second hand, those angry red-faced toddlers trying to bend themselves backwards to escape from the trolley, the intensifying noise levels, low-level whingeing and crying building into a spectacular showdown crescendo played out in full view of checkout staff and other customers.

In the not so distant past, when supermarkets routinely and cynically put sweets and confectionery at the till, this was the typical flashpoint for that all too familiar parent/child battle: '*I want it – You can't have it.*' Nowadays, under pressure from parents who felt that the checkout had become a sugar-trap, sweets have mainly been replaced by useful items such as batteries and magazines. And yet the battles continue. Why?

The nub of the problem is that the typical weekly shopping trip is deeply boring for most children. The first one or two have novelty value; thereafter for most children weekly supermarket shopping is a penance, just as it is for their accompanying adults, who usually have no alternative but to take their offspring with them.

Just think of the routine. They are in and out of the car with all the palaver of baby seats or seat belts at least four times. Just as they are getting interested in something, they are moved on to something different. Waking up, sleeping, dozing, being bundled out of car parks, into lifts and down aisles. They are made to wait in apparently interminable queues, their movements restricted, and generally not allowed to touch anything that seems interesting.

Obviously, these conditions are guaranteed to bring out the worst in any child and it takes only a small catalyst for all hell to break loose. The older they get, the more children realise that the mere threat of a tantrum gives them considerable bargaining, or 'pester', power over the adult. A well-timed demand for a food the child wants but the parent doesn't is often successful. The price many adults pay for 'good behaviour' in this setting is giving in to demands for junk, usually those foods and drinks that are hyped relentlessly on children's television.

We can avoid this trap by taking preventive action.

The first thing to do is to make sure that the children aren't hungry when they arrive in the supermarket. We need to feed them first or, if that is not possible, take some good food and/or drink from home to give them when those predictable demands commence. It's easy to overlook just how much hunger affects behaviour. And, hunger apart, just like adults, children react to boredom by wanting to eat. This way we can make sure they have something we want them to eat, not something we have been browbeaten into buying.

The next thing to consider is changing the nature of the 'sweetener' or bribe for going there in the first place to something more acceptable than junk food. Using the approach described in Sweets, Treats and Bans (pages 91–5), we can tell children that they can choose a treat but that it must be something like stickers, a book, a drawing pad and so on. This gives them something to look forward to but distracts them from food.

As children get older, we can make supermarket shopping much more bearable all round by involving them in the creative side of the process – evaluating food quality and making decisions about what to buy. This participation in the shopping process should give them more feeling of control over what they eat and more inclination to eat what is offered to them. It also gives adults a perfect opportunity to explain to children why they buy some products and not others, and how they assess food quality. (See The Fun and Skill of Food Shopping on pages 221–4.)

For children of all ages, it's important to recognise that small shops are generally much more interesting. The time spent in each shop is shorter and so a typical high-street shopping-parade trip is by definition more varied and stimulating. There is often more one-to-one interaction in small shops and more human contact – children like that. Unlike the supermarket, where car trips are increasingly essential, a variety of small shops can be visited on foot or in a pushchair in a seamless way, without the disrupting 'ins' and 'outs' of the car. In short, small shops are calmer and more intrinsically interesting for children. The Fun and Skill of Food Shopping (pages 221–4) explains in more detail the benefits of small and more specialist shops when shopping with children.

CAR TRIPS

'*Are we nearly there?*' – the classic chant when the car has completed only a fraction of the journey. There is the odd child who likes the car but for the majority such trips are hell, a hell relieved only by the prospect of taking out their grievances on the adults inflicting such torture upon them.

Clearly there are many non-food elements that can make a necessary trip more bearable (the comfort of the car, tapes, stops and so on) but food can loom large on the agenda. Firstly, because boredom makes us all – both adults and children – want to eat. Secondly, because demands centring on hunger and thirst are a great weapon for children who feel like being difficult and venting their exasperation.

Standard children's car fare consists traditionally of a series of 'treats' thought to buy peace, such as sucking sweets. However, although a very chewy toffee may guarantee silence for a minute or two (if only because the child's teeth are stuck together), sugary and salty snacks are more likely to generate hyperactivity than tranquillity and exacerbate the predictable demands for drinks because of the thirst they generate.

Since few non-masochistic adults would ever choose a touring holiday with children, most car journeys are tedious motorway trips. As we all know, the highways of Britain are studded not with wholesome food outlets but with the most rapaciously priced low-grade catering, whose 'child-friendly' repertoire consists of the over-processed junk described on pages 48–52. Rely on this little lot for sustenance and we will be forking out a serious amount of money on horrible food.

How can we make such trips more bearable?

Unfortunately there is no quick-fix solution. The only way to make things better is to get organised in advance and take decent food and drink with you. To give children a change of scene, a major break out of the car, centred on a home-made picnic, is the obvious choice. You can use all the service-station facilities but avoid the food. Picnic menus ideas can be borrowed from Ten Good Packed Lunches (pages 259–62), while ideas for satisfying the seemingly endless demands for snacks generated by long car trips can be found in Twenty-five Good Snacks (pages 237–8).

When travelling on roads that go through real places as opposed to motorway service stations, it can be a good idea to plan a stop for lunch in a restaurant or café which your advance research suggests can offer a reasonable meal. Though adults can cope with long journeys, just stopping for coffee and snacking in the car, children thrive on a change of scene and a short – say, one hour – break out of the car.

Feed them a decent-quality, satisfying lunch or supper, then give them some activity to do in the car and you may not hear a cheep out of them for the next few hours!

BIRTHDAY PARTIES

Birthday parties are the perfect showcase for children's junk food. The food served has to come over as a treat. The birthday child wants his or her friends to like the food and drink on offer, so the pressure is on even the most real-food-minded parent to give in to demands for junky 'children's food' and drink. A child who routinely accepts water as the standard drink may beg that something more 'popular' is laid on that the other children will like. Custom and practice demand a table groaning with mini-sausage rolls, pappy sandwiches, crisps and extruded snacks, trayloads of chocolate crispies and a cake slathered with gooey icing. How should we react?

We can just shrug our shoulders. After all, it's only one day of the year and to hell with any food principles. But why should we give in to the notion that junk food is a treat when we don't even agree with that?

Without remaining entirely rigid, however, we can still lay on only food and drink that we know is good but that children also see as good fun. The first empowering thing to bear in mind is that although children like the *idea* of the classic birthday repertoire they cannot actually eat that much of it. Remember coming back from that childhood birthday party and going straight to bed to lie in a queasy state induced by jelly, ice cream and the like? The fact is that most children like the thought of birthday food more than the reality. That's why the debris from a cut-up commercial birthday cake often amounts to almost the weight of the original cake. Thick glacé icing and sickeningly sweet chocolate toppings may appeal to Roald Dahl's child characters but hardly any real children can finish and truly enjoy them.

The lesson to be learned is that looking good is the most important thing about birthday food. It needs to look like a treat, an exciting spread. Using real, wholesome ingredients, we can achieve this relatively effortlessly as well as giving children something they can actually finish.

Starting with drinks, it is fine to boycott the typical junky children's fizzies. The obvious low-effort alternative is any kind of unsweetened fresh fruit juice mixed with sparkling mineral water. Starting with this standard fruit juice spritzer, we can diversify into home-made lemonade, iced teas, milk shakes, flavoured waters and smoothies. Details of how to make these simple drinks are in Ten Good Drinks on pages 251–8.

When we turn our attention to the food, then what we serve depends a lot on the age of the child.

For younger children, it's a good idea to concentrate on foods that are easy to hold. Instead of the ubiquitous mini-sausage roll, we could serve tiny portions of the mildly spicy Ajwain chicken (see pages 241–2). Good-quality sausages could be halved (simply twist them in the centre to create a new link, then cut) to make a better alternative to the standard chipolata. Home-made mini-meatballs or kofta can be served warm or cold with cocktail sticks or on skewers.

Little sandwiches, cut into shapes or rolled in pinwheels, can be made with smoked salmon, tuna or mackerel pâté (made just with mashed fish, cream cheese or yogurt, seasoning and lemon juice). If sandwiches are already seen as old-fashioned, then mini-bagels or mini-pittas can be filled instead.

On the nibbles front, we can replace the usual salty, fatty, extruded snacks with little bowls of items like soy-roasted nuts and seeds (see recipe on page 271) and interesting dried fruits like cherries and plump raisins.

If we feel that the demand for crisps is too strong to ignore, a visit to any decent wholefood shop will yield more nutritious blue corn tortilla chips. We should also be able to buy there some additive-free crisps with natural seasonings such as cheese and tomato powders or spices rather than the standard chemical ones. All wholefood shops stock corn to pop, too.

Cheese straws, either bought or home-made, offer a more wholesome alternative to 'cheesy' extruded snacks.

A platter of vegetable crudités, such as carrot batons, cherry tomatoes, slices of cucumber and red pepper, served with a yogurt or mayonnaise dip, is fast to prepare and looks great. Similarly, a fresh fruit platter, perhaps with a spiky pineapple top as its glamorous centrepiece, is irresistible for children, as long as it features some exciting fruits: two colours of grapes, melon, strawberries, clementine segments, pineapple chunks and kiwi, for example. Some could be half-dipped in good-quality chocolate for variety.

For traditionalists who like the idea of jelly, individual jellies can be made in ice-cube trays (choose ones with interesting shapes) using real fruit juice, set with an agar-agar-based vegetarian gelling mix (available from wholefood shops). They will be much better than the standard packet jelly, which is basically a mixture of gelatine, sugar and chemical additives.

Fairy cakes can be given a healthier twist by making them to a carrot cake or muffin mixture, with a dab of cream cheese frosting (see below) under the 'wings' if making them into butterfly cakes. Some home-made biscuits, cut with a cookie cutter and made by the child, would be better fun than bought ones. The ingredients will definitely be better too.

When it comes to the birthday cake, it's a bit harder because it is well nigh impossible to buy anything that looks like a child's birthday cake which isn't unbearably sweet and sickly. This is not necessarily a big problem for parents who want their children to eat well generally. Birthdays are only once a year and anyway the chances are that, though they like the look of the cake and will clamour to have their bit, the children won't eat much of it anyway.

Alternatively, if we can bake at all, then this is the obvious annual occasion for our efforts. If we want the children actually to eat the cake, then a fairly simple light sponge made to an airy swiss-roll-type recipe – either plain (vanilla) or chocolate – usually fits the bill. We can hire a cake tin in a shape that children like – teddy, dinosaur, train – to give it a more professional look.

Glacé icings and icing-sugar-based frostings make cakes too sweet for most children so, if used, they should be very thin. Some shops now stock golden icing sugar. This tastes less overwhelmingly sweet than the usual white stuff and has a more fudgy, caramel flavour. It could be beaten with cream cheese or mascarpone cheese and unsalted butter to make a more subtle, less cloying frosting. Spread thinly over the top, it can be dusted with cocoa powder, grated chocolate, toasted almonds or coconut. If we want it to look fancy, we can cut out a stiff-paper template shape (such as leopard stripes or a horse) or simply use a paper doily to produce an interesting pattern.

This type of frosting, thinly spread on top, works well with a fresher filling made with a mixture of whipped cream or thick Greek yogurt. We could grate chocolate into it or flavour it with chopped-up red fruits such as strawberries or defrosted frozen raspberries, or simply spread it on along with good jam or lemon curd. Ready-made stick-on 'birthday greetings', age numerals and candles will finish it off nicely. It will definitely reach the spot that commercial children's birthday cakes just don't reach.

If party bags are still *de rigueur*, we can avoid filling them with sticky sweets and put in items like rubbers, stick-on earrings, marbles, mini notepads, football stickers and balloons instead. If the birthday child insists that some sweets must be included since other children might expect them, 'mini' or even single-mouthful versions of large confectionery items fit the bill.

For older children and teenagers some of these food ideas – such as mini-koftas – will still be acceptable and not seen as too babyish. But in the main they appreciate slightly more sophisticated food that is more hands-on or DIY. In summer, an adult-supervised barbecue would be fun with home-made kebabs and burgers. In winter, baked potatoes with various toppings to choose and assemble, or warmed tacos or tortillas which they can roll and fill, could be served.

They could have their own cocktail bar, complete with shaker and ice bucket, and be let loose on making their own (non-alcoholic) concoctions. They could make their own fondue. A savoury cheese fondue or raclette can be served with baked potatoes, cold meats and crunchy pickles, a sweet chocolate one with fruit to dip. They could run their own ice-cream parlour, making home-made sundaes out of premium ice cream or frozen yogurt, topped with things like grated or melted chocolate, crushed nuts, maple syrup and raspberry purée.

Managing our own child's party is one thing, but what about other children's parties? We can predict with some certainty that children used to a real-food approach are likely to be presented with food and drink they don't get at home which conforms to the junk birthday-food model.

At the end of the day, we have to be philosophical and accept that they will eat or drink some of it. We can, however, minimise that by sending them off well fed: most parties for young children are in the afternoon. The less hungry they are, the more they can pick out the better food and drink on offer.

We can flag up to them in advance some of the usual risks. Deep-frozen sausage rolls, inadequately reheated, are a food-poisoning hazard. We might counsel younger children away from anything reheated and meaty without explaining why – just in case they blurt it out! We can explain why to older children but remind them not to mention this in case it offends the host.

We can explain that even if they see only cola and orange fizz, they can still ask politely for water or fruit juice. For children with certain food allergies and intolerances, the standard party food can be a serious problem. Colourings in icings and sweets and chemical preservatives and flavourings in fizzy drinks can prove to be a real danger. So if we have children with this sort of vulnerability, we need to school them well on how to avoid the most hazardous triggers in food.

Of course, whatever we tell our children, they will probably feel under stronger pressure to go along with everyone else and ignore us anyway. But at least they will have heard our reservations in advance and this will make them a little bit more discerning.

GRANDPARENTS' HOUSES

It's a familiar tale. A child is going to stay with his grandmother. The parent warns her that he isn't very good at eating breakfast and can be awkward. When the parent comes back to pick up the child, the grandmother reports that he ate a good breakfast. Surprised, the parent asks what exactly he ate. 'Well, cherry cheesecake of course!' comes the reply.

The fact is that grandparents almost never have any problems feeding their grandchildren because they say yes to virtually everything the children want. Grandparents like to give treats, and never want to remonstrate with children in any way. The grandparent role is generally indulgent and line-of-least-resistance, of the 'If my little darling wants it, she gets it' variety. Not surprisingly, children often identify their grandparents as a soft touch and make demands on them they know their parents would throw out instantly.

What ought we to do about this, if anything? Parents who are trying to encourage their children to eat real, wholesome food can easily see this as undermining the stance they are taking. On the other hand, what are grandparents for if not to indulge their grandchildren to a degree that makes their parents envious? All depends on how much time children spend with their grandparents. If the grandparent is regularly acting as a childminder and having a major influence on forming their grandchild's food tastes, then parents do have to try to rein them in and establish the kind of food they want their children to eat. What You Can Expect from Childcarers (see pages 169–75) suggests strategies for raising food issues with childcarers, all of which would also be appropriate with grandparents.

We can also ask them to find ways of giving children a treat that doesn't involve food (see pages 94–5).

If time spent with grandparents is just every now and then – say, the odd weekend, holidays or even one day a week – then it is best to be philosophical.

Grandparents are older – we aren't going to change them. If we raise a vexed food issue with them – for example, an endless supply of 'sweetie money' – then chances are they will merely humour us parents anyway, continuing as before but just not owning up to it.

Children can and will learn that different people do things in different ways. Just because they get a packet of biscuits at a time at Grandad's, that doesn't set a precedent for anywhere else.

PART SEVEN

···

CONSOLIDATING YOUR EFFORTS

ENCOURAGING CHILDREN TO COOK

Wouldn't it be marvellous if we could wave a magic wand and instantly transform our children into adults with wide-ranging food tastes, adults who appreciate food quality and revel in the pleasure of eating?

Unfortunately there is no single magic wand at our disposal, but the next best single measure we can use to achieve that end is something that we all have in our power: we can encourage them to cook.

Nowadays the food industry likes to make out that cooking is about as rarefied a skill as making your own clothes. We're told that the pace of modern life means that people are caught up in vital all-consuming activities which mean that they don't have the time or inclination to expend energy on food preparation. This pernicious lore is used as the justification for the many dubious industrial interventions to which much modern food is subjected.

The propaganda is successful. There are now subsequent generations of adults who are ever more divorced from primary foodstuffs in their raw state and whose idea of cooking is assembling several pre-cooked, long-life components from cartons, packets and tins. The consequence is that many adults are increasingly de-skilled in the art of feeding themselves and their families.

Although this erosion of cooking skills is an issue in itself, there is an equally important consequence that is often ignored. Through cooking food, people develop shrewder judgement about its quality. If you cook your own lasagne, for example, you will notice if one butcher's mince is fattier than another's and you'll instantly taste the difference between your own tomato sauce and the starchy, sweetened gloop that you get in a ready-made one. If, on the other hand, all you ever taste is the ready-meal lasagne, you may forget or even never experience the home-made equivalent, so the mass-produced, food-industry offering becomes your only point of reference.

Along with that haemorrhage of skills and lowering of standards comes a loss of pleasure in food. The process of eating becomes much more mechanical, functional and ultimately unrewarding. We get bogged down in a lacklustre world of uniform tastes and limited food horizons, where our points of reference are almost exclusively over-processed, mass-produced food.

By encouraging children to cook simple dishes from the earliest age, we give them the best chance of breaking out of this modern food straitjacket. Being able to cook has the same relationship to food as literacy has to books: it's an essential skill that opens doors and widens horizons.

So where do we begin? We can start by realising what children don't learn at school. Baking is a fairly common activity for nursery-age children but it usually consists of very simple sweet recipes that require no real cooking. Through primary school, food preparation or cooking is generally a very occasional activity, although a certain amount of general food knowledge is often included in the curriculum as part of themed projects or health education.

In the first two years of secondary school, most children still get some blocks of Home Economics, a significant part of which is basic cooking. For children who have not learned at home, this may be the first time they pick up skills like using an oven, how to use a knife safely and a few straightforward recipes.

But this is the last taste of cooking that most children get. Those who drop Home Economics or Food Technology stop there. Those who take it as a certificate subject will be taught very little in the way of cooking; instead they learn about modern technological food processes. Teenagers studying this new discipline of Food Technology will be taught, for example, how to design a production process for a fish finger, not how to cook fish. They will be able to design packaging for ready meals or a vegetarian airline meal. They do not discover how to make their own food at home – vegetarian or otherwise. They may know how to interpret a nutrition label or work out a supermarket's food profit margins. They will not learn how to judge whether, for example, a stone fruit is ripe or a burger is made from safely sourced meat.

Putting it bluntly, parents can't assume that children will have learned any cooking skills by the time they leave school. So if we want our children to become adults who can cook and appreciate unprocessed food, we have to teach them at home.

The earlier we start, the better. Even very young children, from two years onwards, can really enjoy cooking and although they obviously can't follow a recipe through, and will need careful supervision, they will get a lot of fun and satisfaction while 'helping' an adult to cook. Washing potatoes in muddy water, pummelling dough, mixing up and stirring, using a rolling pin, and cutting out shapes are just some activities that children like. Adults, on the other hand, have to take a deep breath and resign themselves to the general mess and uproar in the kitchen. Just keep saying to yourself that this is the price you pay to produce a child who'll be inviting you round for a delicious home-made meal when adult!

By the age of four, with a bit of help, most children can make a simple recipe from start to finish. This process is very satisfying for children, as they see that the whole point of food preparation is that you get something nice to eat at the end of it. Natural curiosity will make them open to tasting what they've made and because they feel responsible for making it they are more likely to think that they enjoy it than if it has been prepared by someone else.

However, we don't have to give children only the classic 'children's recipes', such as rock cakes or chocolate crispies, which tend to be quite limited. For example, crispie recipes usually use hard baking margarine and cheap cake covering 'chocolate', not butter and real chocolate. Many of these old recipes also overdo the sweet ingredients, so we may need to revise them. We also need to make sure that children do some savoury cooking (see Ten Easy Recipes That Children Can Make, pages 270–81) so that their involvement in cooking isn't restricted to sticky, sugary baking.

Once children are of school age and can follow simple instructions it's a good idea to buy basic equipment that makes it easier for them to cook and which they recognise as their special *batterie de cuisine*. For example:

- An electronic scale which gives a visual display of both solid and liquid quantities in both metric and imperial measures. (However much you cherish your antique scales, you have to recognise that these more old-fashioned scales are hard for children to read. A visual display means that children don't have to do any calculations. They resemble pocket calculators and electronic toys, which are user-friendly for modern children.)

- A set of plastic or metal American cup measures. (For children who are too young or can't cope with scales yet, cups are the simplest measures to use. They will also help you to follow any American recipes you might have.)

- Lightweight plastic or metal bowls. (The classic ceramic mixing bowl is too heavy for children to pick up and scrape out.)

- Paper cake cases and pre-cut lining papers for cake tins. (The offerings that emerge in these generally look more presentable. They also save the need for greasing tins, which many children don't like doing and which gets them in a big mess.)

- Wooden spoons and a plastic spatula. (For quieter kitchens and more thorough scraping out.)

- A rolling pin. (They will roll dough to death but they'll have fun.)

- Plastic or metal cutters in fun shapes. (They can use these to cut out the sticky mixture they've rolled out.)

- An apron that fits. (To promote a more 'professional' attitude and to save a lot of washing of clothes after.)

- A solid and stable chair or stool. (The child can stand on it to get up to kitchen-unit height without stretching.)

As children grow older, more sophisticated kitchen equipment can be introduced. From about nine years on, most children will enjoy using a food processor and seeing all the various operations it can perform. But they will need strict supervision. Children wrench off covers rather than turning them according to manufacturer's instructions, so watch what's going on all the time. Also, food processors have sharp blades. You will have to wash and assemble these yourself.

From the age of eleven, if carefully shown how to do so, children can be expected to turn on the oven to the right temperature, take foods in and out of a hot oven using oven gloves and operate most electrical appliances. This opens a whole new world of more ambitious cooking for children. A huge range of both sweet and savoury dishes can be made quickly in a food processor. Liquidisers, blenders and juice extractors offer endless hours of noisy experimentation.

Whenever children have made a couple of dishes successfully, it's time to reinforce their independence in the kitchen by giving them their own personal recipe book and encouraging them to write down the recipes themselves. Being able to cook independently is not only about using kitchen equipment but also about being able to follow a set of instructions from start to finish. When children write a recipe out for themselves, having made it a couple of times, they will be more likely to follow it again when they return to it later. A personal recipe book is also a confidence-building exercise which lets children see the progress they have made through the number of recipes they have mastered.

Special cookery books aimed at children can be a mixed blessing. They can be easy to follow and do appeal to children, but many simply contain primarily sweet recipes which consist of sticking sweets in icing on top of bought-in biscuits. Very few contain many savoury dishes and the end results are not that likely to appeal to adults. In the long run, it is probably best to select easy recipes from your own books and write them out in larger, bolder print. If they go down well, children can then copy them into their own personal recipe book. You will be reinforcing the important principle that children's food is not distinct from adults', and building in the expectation that they potentially like *all* food, not just special children's recipes.

THE FUN AND SKILL OF FOOD SHOPPING

When children have begun to show some interest in cooking and can make a couple of simple dishes with a bit of help, it's a good idea to get them involved in choosing ingredients too.

On pragmatic grounds alone, many parents and childcarers end up having to take children with them while they shop for food, at least occasionally. All too often this is on sufferance from both parties. So if we can get children more interested in the decision-making process of food shopping, then shopping trips are a lot more bearable for everyone concerned.

Children who have a say in what they eat – by being allowed to choose ingredients and suggest what's on the menu – feel consulted and involved, so they are much more likely to eat what's given to them. Viewed long-term, if children are to be interested in food and thoughtful about food quality in later life, the abilities to select good ingredients and shop well are as important as learning cooking skills. The sooner they participate in food shopping, the better.

Just as communal meals are a perfect opportunity to pass on your love of good food to children, so food shopping is a ready-made vehicle for showing them that food doesn't just magically materialise in your kitchen. Every food product has a production history and some are much more appetising than others.

It's also the perfect occasion for making explicit your personal food shopping rationale. If you think out loud when you shop with children, they are more likely to understand why you buy some products and not others. When children rush up and clamour, '*That looks great, can we buy that?*', brandishing the latest gimmicky kids' food, you can explain to them why you don't.

You can show them what there is to be gleaned from reading labels and justify your purchases accordingly. You might explain, for example, that the new, attractive-looking orange drink with the cuddly cartoon name has colourings and sweeteners and why you prefer just the straight orange juice you normally buy. You can use this opportunity to instil cynicism in them about the 'child-friendly' packaging that appears on widely hyped junk foods. If you look out for organic food, you can describe why you buy this in preference to conventional food. If you always buy free-range, you can explain why this is kinder to animals and why that matters to you. You might tell them that even though they use margarine in school, you think butter has a better flavour and so on.

Obviously, the subtlety of the message varies according to the age of the children. But from as early an age as possible, it is helpful to voice your shopping strategy and show that when you say no to certain foods and yes to others you can justify that choice. Children of all ages are often surprisingly interested in food quality and safety issues and extremely receptive to learning about them.

One mechanism for motivating children to take a special interest in shopping is to let them choose from a magazine or recipe book a meal or food they like the idea of eating and then come with you to do the shopping for it. Another approach is simply to tell them that they can choose, say, any three ingredients they fancy and you can jointly try them out at home. You can let them choose what's on the menu for a meal. Alternatively you can give them a modest budget to spend on the ingredient or dish of their choice.

Although they like the idea of being consulted, often children can't actually cope with this choice and will fall back on you for guidance. But even if it ends up being you who really decides what you're buying and cooking, they will feel that they have participated in that decision and will be much more inclined to eat the end product.

Provided they choose something that does have real ingredients – not a ready-prepared meal or widely hyped junk food – then you can agree to buy whatever they choose and help them to prepare it or, better still, let them do so themselves.

The whole point of this exercise is to give children some proprietorial interest in the food being served in their house. So when you eat it, it needs to be billed as their thing – *'This is the pasta that Jessica chose and she made it too!' 'Nick made all the main course tonight and he decided what it would be too!'* and so on. Lay on the praise with a trowel to encourage some pride and a feeling of accomplishment. In the unfortunate event that the end result turns out to be less than appetising, salvage the situation by blaming the recipe – *'We'll know not to trust that magazine next time, won't we?'* – and suggest a tried and tested success for the next attempt.

When children are first allowed to choose food ingredients, you may well find that they go for something gooey and sweet which involves, for example, lots of melting of chocolate and golden syrup and bashing up of digestive biscuits. But that doesn't really matter. It's quite likely that they will discover that they liked the idea of those ingredients better than the reality. Over time, and with a bit of experimentation, children who are used to being given real food at home will start selecting more sophisticated dishes that appeal to them, especially if you show them recipe books and magazines with tantalising pictures.

Offering a degree of involvement in food selection is a useful strategy not just for adventurous eaters but also for managing those children who have a habit of telling you they don't like what you are offering. You can put the ball back into their court by effectively saying, *'Okay, you don't like what we had last night, so tell me what you do fancy and I'll cook that later this week.'* This reaction appears to respect their preferences and offers an accommodating response. But it does not, however, allow them to adopt a blanket negative veto on food.

Whether you take children shopping because you have no other choice or because you actively want them to get involved, here are some ways to keep them interested:

- Don't assume that supermarkets are best. Although supermarkets carry a huge number of lines, the supermarket shopping experience can be exceptionally boring, for both children and adults. It is easy to settle into a fixed, repetitive way of shopping there which becomes very dull indeed. Also, there is no real human interaction in large stores and, although they may be freer to move about, children often prefer the human contact you get in small shops where there are 'real' people and sometimes familiar faces.

- Give them jobs to do. For older children this might include a list of ingredients to find, a checklist of things to remind you to buy, letting them choose and bag loose produce, telling them to look out for 'loyalty' or 'reward' points, sending them back several aisles for items you've forgotten.

- Take them to interesting small shops where there are unusual things to look at. Obvious places include Chinese supermarkets and other ethnic shops, greengrocers selling exotic or just interesting seasonal produce, specialist cheese shops (especially if they offer tastes of food), wholefood shops with sacks of grains and so on sold loose, pick-your-own farm shops and traditional fishmongers with a good fresh display. Be prepared to buy almost anything they'd like to taste, provided it's real food not junk.

THE FASCINATING WORLD OF RESTAURANT FOOD

Restaurants are potentially fascinating establishments for children. While 'improving' expeditions such as visits to museums and galleries can all too quickly come over as a boring imposition, for most children there's something intrinsically exciting about a visit to a restaurant – the idea of chefs, cooking, menus, waiters, prettily arranged tables with tablecloths, candles and glittering glassware. A special visit to a swanky restaurant has many of the hallmarks of Christmas for a young child: special rituals and treats in store.

Yet relatively few British children get taken to 'real' restaurants – that is, restaurants whose *raison d'être* is first and foremost serving good food to adults. Instead, many children's experience is confined to the self-styled 'child-friendly/family' restaurants described on pages 48–52, which specialise in the usual children's junk-food repertoire. This is mainly because we anticipate all sorts of difficulties attached to adult restaurants, which in the event might or might not be experienced. We worry that the children will behave badly and that this will be embarrassing. We predict the disapproval of other diners and staff at the first sign of restlessness. We don't like the idea that our adult treat will be spoiled by the stress of supervising potentially troublesome offspring. We dread them not finding anything they want to eat. We resent the idea of spending a lot of money on food that the child won't like and might reject.

So, rather than face all that, we chicken out and consider taking them only to an anonymous fast-food joint. If they throw a major wobbly, or don't eat anything at all, it doesn't really matter and the financial damage will be limited too. We rationalise our reactions by saying that, like learning to drive and seeing X-rated films, 'proper' restaurants are an experience reserved for the over-eighteens.

Clearly, age does make a difference to how well a child will tolerate a restaurant and there is, of course, a difference between taking a baby and a child out to eat. A visit to a restaurant with a baby can be a hit-or-miss experience. If you are lucky, the baby will sleep peacefully in a pushchair or baby carrier, stirring only to blow sweet bubbles at the doting elderly couple at the next table. Dream babies like this can fit into any type of restaurant. If you are unlucky, the baby will literally bawl his or her head off, demanding a restless tour of the corridors and streets outside, never to give up until plonked prematurely in the car to be driven home. Babies in this mood do tax even the most indulgent management and the most relaxed parents.

Sometimes we just have to take babies to restaurants for reasons of expediency – on holiday, for example, when there is no babysitter and we want to eat out. On a routine basis, however, taking babies to restaurants does put parents under some pressure and probably doesn't add significantly to the baby's learning experience.

However, if we want our children to learn to appreciate a wide range of wholesome food, from toddlerhood on, trips to restaurants – even only occasionally – offer a ready-made learning opportunity to extend their good-food horizons.

It is the perfect way to get them to think big and open about food, to move on from the familiar foods they are given at home. The broader the menu they encounter, the more varied and diverse the dishes, the better. A visit to a real restaurant is yet another effective tool to counter the 'tunnel effect' described on pages 71– 3, which can drastically limit children's food horizons. By contrast, visits to the typical 'child-friendly' restaurant with its cynical bill of 'kiddies' fare' reinforce the tunnel effect and connive in narrowing children's food tastes.

Although the UK is not exactly a child-welcoming culture when it comes to public space, it's worth remembering that the difficult phase is actually quite short-lived and that the older children become, the easier eating out with them gets. Quite soon you will be able to rely on them not to get a breadstick stuck up their nose or get barricaded into the toilet, for example!

But even quite young children, when they are in the right mood and the right restaurant circumstances, can stun adults with their ability to rise to the occasion. They may behave excellently. They may eat food they would never countenance at home. They may defy all our conservative predictions because they want to demonstrate that they can live up to the more sophisticated adult role they have been given, displaying the civilised behaviour we have unsuccessfully sought from them during meals at home. But in the wrong mood, the whole thing can turn into a disaster all round. So how can we handle restaurant visits so that they turn out well?

The single most important factor in the whole equation is the mood of the child. The idea of going to a restaurant is exciting for children but, like all exciting treats, it can make them overwrought. It is easy to forget that this is much more likely to happen when a child is tired, below par for some other reason such as illness, or, quite simply, too hungry to start with. This is especially true of younger children.

So ideally, when eating out with children, plan ahead wherever possible, or at least take a rain check on their mood before setting out. As adults, the idea of eating out may appeal to us simply because we are tired and can't face cooking. But if we are tired, chances are the children are too, and this might not leave them in the best frame of mind for a restaurant outing.

If at all possible, try to see that children are well rested in advance and are in good form physically. For very small children, a lunchtime meal is often the most realistic, as their mood often deteriorates as the day goes on. If you want to eat out in the evening, a decent afternoon nap beforehand is sensible. Obviously, a tired four-year-old with an irritating cough that keeps him or her awake at night just isn't going to last the pace of the typical adult dinner, which is usually protracted and drawn-out by children's standards.

The next thing to bear in mind is how hard children find it to keep going when they are hungry. We may serve a light, snacky lunch and nothing much else in the afternoon because we know that we are eating out that night. But children have more efficient metabolisms than we do and it's unlikely that they will have had enough to keep them going. We may forget that although the booking was reasonably early in restaurant time, say 7 pm, very little food might appear for at least half an hour – and that might just be the bread basket.

So even though we expect children to satisfy their hunger when they are in the restaurant, we may have to give them a substantial snack earlier in the day to take the acute edge off that hunger. Made to wait too long, many children simply become too bad-tempered to eat, or wolf down the first nibbles so fast that it's only a matter of time until they are complaining of stomach cramps and refusing to eat anything further.

When potential tiredness or hunger has been forestalled, the next factor to consider is boredom. What can seem to an adult a reasonable wait for food can be interminable for a child. So it is not a bad idea to bring with you some small diversion – a notebook and pencils, a book, a pocket-sized toy or game – to offset boredom before it leads to more cantankerous behaviour.

With children equipped to enjoy the experience of dining out, we need to turn our attention to the right sort of restaurant.

One good scenario for unremarkable but nevertheless perfectly satisfactory eating is unpretentious – and relatively affordable – independently owned restaurants. A few of the better chain pizza outlets also fit the bill. This type of place, be it the neighbourhood Italian, Indian, Thai or Chinese restaurant, doesn't cultivate a stuffy image and this makes them more approachable for people with children. However, because they are there primarily for adult diners the food will be less formulaic and much more varied and interesting. Usually the range of dishes on offer is popular enough for both adults and children to find something they like to eat. In the more adventurous places, where the menu might seem off-puttingly complicated for children, the best idea is to order a selection of dishes and let children select the elements they like when it arrives.

Most restaurants of this type won't make a bureaucratic fuss about being asked for three pastas with four plates or a double order of pancakes to go with the Peking duck. The potential problem of finding one thing on the menu that a child agrees to eat can be avoided by a communal order. The galling scenario where a child orders a particular dish then refuses to eat it can't happen under these circumstances. The child is not put in a 'succeed or fail' eating situation. Instead, everything she or he does eat will be seen as a bonus, which means less pressure all round.

Formal, upmarket special-occasion restaurants can be more intimidating for adults with children, but under certain circumstances we may nevertheless want to take children to them: birthdays, weddings and holidays are just a few of the likely occasions that spring to mind. For the more cowardly, the soft option is to go for lunch rather than dinner. Many serious establishments are more child-tolerant at lunchtime and offer cheaper menu packages. If it has to be the evening, it's worth finding out what you can about the place in advance. Do they serve starter portions of main courses? Are there dishes on the menu that are likely to appeal to children as well as adults? Can a child simply share the adults' food? How relaxed do they seem to be about child diners?

If possible, check that the service isn't too leisurely (or take your children there on a quiet night), otherwise small children will get bored between courses and will want to get down. When you book, tell the restaurant that you are bringing children with you.

A phone call or drop-in visit can offer an illuminating insight into the management's attitude. The more upmarket the establishment, the better it ought to be at coping with children, if for no other reason than that the front-of-house staff should be better trained to deal with the eccentric needs of a variety of diners, whatever their age!

If you are going to spend a lot of money on a special eating-out occasion with children in tow, use your impressions to make a good choice. Get it wrong and you'll end up feeling uncomfortable while you are there and hard up when you leave. Get it right, by finding a restaurant that treats children like little emperors and woos them into astoundingly good behaviour with delicious dishes, and it could be one of the best eating-out experiences both adults and children can have.

Whatever kind of restaurant you visit, it's not a good idea to insist that small children eat something there; instead, just gently encourage them to do so. The most important goal at first is to get into their heads the notion that they like eating out (even if in reality they eat very little) and feel at ease in an adult restaurant environment. As they grow older and make more restaurant visits, they will gradually become intrigued by what everyone else is eating and want to try it too.

When we decide to make 'real' restaurants the focus of children's eating-out experience, what scope, if any, is there for the typical 'child-friendly' fast-food joint? How can we react to children who demand to be taken there?

We can start by recognising that such demands are both predictable and natural given the millions of pounds that are spent by fast-food outlets on advertising targeted at children. It is inevitable that even children who are fed wholesome, unprocessed food at home are going to want to visit such restaurants. The younger they are, the more likely they are to be lured by the idea of gifts and believe that they will like the food served.

Even if fast-food outlets don't fit in with our idea of delicious, appetising food, there is no point in refusing to visit them. So the best tactic is to say that you will take the child to one *once*, so he or she can see what they are like, but that you personally don't like the places. You can explain your objections using the strategies outlined in Getting the Message Across (see pages 61–6), such as telling them what's wrong with junk and enthusing about real food.

You can explain to them that the idea of these places is much better than the reality and that when they have tried one you think they will probably prefer to eat in a better, more 'grown-up' restaurant.

When visits to real restaurants are on offer as an alternative, few children are likely to maintain their apparent loyalty to a fast-food joint for very long.

EXERCISING JUNIOR TASTEBUDS

It's hard to imagine a child who would agree to eat absolutely anything that was put before him or her – even the most adventurous. However, most children have a natural curiosity about the taste of food and are prepared to sample a given food even if that is just a token concession before rejecting it.

Often when we are trying to get children to eat something, we appeal to them to 'just try a bit', but by then it is often too late because they have already decided they don't like it and won't eat it. But when tasting is separated from routine eating, with no strings or obligations attached, most children will find it good fun and feel inclined to go along with it. This openness to sampling food is something we can exploit, both to extend children's food horizons and to heighten their appreciation of quality.

The easiest way to capitalise on it is to make tasting into an occasional game, where the children have been appointed as judges. Just watch. They love it.

This is how it works. Ask each child to bring along a friend (everything is more fun with a friend). Give them all a sheet of paper and pencil if the tasting is long and complex, or just ask them for verbal comments otherwise. All sorts of food comparisons can be made into a game. For example, we can ask them to compare:

- diluted orange drink, fresh orange juice from a carton and freshly squeezed juice

- different brands of the same biscuit, say oatcakes

- different types of plain yogurt (full-fat, Greek, low-fat)

- milk and dark chocolate or different dark chocolates with varying cocoa-solid contents

- a shop-bought scone and a home-made scone

- big old carrots and new baby carrots

- different olive oils on bits of bread.

The possibilities are infinite. We can take things a bit further by holding blind tastings (where the identity of the food is unknown and revealed only after the children give their rating) or even where they are literally blindfolded and ask to identify foods. Spices are obvious candidates for this treatment. Part of the game is for the children to sniff them all first, then see if they can identify them blind, by holding in their head the memory of each spice's distinctive aroma.

Of course, a tasting doesn't have to be complicated, comparative, or even blind; it could simply have a theme. An obvious one is 'things we haven't tasted before' – preferably selected by the children. We could buy, for example, unusual fruit – such as a blood orange or a papaya – and ask the children what they make of it.

You can more or less predict in advance the children's reaction to any tasting. They will adore being consulted and giving opinions. One will like one item and hate another. Some reactions will be shared, others quite divergent. Whether or not they like what they taste is largely irrelevant, as is what they are tasting. The whole point of this exercise – quite apart from being a good diversion for rainy days – is that we are getting children to think about what they put in their mouths, something that many children (and adults for that matter) are not that good at.

When we present food to children in a comparative framework rather than in isolation, they can focus on those tastes and this enhanced awareness will help them notice differences within the category. They will be able to pick up, for example, how a processed 'chocolate' pudding doesn't taste of chocolate when tasted blind, how much saltier one breakfast cereal is than another, the difference between red and green grapes, the distinctive characters of different vinegars such as wine, sherry and balsamic. This hones their tasting skills, which will help them make qualitative choices about the foods they eat and, when good, wholesome foods are being sampled, it provides them with real-food benchmarks against which to appraise other food. It also gives us an ideal opportunity to talk to them about the differences they have noticed and explain why they occur. We can look at a label with them and raise issues about how that food has been produced or what it contains.

Tastings also get children accustomed to handling a wide range of diverse foods they would be unlikely to encounter otherwise. Once more this helps to extend their horizons and counter the 'tunnel effect' described on pages 71–3. It flags up to children that a vast and exciting world of food exists beyond the narrow limits of the ubiquitous 'children's foods' they see all around them and it makes them feel more confident about handling and discussing these foods.

In this way, tasting can extend children's food literacy and, in turn, their willingness to be open-minded about eating. Just as young readers are likely to become keener when they learn their way round a library, so with food sampling young eaters can be motivated to explore food in all its varied and interesting forms.

Last but not least, in the process of tasting, children may discover that they like the taste of, say, that blood orange, even though they thought they wouldn't. Few children will keep up a consistent 'don't like' response to a no-strings-attached fun tasting. Most will discover something surprising that they like. And this is one more thing than they liked at the outset. With a bit of luck, they will ask us to buy that new food find for them and feel enthusiastic about discovering others.

PART EIGHT

....

NITTY-GRITTY IDEAS AND RECIPES FOR INSPIRATION

TWENTY-FIVE GOOD SNACKS

- Oatcakes, ricotta, cottage or cream cheese and grapes
- Natural yogurt, honey or maple syrup and fresh fruit
- Carrot and cucumber batons with dip (bought or home-made)
- Mini-naan breads filled with dressed crab or smoked mackerel pâté and yogurt
- Fresh fruit platter (assorted cut and prepared fresh fruits)
- Fruit and nut platter (assorted dried fruits such as cherries, cranberries, apricots and raisins, with nuts and seeds, such as peanuts, pumpkin and sunflower)
- Bread, olive oil and Dipping Crunch (see recipe on pages 272–3)
- Pitta bread, split, filled with thin slice of cheese, then toasted
- Slice of Parma or other cured ham with crisp fruit (apple, pear) or melon
- Half and half brown- and white-flour scones (see recipe on pages 277–9) with a little butter or jam
- Italian breadsticks with bought or home-made hummus or tsatziki (cucumber and yogurt dip)
- Home-made or good-quality bought carrot or banana cake
- Thick slices of Irish soda bread (see recipe on pages 279–80) with a little butter or jam

- Guacamole (see recipe on pages 270–71) with pitta bread or breadsticks

- Wholemeal bread with smoked salmon

- Cherry tomatoes, crackers and half mayo–half natural yogurt dip

- Bowl of home-made or bought unsweetened muesli (see recipe on pages 280–81) with milk

- Mini-rice cakes with bought or home-made olive spread or peanut butter

- American blue corn tortilla chips (from wholefood shops)

- Soy-sauce Nuts (see recipe on page 271)

- Mashed banana on warm toast

- Warm foccacia or ciabatta bread spread with pesto

- Mini-mozzarella cheeses with cherry tomatoes and vinaigrette dressing

- Fruit kebabs (see recipe on page 277) with natural yogurt

- Thin slices of cooked poultry or meat with vegetable batons and chutney or pickle

TEN MAIN COURSES THAT BOTH ADULTS AND CHILDREN LIKE

Good Food That Children Like (pages 96–101) describes the wide categories of food that many children tend to enjoy and which are more than acceptable for most adults. Here are some more specific recipes and recipe ideas for savoury dishes that should appeal to everyone in a household, irrespective of age. These are good candidates for popular communal meals. Some are so easy to prepare that older children can make them themselves.

The quantities for some dishes are quite flexible, which is why fairly loose measurements are given. Where precise measures are essential, strict quantities are provided.

All recipes with precise quantities make four adult or six children's main-course portions.

Smoked fish chowder

4 undyed smoked haddock or cod fillets, skinned and cut into large chunks
1 large leek, finely chopped
1 large onion, finely chopped
2–3 carrots, diced
3–4 potatoes, chopped (skins left on if organic)
1 celery stick, chopped, or ½ fennel bulb, chopped (optional)
2 bay leaves
250ml single or whipping cream
1 litre whole, unskimmed milk
200g sweetcorn (fresh, frozen or drained from a tin)
finely chopped parsley (optional)
black pepper to taste (optional)

Put all ingredients except the corn, parsley and black pepper into a very large saucepan or casserole. Bring to the boil, and then reduce to a simmer. Do not cover. Simmer only until the hard vegetables are soft but not mushy. If the corn is fresh, add it while the potatoes are just beginning to soften; if frozen or tinned, add just before serving and cook for 2 minutes. Sprinkle over parsley and season with pepper (or leave this to be done at table) and serve. No added salt is needed because smoked fish is salty enough to start with.

For children who say they don't like 'bits' in soup, this is also good liquidised.

Serve with warm, crusty bread.

Salad plate

Use your biggest and most attractive plate or a shallow ceramic serving dish. (Flat plates are out. It needs to have a low edge to keep everything on.)

Choose any selection of items from the following list of possibilities:

- thinly sliced crunchy Little Gem or romaine lettuce
- any salad leaf, broken up small
- sliced cucumbers (rounds or batons)
- whole cherry tomatoes
- thinly sliced mild red onions
- cooked sweetcorn
- julienned or coarsely chopped carrots
- new potato salad (in mayonnaise)
- thinly sliced red or yellow peppers

- finely chopped celery

- radishes

- chopped cooked beetroot

- hard-boiled eggs, cut in half

- tinned tuna

- thin slices of cured ham

- anchovies

- black olives

- tinned chickpeas or other beans, drained.

Arrange a combination of what you have and what you fancy in sections around the plate, placing each judiciously to give the most dazzling colour contrast. It should look fantastic.

Serve with a good quantity of either:

- a mustardy vinaigrette (5 tbsp extra virgin olive oil, 1 tbsp red wine or sherry vinegar and 1 tsp smooth Dijon mustard); or

- a dip (e.g. half and half Greek yogurt and mayonnaise flavoured with fresh herbs).

Children can attack the salad plate without any dressing if they prefer, or help themselves to it liberally.

Ajwain chicken

This is my variation on Madhur Jaffrey's blindingly simple but
delicious recipe. I find that children really go for Indian flavours,
provided they aren't chilli-hot. These succulent bits of chicken can
be served as they come sizzling from the oven or threaded on to
skewers like kebabs. They are good eaten cold for packed lunch,
picnics, at children's parties or as an after-school snack. When hot,
they can go inside toasted pitta bread with some minty yogurt raita
or be accompanied by rice, potatoes or grains, plus almost any
vegetables or salad.

4 free-range chicken breasts, boned and skinned
¼ tsp ground turmeric
1 tsp ground cumin
½ tsp ajwain seeds (or use cumin seeds)
½ tsp salt
1 garlic clove, crushed
3 tbsp extra virgin olive oil

Preheat the oven to 180°C/350°F/Gas Mark 4.

Cut the chicken breasts into thin strips. Place in a wide, shallow
bowl with all the spices, the garlic and 1 tablespoon of the oil. Mix
well to coat and leave to marinate for 15–30 minutes.

Take a frying pan (preferably one that can later be put in the
oven) and warm it up until it reaches a very high heat. Pour in the
remaining oil, which should sizzle, then add the chicken. Pat it down
firmly and do not move it around until it is well browned underneath.
Flip the slices over and do the same on the other side. The chicken
should look brown and crunchy on the outside. Take the pan off
the heat and cover with a layer of baking parchment, needs to sit
only lightly on the top.

Transfer the pan to the oven and bake for 10 minutes. (If you don't have an ovenproof frying pan, transfer the chicken to a baking tray and cover with parchment, then bake.) Remove and eat.

Filled crêpes/tortillas/tacos

Children who dislike thin, French-style crêpes, pliant Mexican tortillas or crunchy taco shells are few and far between. Somehow or other, the idea of having a vehicle that can be filled with a selection of different foods is appealing. And the hands-on, rolling-up nature of the dish seems to make children more inclined to eat it.

Whether you start with your own home-made crêpes made to a standard recipe or simply buy ready-made tortillas or tacos, the fun is assembling them.

Along with the warm crêpes/tortillas/tacos, serve any combination of the following, depending on your whim, people's preferences and what you find in the fridge:

- grated firm cheese or small cubes of melting cheese like mozzarella

- mashed avocado or guacamole (see recipe on pages 270–71)

- warm grilled meat in thin slices

- ratatouille, vegetable stew or warm tomato sauce

- cold meats and ham

- left-over chilli con carne or bolognese sauce

- stir-fried vegetables

- soured cream or Greek yogurt

- tahini paste thinned with lemon juice and water and flavoured with garlic.

Autumn salad

This salad has a theme – everything that's seasonal in autumn. It appeals to that common liking amongst children for a variety of different ingredients from which they can make a selection. Each element is small and dainty and there is a good combination of textures and colours, too. The old alliance of fruit and nuts is exploited. Served with good wholemeal bread, with nuts in if this is popular, it makes a pretty good supper dish to follow, say, a light soup.

1 heart of cos lettuce or 2 hearts of Little Gem, roughly torn
½ softer-textured lettuce, red if possible, e.g. oak leaf
a handful of watercress, coarse stems removed
a small bunch of grapes (a mixture of red and green is perfect)
2 ripe pears or crunchy apples
a handful of fresh-tasting (not bitter) nuts (pecans or fresh walnuts for preference)
2 small goat's cheeses, or a slice weighing around 125g, cut into small cubes
a handful of sunflower or pumpkin seeds

Arrange the salad leaves attractively on a large serving platter, mixing them up. Put the other ingredients on them in little piles.

Dress with a good vinaigrette (see page 241). If nutty flavours are in vogue in your household, replace 1 tablespoon of the olive oil with cold-pressed nut oil. Let people help themselves to vinaigrette if they want it or leave it if they don't.

Spinach and ricotta gnocchi

A child's response to spinach is unpredictable. Some like it; others approach it as vampires do garlic. It can be a tricky vegetable to market. This recipe, however, my version of a Jane Grigson one, is a long-standing favourite in our house. Perhaps it's because the spinach is soft, with all its mouth-puckering iron quality cooked out. Ricotta cheese is light and slips down a treat. When the two are united under a silky tomato sauce, the combination meets a surprising degree of favour even with children on record as spinach-haters.

The amount of spinach you will need depends on how much waste there is. If you are using unprepared spinach you will need more; pre-washed and packaged, less.

750g–1kg fresh spinach
370g ricotta cheese
2 large eggs
200g plain white flour, plus extra for dusting
80g Parmesan cheese, freshly grated, plus extra for dusting
salt, pepper and grated nutmeg
a large quantity of smooth (liquidised) tomato sauce

Wash the spinach if necessary. Place in a large saucepan with just enough water to cover the base of the pan, then put the lid on and bring to the boil. The spinach will wilt and turn dark green. Strain it into a colander and leave to drain, squeezing occasionally, for at least an hour.

Take the spinach out of the colander and squeeze firmly again with your hands. Place on a chopping board and chop finely. Transfer to a bowl and mix with the ricotta. Then add the eggs, flour and Parmesan, mix well and season generously with salt, pepper and nutmeg. Refrigerate for at least one hour.

Preheat the oven to 190°C/375°F/Gas Mark 5.

Pour the tomato sauce into a shallow ovenproof dish. Bring a large saucepan of water to a rolling boil. Put some flour for dusting in a shallow dish.

Using a dessertspoon, form the chilled mixture into oval dumplings. The mixture will be soft and sticky, so drop the spoonfuls into the flour from your spoon, then turn them on all sides to coat them lightly in the flour. Drop them into the boiling water in batches, no more than eight at a time They should have lots of circulating water about them, so don't pack them in. They will fall to the bottom, then gradually rise up to the surface. They are done when they float to the top and feel just slightly firm to the touch. Scoop them out with a draining spoon and put them into the dish with the tomato sauce as they are ready, turning them over in the sauce to coat. Add a little water if the sauce is too thick. Dust generously with Parmesan and bake until bubbly and brown on top. Serve with warm ciabatta or airy continental bread and more Parmesan and black pepper.

Crispy Chinese fish

This offers some of the attractions of deep-fried fish without the batter but it is much more interesting and exotic. Go for a firm white fish, preferably monkfish – its resilience and firmness in the mouth appeal to children. But since this fish is very pricey, thick fillets of cod or haddock are a more affordable option.

The sauce gains a large part of its appeal from the mirin–Japanese rice wine. It is naturally quite sweet and has a pleasant viscosity which gives an agreeable roundness to any dish. In my experience, children love it. You can find it in good wholefood shops nowadays as well as oriental food shops.

500g white fish fillets, skinned, any bones removed
coarse sea salt
fine polenta or cornflour for coating
groundnut or sunflower oil for frying
spring onions, finely chopped, to garnish

For the sauce:
1 tbsp fresh root ginger, pounded to a paste
2 tbsp mirin
2 tbsp water
2 tsp toasted sesame oil

Cut the fish into slices about as thick as a thumbnail. Rub with coarse sea salt and leave for 30 minutes. Put the fish on absorbent kitchen paper and pat off any excess salt, then dip it in polenta or cornflour to coat lightly.

Warm just enough oil to shallow-fry the fish in a frying pan until it is almost sputtering. Add the fish and pat down. Do not try to move it until it becomes crispy on the bottom and the top is starting to turn opaque – a few minutes. Turn it over and repeat for the other side. When the fish is crisp on both sides and firm but still springy, transfer it to a warm serving plate.

Put the ginger into the frying pan and stir-fry for about half a minute, taking care that it does not burn. Pour in all the remaining sauce ingredients and allow them to bubble up and then evaporate slightly. Pour this over the fish and garnish with spring onions.

Serve with lightly stir-fried Chinese-style cabbage that is still crunchy, plus rice or noodles.

Pasta alla crudaiola

My mother's spirit of adventure for good food never diminishes, even though she is now in her seventies. This is a blissfully easy recipe she picked up only recently at Monica Cuniberti's cookery classes in Bologna.

Pasta is one of the foods that almost all children like, but very often they get it in only a limited number of familiar (often over-cooked) forms: with tomato sauce, bolognese sauce or carbonara. This recipe, which combines more challenging fresh, cold ingredients with warm pasta, is somewhere between a hot pasta dish and a pasta salad.

The basil scents the warm pasta in an aromatic way. Even if children pick out some of the 'bits', such as the capers or basil, they feel familiar with the tuna and eat surprisingly respectable amounts of other ingredients such as olives, too.

6 sweet, red tomatoes or the equivalent in cherry tomatoes, chopped
100g tinned tuna in oil, drained and flaked
15 unvinegary black olives, stoned and roughly chopped
300g mozzarella, cubed
50g capers (preferably in salt, not brine), soaked in warm water for 10 minutes, then drained
a handful of basil leaves, finely chopped
salt and pepper
extra virgin olive oil
500g pasta (penne, garganelli, spiralli, fusilli, conchiglie)

Combine all the ingredients except the pasta with enough olive oil to coat them generously and leave a bit at the bottom of the bowl. Allow to stand for 30 minutes.

Cook the pasta in boiling salted water until *al dente*, then drain well. Mix with the cold ingredients in the oil.

Serve with a bottle of extra virgin olive oil on the table for those who want more.

Shepherd's pie

This traditional dish is the classic carnivore's comfort food. Most children like mince-based meaty sauces and go for mash in a big way. Many adults have bad memories of undistinguished versions of shepherd's pie, with a dull meaty flavour, made with greasy mince and gravy browning.

The food writers Sue Lawrence and Josceline Dimbleby have both reworked the basic idea and put a new spin on it which makes it much more interesting to adults. They both make the topping with a mixture of sweet potato and ordinary potato. Sue sometimes uses parsnips and adds a little grated cheese or Parmesan. Josceline sprinkles sesame seeds on top before cooking to add crunch – they look good too. Sue's base is basically British: a well-browned lamb mince with onions, cooked with Worcestershire sauce, a little stock and a splash of red wine – if there's a bottle open. Josceline's base is Middle Eastern in approach. She uses lamb, fresh tomatoes, carrots, onion and garlic, spiced with ground cumin and coriander and freshly chopped coriander stems. Both versions of this new-look pie are great served with a good green salad.

When the vegetables in the meat layer are chopped small and cooked to a luscious softness, vegetable avoiders don't notice them. Sweet potato or parsnip served on its own could be hit or miss. Some children like the sweetness; others find it too much. Cooked in with basic spuds, however, neither constituency is likely to complain.

Ricotta crêpes baked with tomato and mozzarella

Pancakes in any shape or form are a winner with children but they need to be served with nutritious ingredients if they are to be anything other than stodge. This dish fits the bill.

Mix together ricotta cheese, small cubes of mozzarella, grated Parmesan, salt and pepper and use as a stuffing for crêpes. Place the filled, rolled crêpes in a greased baking dish. Pour over a smooth (liquidised) tomato sauce to cover. Dot with a few knobs of butter and dust generously with Parmesan. Bake in a moderate oven (180°C/350°F/Gas Mark 4) until bubbly and browned on top.

TEN GOOD DRINKS

As discussed on pages 103–7, water ought to be the standard drink that children consume regularly throughout the day. But there are times when we want to offer them something a little more interesting and special, something that can compete in their minds with the much-hyped, ubiquitous fizzy drinks.

When every other child around seems to be allowed to drink cola, lemonade and sweetened 'fruit' drinks, children given only water as an alternative can easily feel that they are being deprived. We have to anticipate that feeling and prevent it by coming up with drinks that appeal to children but which fit in with real-food thinking.

Here are ten versatile ideas for cold and hot drinks that should appeal to children. Be ruthless – give them gimmicky and fanciful names targeted at the desired age group to add to their appeal! Think of attractive ways to garnish them, too. Mint leaves, edible flowers, cucumber or fruit slices and generous quantities of ice all add child appeal. In hot milky drinks, the merest sprinkling of cocoa powder or grated chocolate or the thinnest drizzle of runny cream can help to sell the package.

All of these drinks require a small amount of 'hands-on' preparation and children can be encouraged to make them on a DIY basis as soon as they have mastered simple kitchen operations like whizzing a blender, boiling the kettle or heating milk. The more involved children are in the preparation of drinks, the more likely they are to want to consume them. Making drinks can be good fun!

Fruit juice spritzer

Combine any unsweetened fruit juice with twice or three times the quantity of sparkling mineral water.

The mineral water dilutes the potentially tooth-rotting fruit sugar and acid present in the juice and lends the attractive fizz of so many soft drinks. The fruit juice is a good source of vitamins, especially if freshly squeezed or pressed.

Most supermarkets have a wide range of unsweetened fruit juice these days. Wholefood shops also stock more unusual and interesting juices such as carrot, beetroot and prune. By varying these juices and exploiting the possibilities of cocktail terminology, there are endless variations on the spritzer theme, such as:

- Caribbean ('tropical' blend containing mango, pineapple, lime and so on)

- Pink Lady (cranberry)

- Koala (prune)

- Peter Rabbit (carrot)

- Amethyst (beetroot)

- Ruby (blood orange).

Home-made lemonade

Most manufactured lemonade is of the clear, fizzy variety and contains no real lemon whatsoever, only flavouring. Recently, apparently healthier lemonades have come on the market which purport to be 'traditional', 'old-fashioned' and so on. This image is deeply misleading, because although they do contain some real lemon juice the quantity is terribly small in a comparison with the vast amounts of sugar and/or sweeteners in them. Instead, a genuinely home-made lemonade can be prepared quite easily by simply combining freshly squeezed lemon juice with sparkling mineral water and white or golden sugar. Even allowing for a fairly generous amount of sugar to make the acidic lemon palatable, this will still end up being considerably less sweet than commercial lemonades and will definitely contain more lemon, which is an excellent source of vitamins.

If you want to vary lemonade a bit, you can make a sugar syrup infused with fresh lemongrass: bring 500ml water to the boil with 350g sugar and some finely sliced lemongrass, stirring until the sugar has dissolved, and simmer for a few minutes. You could also infuse the sugar syrup with root ginger for a ginger version. Some lime juice and zest adds a tropical taste.

If you are short of time, you can buy chilled fresh lemonade, made with just sugar, water and lemons, in supermarkets. But it is a good idea to cut this with some fizzy mineral water because they do tend to be sweeter than true home-made versions.

Iced tea

Iced tea drinks are one of the newer categories of sickly-sweet soft drinks that have appeared on our shelves in recent years. They appeal especially to older children and teenagers. A much less sweet home-made version can be made by chilling interestingly flavoured teas, adding a very small amount of sugar or honey and then mixing the tea with a generous proportion of water and ice.

Iced tea can take on many forms using characterful teas. The possibilities are endless but they could include:

- Moroccan mint (an infusion of mint leaves)

- Jasmine

- Fruit-flavoured black teas (mango and passion fruit)

- Lemon tea (with fresh lemon slices)
- Lemon balm tea (with fresh or dried leaves).

Milk shakes

The typical milk shake served in school canteens and cafés these days is made by combining a dry mix of milk powder, sugar, thickeners, flavourings and colourings with water. But it is easy to make a proper milk shake simply by whizzing up fruit and milk in a blender. The colours are naturally attractive and, drunk quickly, it will still be bubbly, which adds to its appeal. Better still, most children really like being let loose with a blender to experiment to their heart's content.

If sweet fruits like banana or strawberries are used, there will be no need for a sweetener of any kind. A decent milk shake consists only of fresh fruit and milk – a nutritious combination. When fresh fruit is seasonally limited, frozen fruits like raspberries and blueberries are perfect for this purpose.

If a thicker milk shake is in demand, some natural yogurt can be added. Small amounts of flavouring can be incorporated judiciously according to the type of fruit. A small teaspoon of cocoa powder could be mixed in with banana and milk, for example, or some natural vanilla extract.

Flavoured water

Even ordinary tap water can be made more interesting by serving it in a glass with a flavouring of some kind. Obvious candidates include lemon, lime or orange slices, fresh herb leaves such as mint or lemon balm, or finely chopped aromatic roots such as ginger or lemongrass. Generous quantities of ice cubes add to its appeal.

Smoothies

Smoothies are American inventions. The basic concept is similar to a milk shake except that yogurt and crushed ice are generally used as well as fruit and milk.

Put equal quantities of natural yogurt and milk in a blender along with about half that quantity again of fruit and ice combined. Whizz the lot and serve. Quantities are very flexible and children can be encouraged to experiment with different proportions of the various elements.

Since very few households possess the equipment to crush ice, this element can be dispensed with. Or you can put some ice cubes in a plastic bag, seal it and bash the ice with a rolling pin. Be careful not to let children loose with ice cubes in a blender, unless you want it totally wrecked. When crushed ice is not available, frozen fruit and frozen yogurt can be used instead of fresh to give a very similar effect.

Depending on what you put in them, smoothies can be quite substantial. Add a little wheat germ or bran, for example, to make a healthy and nutritious breakfast or substantial snack which particularly appeals to teenagers. Smoothies are also a clever way to use up fruits with a good flavour but a mushy texture, such as disappointing apricots, pears or nectarines.

Some smoothie possibilities include:

- Breakfast smoothie – yogurt, milk, banana (frozen if no ice is available), wheatgerm, ice

- Berry smoothie – yogurt, milk, fresh or frozen raspberries/blueberries/blackcurrants, a little lemon juice (optional), ice

- Peanut butter smoothie – yogurt, milk, a little unsalted peanut butter, a very little honey or maple syrup, ice

- Coconut smoothie – yogurt, half milk and coconut milk, a little lemon (optional), frozen tinned mango juice (optional), ice

- Mocha smoothie – yogurt, milk, frozen coffee, a little unsweetened cocoa powder, a sprinkling of sugar, ice

- Stone fruit smoothie – yogurt, milk, fresh apricots/peaches/nectarines/cherries, a little lemon juice and/or sugar to taste, ice.

Real cocoa

Old-fashioned cocoa has been superseded these days by commercial processed chocolate drinks which are little more than milk powder laced with additives and loaded with sweeteners. Proper cocoa made with unsweetened cocoa powder, milk and sugar to taste is a comforting, healthy and attractive alternative for children. To vary the flavour, a drop of natural vanilla extract can be added.

For one mug of cocoa, simply bring just under a mug of milk to the boil. Meanwhile spoon a heaped teaspoon of cocoa powder and a level teaspoon of sugar (muscovado or other unprocessed brown sugar for added flavour) into the mug and blend with just enough water to make a paste. Pour on the hot milk, stir well and serve.

Real hot chocolate

Another healthy home-made alternative to the commercial chocolate drinks discussed above. This is the traditional way to make hot chocolate, using a good-quality dark chocolate bar (50–70 per cent cocoa solids).

This type of hot chocolate appeals to children because they like the idea of chocolate bars. If you use quality dark chocolate, it will have little sugar, only natural cocoa butter and a good complement of useful vitamins. Combined with milk, this is a nutritious drink. Simply bring milk to the boil and whisk in two squares of chocolate

with a balloon whisk, lowering the heat if necessary, until the chocolate has melted. Add a sprinkling of sugar to taste. For a more Aztec
or Inca flavour (the ancient peoples who discovered chocolate) add
a drop of natural vanilla extract, or a dusting of cinnamon or nutmeg.

Herbal and fruit teas

Although these teas are usually offered to adults, they often appeal
to children too because of the sheer variety of flavours and tastes on
offer, the exotic names (Dazzler, Bracer, Rosehip, Tranquillity,
Melissa and so on), the pronounced flavours and, last but not least,
pretty and eye-catching packaging.

Teas of this type form a huge and varied category which appeal
to that familiar 'collector' tendency in children. Just as endless variations on the same doll or tiny toy creature seem to enthral children,
they can take surprisingly well to the extended family grouping of
herbal and fruit teas, testing out the various names, colours and
types, choosing their favourites. Recognising this, some manufacturers are now selling special herbal 'children's tea', available in
wholefood shops.

Herbal teas should not be confused with herbal 'drinks' aimed at
babies which generally contain large amounts of sugar or other disguised sweeteners. Herbal and fruit teas are straight infusions, usually in teabag form but sometimes loose.

From a parent's point of view, herbal teas represent a good way
of getting a child to drink more water, they contain no calories and
no sugar or sweeteners of any kind and some have positive health
benefits. Camomile can sooth a child, while mint or ginger can help
a sore tummy. Although some fruit-flavour teas do contain rather
aggressive synthetic flavourings (which must be declared on the
packet as 'flavouring'), most teas in the herbal range contain only
natural ingredients.

For older children, black teas such as Earl Grey, served quite weak, should not be overlooked. Although they contain caffeine, which does act as a stimulant, the amount is negligible.

Another very healthy choice is Japanese green tea, which is caffeine-free, full of vitamins and now attributed with bestowing many health benefits, especially for the circulatory system and the heart.

From the time that a child can hold a cup of warm liquid safely without spilling it, parents can offer lukewarm teas of this kind. Older children can be encouraged to experiment with them at will as soon as they seem to be able to boil a kettle and pour out the water safely.

Miso soup

Children may sometimes feel in the mood for a warming, clear, savoury liquid. The classic children's drink usually offered is the brown and sticky sort with a meaty flavour, made from yeast extract. The major shortcoming of these drinks is that they are extremely salty.

A much better alternative is miso. Miso is the name for soya-bean paste which is a by-product of soy sauce production. It has a savoury flavour and is extremely healthy because, if not boiled, it contains beneficial enzymes which help digestion. Miso soup is now sold in instant sachet form in wholefood shops and some supermarkets.

TEN GOOD PACKED LUNCHES

There's something about packed lunches that defeats lots of parents. Is it staggering around the kitchen in the morning, half-asleep, trying to assemble them? Is it the day–in–day–out necessity for them? Might it be that all-too-frequent realisation that the fridge is bare and there is little or nothing with the makings of a packed lunch, or the dispiriting observation that half of it is coming home uneaten anyway? No wonder so many of us fall back into a set formula meal, thrown together from familiar component parts. A standard sandwich of some sort, a packet of crisps, a chocolate sweet of some kind, an apple, a carton of juice . . . day after day after day.

But children, perhaps even more than adults, get fed up with repetition. If we stick to one packed lunch structure, they will end up eating less and less. And as soon as they have any money to spend, they'll be supplementing it with junk from the sweet shop. If we vary their lunch, they will eat more. Yet by the time we reject the foods we think they don't like and search for creative food alternatives which we can provide, it can often seem that we don't have a lot of room for manoeuvre.

When your ideas for packed lunch dry up and you need inspiration, cast your eyes down the formulas that follow: two school weeks' worth of lunches. Most of these are just twists on sandwiches or 'wraps', but they vary the bread component of the basic sandwich idea. It's easy to get into the habit of using the same kind of bread all the time, but by varying it using all kinds of bread and all types of roll, we can make essentially the same fillings seem quite different.

All of these lunches include fresh fruit and vegetables in forms that many children will find appealing.

Salads can be served in plastic tubs saved from yogurt or cream cheese, for example, or in steel *thali* dishes with lids, sold in most good kitchenware shops.

By investing in a plastic water bottle, we can save money on juice and encourage them to drink water. The space created in the lunch box by leaving out the juice leaves more room for fruit in a fresher, unprocessed form.

FORMULA 1

Tuna pasta salad (pasta, tuna and tomatoes/cucumber/celery/ olives/red onions in half-and-half mayonnaise and Greek yogurt)

Home-made or good-quality bought banana or carrot cake

Bag of grapes

FORMULA 2

Salad roll (wholemeal bap filled with cucumber, crunchy lettuce and tomato, smeared with mayonnaise or hummus)

Greek yogurt with honey

A stone fruit (nectarine, peach, plum) or banana

FORMULA 3

Crêpe or bought chapati (either buttered or smeared with a dip or spread, filled with shredded cheese/ham/lettuce/carrot, rolled and cut in small sections)

Flapjack/muesli/sunflower bar

Small tub of fruit salad

FORMULA 4

Couscous or cracked wheat salad (with chopped cucumber/pepper/ tomatoes/olives/carrot dressed with olive oil/lemon juice or vinegar flavoured with mint)

Buttered scone/mini-croissant

Honeydew melon chunks in tub

FORMULA 5
Breadsticks and vegetable crudités with dip (a pile of grissini, batons
of carrot/cucumber/pepper with tzatziki or cream cheese or half
hummus-half peanut butter dip)

Home-made flapjack or brownie

A pear

FORMULA 6
Stuffed pitta bread (filled with left-over cooked meats, such as
Ajwain chicken [see recipe on pages 241–2] with shredded lettuce/
chicken smeared with raita/meats with bought teriyaki or hoisin
sauce)

Tub of Greek yogurt with strawberries

Mixed nuts, seeds and dried fruits

FORMULA 7
Mediterranean ciabatta (ciabatta filled with thin slices of mozzarella,
tomato and red onion/roasted peppers/crunchy cooked green beans,
spread with basil pesto or olive paste, squashed flat)

Tub layered with Greek yogurt, fresh fruit/maple syrup/honey and
muesli topping (see recipe on pages 280–81)

FORMULA 8
Bagel with cream cheese and cucumber or peanut butter

Slices of rolled Parma-type ham or carrot sticks

Fresh pineapple chunks

FORMULA 9

Tuna nutty rice salad (nutty brown, Camargue, wild or mixed rice, tuna, tomatoes/cucumber/red onions/olives/celery, dressed with mustardy vinaigrette)

Soy sauce nuts or seeds (see recipe on page 271)

Clementines

FORMULA 10

Seafood roll (moist wholemeal or rye roll filled with smoked salmon, lemon and butter or prawns in half mayonnaise-half yogurt with shredded crunchy lettuce

Small tub of fruit salad

Flapjack or brownie

TEN WAYS TO GET CHILDREN TO EAT VEGETABLES

Children's objections to vegetables are not as all-embracing as they often seem and generally centre on the matter of texture, not flavour. In a nutshell, they like crunch. That's why lots of children will eat raw but not cooked vegetables. The most common example of this is cabbage. Raw in coleslaw, many children will eat it. Cooked, though, is a different matter. So, offering raw vegetables is the most certain way to break down a vegetable veto.

If a child only ever eats raw vegetables, then it can be a drag. But on health grounds, we can't complain: that's the most nutritious way to eat them.

Many children – and quite a few adults – have problems with classic British boiled vegetables. Watery carrots and cabbage, mushy sprouts and flabby green beans are a national staple. Who can blame anyone for disliking them? Vegetables cooked this way are the worst of both worlds. They have lost any crunch, yet they still retain their original shape. By contrast, properly slow-cooked, really soft vegetables, such as those in puréed soup or sauce or baked in the oven, meet with far fewer objections. In fact, they can often be quite popular.

The motto with children, therefore, is to cook vegetables long and well or very briefly – or, better still, not at all!

What follows is a list of ideas for vegetables in forms that often appeal to children.

Crudités

Take any raw, firm vegetables and cut them into smallish, manageable batons, julienne sticks, discs, wedges, cubes, strips and so on.
Choose as wide a selection as possible – e.g. grated carrot, thin
cucumber slices, finely shredded crisp lettuce, halved cherry tomatoes, diced celery, grated raw beetroot – and arrange them to show
off their contrasting brilliant colours. See the recipe for Salad plate
on pages 240–41.

Crudités with dip

Children who show no interest in raw vegetables may well get
enthusiastic and consume several when they are accompanied by a
dip. Good candidates include mayonnaise, or mayonnaise and yogurt,
tzatziki, hummus and guacamole (see recipe on pages 270–71).

Raw in salad with fruit and nuts

Children who aren't keen on the idea of vegetables will often eat a
reasonable amount of them if they are teamed up with fruit and nuts
in classic combinations such as Waldorf salad (apples, celery and
walnuts in creamy dressing) or carrots, peanuts and raisins.

Sugarsnap peas and mangetout

Steamed for two minutes, the odds are high that these crunchy
greens will get the thumbs-up.

Green beans

Steam the beans for four minutes until vividly green and still crunchy. Drain, then place in ice-cold water with ice cubes in it for two minutes to halt cooking. Drain well and dress lightly with flaky salt, lemon juice and extra virgin olive oil. Serve as a salad.

Crunchy steamed vegetables with garlic butter

Lightly steam green beans, broccoli, carrots or cabbage, leaving them crunchy. Top with a melting, oozing dollop of freshly made garlic butter with some finely minced parsley in it.

Root vegetables in mash

Most children love mashed potato. Incorporate a small quantity of boiled or baked root vegetables such as squashes, turnips, sweet potatoes or parsnips (see Shepherd's pie on page 249). If you meet with no objection, increase the quantity gradually.

Any vegetable liquidised in soup or sauce

Getting the thumbs-down for vegetables such as tomatoes, celery, watercress, leeks, courgettes, spinach or mushrooms? Liquidise them in soup and give it a non-vegetable name like 'hunter's soup' or that old tag 'cream of garden'.

It's amazing how many children will eat a liquidised sauce made from tinned tomatoes but not a bashed-down one with 'bits' still visible. Vegetable chunks in a stew or casserole can be passed through a sieve and returned to the gravy to be eaten with the meat and, say, a starchy food like potatoes or rice.

Most vegetables liquidised in a juice extractor

A proper juice extractor machine can turn vegetables like carrots, celery, beetroot and cucumber into an attractive-looking frothy drink. These are most likely to appeal when they are teamed with juiced fruits such as apples, kiwis, pears and oranges. In nutritional terms, these juices are excellent and make it well worth investing in a proper juicer. Older children and teenagers enjoy using them and can do so without adult supervision once they know how.

Roasted or stir-fried vegetables

Vegetables cooked this way are firm, not watery. Stir-fried vegetables such as peppers or beansprouts still have that essential crunch. Roasted vegetables such as carrots, parsnips, peppers or squashes are softer, but agreeably so, with a more concentrated gooey sweet flavour and those compulsive sticky blackened bits.

TEN IDEAS FOR MAKING EATING MORE FUN

We are often told that children have to be psychologically manipulated if we want them to eat. This is why it's not uncommon for parents with 'picky' children to think that they must become singing, dancing entertainers-meet-stand-up comics in order to induce their offspring to eat. Dress as a waiter. Make aeroplanes out of spoonfuls of food. Crouch under the table and make slices of toast beg to be eaten in a funny voice. Tell them to eat that morsel which is cunningly hiding the picture of that lovable bunny on the bowl . . . just a few of the desperate devices suggested to get food inside them. But if we want our children to eat a good, wide range of wholesome food, they have to realise sooner or later that mealtimes aren't a toe-tapping, side-splitting entertainment extravaganza.

What parents who are not card-carrying Equity members can keep it up indefinitely anyway? And how can we endlessly dream up something ever more novel to tempt? Long-term, integrating children into communal household eating (as described in The Real-food Approach, pages 55–60, and Eating Together and Why It Matters, pages 74–7) seems a more effortless solution – one that is definitely more sustainable and probably more effective in the end.

But if we hit a bad patch with children's eating and feel that some new input is required, or simply want to try to move children on from a small, safe selection of foods to something more challenging and unfamiliar, there is no harm in occasionally employing a few devices to set the scene.

Here are some ideas which might work without putting any oppressive burden to entertain on adults:

- Switch off the main lights and light the candles. The more the merrier in the centre of the table; hanging, safe individual night-light candles in glasses of water for smaller children. Candles make meals special as well as being soothing.

- Dictate the evening's menu to a child who can write. Get her or him to announce it to everyone else with a description of ingredients. Also known as 'verbally proposing' a menu in some pretentious restaurants. This harnesses a child's energy and encourages them to take an interest, even feel slightly proprietorial about what's being served.

- Play some 'mood' music: Indian, French, Chinese, Italian themes. Corny, yes, but it helps set the scene for food that might seem exotic and it may make them less inclined to want to leave the table instantly.

- Serve food outside on a tablecloth on the ground or at a low table. Everyone likes al fresco eating, children included. They even like it when it's freezing cold!

- Get the children to write out attractive menus on stiff paper with food illustrations. Keeps them busy and adds to the idea that the meal is in a swanky restaurant.

- Buy a cheap paper tablecloth and either write yourself, or better still get them to write, the menu on it with drawings. Gives them something to do while waiting to eat and appeals to their anarchic spirit. Writing on tablecloths is usually a no-no.

- Change the serving utensils and crockery. Set out chopsticks, Chinese soup spoons and bowls when Chinese or Thai food is on the menu, with forks as backup. Serve an Indian meal in little steel *thali* dishes on trays. Buy some banana leaves and serve curries directly on a section of one. Let them eat with their fingers as they would in India. Get out your 'best' adult crockery or fancy glasses for special or even just slightly special household occasions. Children may be inclined to eat more just because they like the idea of the bowls or the banana leaf. They also appreciate being treated as civilised people.

- Get the children to cut out and write placecards for each member of the household or guest and decide where she or he will sit. A diversion which occupies them and may make them feel more involved in the meal.

- Buy a cheap restaurant order pad from an office supplier and ask them to note down orders from a small selection of items you can handle and consider acceptable – a sort of *menu du jour*. Mildly diverting and 'restaurants' can turn into a long-running game. Children also like to feel they have been consulted about what they are eating.

- Give them little pads and paper and ask them to be restaurant critics, marking each dish out of ten and giving comments. Makes them think about what they are eating rather than just swallowing it, and all but the most remorseless children feel obliged to give the poor old cook some encouragement.

TEN EASY RECIPES THAT CHILDREN CAN MAKE

The recipes in this section are all simple for children to prepare, either totally independently or with a degree of supervision and help, depending on age. Adults might need to help out, for example, by taking things in and out of a hot oven and showing children how to use a knife safely. A little time spent showing them how to use a food processor will pay off very quickly. See pages 215–20 for more ideas about how to get children cooking.

Guacamole

Some children don't like avocado, but those who do go for it in a big way. Older children often enjoy a straightforward guacamole, which is quick to make and perfect for an after-school snack with some toast, blue corn chips or cut-up raw vegetables. Vinegar might prove more popular with children than lemon juice.

2 ripe avocados, peeled and stoned
lemon juice or wine vinegar
1 ripe red tomato, chopped small
1 garlic clove, crushed
salt and pepper
a pinch of cayenne or chilli (optional)
a little finely chopped red onion (optional)
finely chopped fresh coriander (optional)

Mash the avocados with a fork, then flavour to taste with lemon juice or vinegar. Add the tomato, garlic, seasoning and any of the optional ingredients to taste. If making it in advance, cover tightly with clingfilm to help prevent discoloration.

Soy sauce nuts

When the soy is sprinkled over the roasted nuts or seeds they sizzle, turn brown and cool to a crunchy, savoury salt-sweet deliciousness. From the taste point of view, the very best nuts to use are cashews, but they are expensive. However, you can get the same effect with cheaper nuts, such as unsalted peanuts, or with seeds. I prefer to use the Japanese version of soy sauce, shoyu. It is often more naturally made and doesn't usually contain unnecessary additives such as caramel.

**skinned nuts (cashews, almonds, peanuts) or seed kernels
   (sunflower, pumpkin)**
shoyu (soy sauce)

Preheat the oven to 180°C/350°F/Gas Mark 4.

Bake the nuts or seeds in a roasting tin until they are toasted and golden – about 20–30 minutes for nuts, 15–20 minutes for seeds. As soon as they come out of the oven, sprinkle over enough shoyu to glaze them and turn them darker brown. Don't overdo the shoyu. The warm nuts or seeds will absorb it quite quickly and no liquid will remain after a few seconds.

Dipping crunch

This is my combination of Claudia Roden's recipe for the Egyptian dipping snack *dukkah* and that wholefood stalwart *gomasio*. The flavour of highly nutritious toasted ground sesame seeds is wonderfully savoury and satisfying and makes a change for children from the more familiar taste of peanut butter. Anything crunchy usually goes down a treat with them. The nuts are toasty and the flavour of the spices is there, but not too pronounced.

This dipping crunch can be served, as Claudia suggests, by first dipping little bits of bread in extra virgin olive oil, then dipping them into the crunch. Most children like dips of all kinds and some really like olive oil on bread (if given the chance to taste it). Those who don't go for the oil might be more attracted by dipping the bread first in sweet balsamic vinegar or even a mixture of mirin (sweet Japanese rice wine) and shoyu (soy sauce).

This is easy to make if a child can weigh and has been shown how to use a food processor.

125g sesame seeds
1 tsp coriander seeds
125g skinned hazelnuts
1 tsp ground cumin
½ tsp salt, or to taste

Preheat the oven to 180°C/350°F/Gas Mark 4.

Put the sesame and coriander seeds on a baking sheet and bake until they begin to smell and look nicely toasted. Pour them (with a funnel if necessary) into a food processor.

Spread the hazelnuts on the baking sheet and bake until golden brown. Allow to cool, then add to the food processor. Process everything until it is finely crushed but do not overdo it and allow it to become an oily paste. If in doubt, err on the crunchy side. Add the ground cumin and season with salt.

Serve as above and store in an airtight jar in the fridge.

Potato wedges in a paper bag

Most adults like chips: those who say they don't are mainly fibbing. All children love them and generally tell us so frequently. But we know they often eat too many. This is a better and healthier alternative to chips which has some of the same appeal, doesn't involve scary deep-frying and tastes a million times better than the standard 'oven chip'. It makes an interesting change from baked potatoes too. The paper bag casing is not entirely a gimmick. It produces potatoes that are soft in the middle and crisp on the outside and the bag, when opened, has a savoury smell to compete with the chip shop. A few garlic cloves or a sprig of rosemary or thyme make it smell even better.

I would leave the nutritious and tasty skins on if the potatoes are organic but peel them off if not, to avoid residues of any post-harvest chemical treatment.

largeish potatoes
extra virgin olive oil
whole, unpeeled garlic cloves (optional)
sprig of rosemary or thyme (optional)
sea salt

Preheat the oven to 200°C/400°F/Gas Mark 6.

Cut the potatoes into large wedges, shaped like segments of melon. Keep them thick. A big potato will produce six, a medium-sized one four.

Tear off a long piece of baking parchment, about two and a half times as long as is needed to accommodate all the potatoes in a single layer. Place this on a baking sheet. Brush the potato wedges with oil on all sides and lay them on the parchment. Add the garlic and herbs if using, then sprinkle generously with flaky sea salt. Wrap the paper over the potatoes to form a paper bag, keeping the wedges in one flat layer as much as possible. Fold down and tuck in any parchment edges that would allow steam to escape.

Bake for at least an hour, by which point the potatoes should smell marvellous and emerge all crusty and ever so slightly burnt at the edges. Open the bag at the table so everyone can smell the aroma.

Spare ribs

I don't know any non-vegetarian children who don't like spare ribs. The hands-on way you have to eat them and the process of nibbling the little sticky, slightly sweet bits of meat off the bones appeals.

Children are rarely given meat on the bone, because of the anticipated 'Yuck' reaction discussed on pages 86–90, and they usually end up eating meat in disguised processed forms like burgers or Kievs. It's even rarer to see a 'children's recipe' with meat that isn't a burger or meatball.

This recipe shows carnivore children just how easy it is to transform unlikely bits of meat into something good to eat. The mixing up of the marinade ingredients has all the appeal of those washing-up liquid, egg, milk and ketchup 'mixtures' that children are so fond of playing with – except, of course, that it is edible. It also introduces children to unusual and exotic ingredients in the context of a dish they think they will like.

When using pork ribs, I'd want them to be at least from outdoor-reared pigs, or, better still, organic – first, because they taste better and second, because they have been humanely reared. This way I could defend myself against any potentially tricky animal welfare questions.

1kg pork spare ribs
4 tbsp sunflower or groundnut oil
3 tbsp dark muscovado sugar or 3 tbsp maple syrup
3 tbsp shoyu (soy sauce)
1 tbsp sun-dried tomato paste or 2 tbsp tomato paste
2 tbsp mirin (sweet Japanese rice wine), rice wine or dry sherry
1 tsp toasted sesame oil
2 garlic cloves, crushed, or garlic paste
2 tsp fresh root ginger, crushed, or ginger paste

optional:
1 tsp finely chopped inner stalks of lemongrass, or lemongrass paste
1 tbsp bought teriyaki sauce
1 tsp Thai fish sauce (*nom pla*)
a large pinch of Chinese five-spices powder

Spread the ribs out in a large, shallow roasting tin. Mix together all the remaining ingredients and pour them over the meat. Refrigerate, turning the ribs over in the marinade, for half a day or, better still, overnight.

Get the oven really hot and toast the marinated ribs until dark and sticky (about 45 minutes), turning and basting about every 15 minutes.

DIY pizza

Nearly all children like pizza but, although in theory it can be a nutritious food, in practice it is all too often made with over-processed ingredients.

Home-made pizza dough is quick and easy to make . . . according to those who find it quick and easy to make! For those who don't, this cheat's version – a baked form of cheese on toast – is a reasonable compromise, with the added benefit that we can select a nutritious bread for the base. Children can have fun assembling theirs and trying out possible combinations.

Ingredients for one child:
2 slices of good wholemeal bread (organic, for preference)
or
a decent roll, split in half
or
2 slices of ciabatta or pugliese bread
or
2 slices of pain de campagne or sourdough bread
extra virgin olive oil
sun-dried tomato pesto
basil pesto
mozzarella cut into cubes or firm cheese, grated

any or none of the following, according to preference:
ham (cooked or cured)
raw or cooked vegetables
olives
tuna
dried herbs such as oregano

Preheat the oven to 200°C/400°F/Gas Mark 6.

If the bread is springy, roll it as flat as possible with a rolling pin. Grease a baking sheet with a little oil. Sprinkle oil on each piece of bread and then lay it on the baking sheet. Thin down each pesto with a little olive oil. Spread one piece of bread with the tomato pesto, the other with the basil. Top with cheese and any other ingredients you fancy.

Bake until the bread is crisp and the cheese is bubbly. Eat at once, with a salad.

Fruit kebabs

Children like the idea of anything on a stick and they usually like fruit too. These simple kebabs are fun to make as children can vary the order of the fruit on the stick as they fancy. The kebabs require only a little adult supervision under the grill. Serve with a tub of Greek yogurt to dip them in.

Don't use metal skewers, because these can get exceptionally hot and tend to have sharper ends, which could cause cuts. The wooden kind are safer for children. Soak them in water for 15 minutes before threading the fruit on; this prevents them burning.

a selection of at least two different kinds of soft, fresh, but not too watery fruit (e.g. pineapple, grapes, peaches, nectarines, oranges, bananas, apricots, plums, mango, kiwi)
runny honey or maple syrup
wooden kebab sticks (from Chinese supermarkets or kitchen shops)

Peel any fruits that need it and chop them into chunks, not slices, so they don't fall off the sticks. Thread the fruit on to the sticks, alternating them so as to highlight their different colours. Brush with honey or maple syrup and grill for a few minutes, turning once, until the fruit is beginning to be hot and the honey or maple syrup begins to look caramelised.

Scones

Real home-baking has gone a bit by the board in recent years as the food industry tells us we don't have time to cook, let alone bake. Yet time-honoured baking recipes can be very quick (this recipe takes about 10 minutes to prepare, 5 minutes to clear up and 15 minutes to bake) and offer tough competition for the packets of biscuits, crisps and sweets that children might otherwise crave. Scones can be much more nutritious than the typical children's snack and many children will be quite happy eating them without any topping, as long as they are still warm.

Children generally like baking scones too and can't resist eating them when they have made them.

Makes 12 small scones

125g wholemeal self-raising flour (organic, for preference)
125g white self-raising flour
50g cold unsalted butter, cubed
1 large egg
3 tbsp milk, plus extra to glaze
then either:
25g golden caster sugar
and
50g dried fruit (raisins, sultanas, cherries, chopped apricots)
or:
50g Cheddar, grated
and
1 tsp Dijon mustard (optional)

Preheat the oven to 220°C/425°F/Gas Mark 7. Grease a baking sheet.

Put the flours and the sugar, if using, into a large bowl and work in the butter with your fingers until it resembles breadcrumbs. Now add the fruit or the cheese. Combine the egg, milk and mustard, if using, and add to the dry ingredients. Stir with a spoon and work lightly with your fingers until the mixture just forms a dough and no more. Turn out the dough on to a floured surface and pat down gently until it is about 2–3cm thick. Cut out scones with a small pastry cutter, flouring the cutter between each scone.

Space out the scones on the baking sheet and brush the tops with a little milk. Bake on the top shelf of the oven for 10–15 minutes until well risen and golden brown.

Irish soda bread

My grandmother used to make soda bread with me. It was so gorgeous, it was hard to wait until it cooled down enough to eat it with butter and home-made jam. But she never measured anything and when I tried to make it on my own it was never the same. Years later I discovered this recipe from the kitchens of the Avoca Handweavers, in County Wicklow, Ireland. I varied it slightly and it tastes as good as hers did. Like hers, it uses ordinary milk, not buttermilk, which is often hard to find.

300g wholemeal flour (organic, for preference)
230g plain white flour
3 handfuls (small for adults, large for children) bran (organic, for preference)
3 handfuls (as above) wheatgerm
2 heaped tsp baking powder
1 tsp salt
700–900ml full-fat milk
2 tsp honey or treacle or 1 tsp raw cane sugar

Preheat the oven to 240°C/475°F/Gas Mark 9.

Mix all the dry ingredients together in a large bowl. Combine the milk and the honey or treacle, if using. Stir most of the milk into the dry ingredients and mix well until the mixture is soft and moist but not too sloppy (this depends a bit on the flour you are using).

Thoroughly oil and then flour a large (1·5kg) loaf tin and add the mixture.

Bake the loaf for 15–20 minutes or until it has risen. Lower the heat to 150°C/300°F/Gas Mark 2 and bake for a further hour. Turn the bread out of the tin. If the base sounds hollow when tapped, it is cooked. If not, return it to the oven for 10 minutes.

Muesli

So many children's breakfast cereals are little more than over-refined grains stuck together with sugar. This home-made muesli is so flavoursome in itself because of the toastiness of the grain and the generous amount of dried fruit that it needs no sugar. Children like its crunchy, varied texture and they can mix it together with their hands. Needless to say, it is packed with brilliant nutrition. Morning, noon or night, this is a perfect snack for any child.

These quantities and proportions are flexible. Vary them according to your household's preferences. This recipe fills two large storage jars.

1kg porridge oats
500g flakes of different grains such as barley, rye, wheat, spelt
200g sunflower seeds
100g pumpkin seeds
100g sesame seeds
100g hazelnuts or almonds
100g pecans, coarsely chopped
200g dried fruit (such as raisins, sultanas, cherries, blueberries, chopped apricots)

Preheat the oven to 180°C/350°F/Gas Mark 4.

Put everything except the pecans and dried fruit in a large roasting tin. Bake for 20–30 minutes, stirring occasionally, until the nuts are brown and toasted-looking and the kitchen begins to smell of toasting grain. Allow to cool, then stir in the dried fruit and pecans.

Serve with ice-cold milk and any nice fruit that's in season – blueberries, red fruits and grapes work especially well.

APPENDIX: CHECKLIST OF ADDITIVES TO AVOID

What follows is a list of commonly encountered additives which are best avoided, either because they are associated with adverse reactions in sensitive people or because they could have a negative impact on the health of those who consume them.

They turn up frequently in the ubiquitous children's junk foods, so the typical modern child is likely to be exposed to them in some quantity. The total effect of this additive cocktail on children has not been adequately researched yet, but it makes sense in health terms to limit children's exposure to additives as much as possible.

When there is an 'E' prefix before an additive number, this means it is permitted throughout the EU and has passed safety testing. Those without an 'E' prefix have not, and may at some point be reviewed and banned.

However, none of these additives can be considered as positively beneficial for human health. What's more, we are not obliged to eat them or let our children eat them, because there is always a safer, more benign alternative, so their use is not strictly necessary. When we let children eat them, we are running a risk with their health that we do not have to run.

COLOURS

E100 Curcumin, E102 Tartrazine, E104 Quinoline Yellow, E107 Yellow 2G, E110 Sunset Yellow, E120 Cochineal, E122 Carmoisine/Azorubine, E123 Amaranth, E124 Ponceau 4R, E127 Erythrosine BS, E128 Red 2G, E131, Patent Blue V, E132 Indigo Carmine, E133 Brilliant Blue FCF, E142 Green S/Lissamine Green/Acid Brilliant

Green, E150 Caramel, E151 Black PN, Brilliant Black BN, E153 Carbon Black, Vegetable Carbon, E154 Brown FK, E155 Brown HT/Chocolate Brown HT, E180 Lithol Rubine BK/Pigment Rubine

PRESERVATIVES

E210 Benzoic acid, E211 Sodium benzoate, E212 Potassium benzoate, E213 Calcium benzoate, E220 Sulphur dioxide, E221 Sodium sulphite, E222 Sodium hydrogen sulphite/Sodium bisulphite, Acid sodium sulphite, E223 Sodium metabisulphite/Disodium pyrosulphite, E227 Calcium hydrogen sulphite/Calcium bisulphite, E230 Biphenyl/Diphenyl, E231 2-Hydroxy-biphenyl/O-phenyl phenol, Orthophenyl phenol, E232 Sodium biphenyl-2-yl-oxide/Sodium orthophenylphenate, E239 Hexamine, Hexamethylenetetramine, E249 Potassium nitrite, E250 Sodium nitrite, E251 Sodium nitrate, E252 Potassium nitrate

ANTIOXIDANTS

E310 Propyl gallate/Propyl 3, 4, 5, trihydroxybenzene, E311 Octyl gallate, E312 Dodecyl gallate, Dodecyl, 3, 4, 5, trihydroxybenzene, E320 Butylated hydroxyanisole BHA, E321 Butylated hydroxytoluene BHT

STABILISERS

E407 Carageenan/Irish moss

FLAVOUR ENHANCERS

E621 Monosodium glutamate/Sodium hydrogen L-Glutamate/MSG

GLAZING AGENTS

E900 Dimethyl polysiloxane/Simethicone/Dimethicone

IMPROVERS (USED TO BLEACH FLOUR)

925 Chlorine, 936 Chlorine dioxide

FLAVOURINGS (ARTIFICIAL)

Unless prefixed with the word 'natural', these are totally synthetic chemical flavourings whose tastes have absolutely nothing to do with anything natural. 'Nature-identical' flavourings are also products of the science lab but the flavouring industry argues that these are indistinguishable from natural flavours. There are literally thousands of artificial and nature-identical flavourings but they are not individually listed on food labels and do not have E numbers, so there is no way of knowing what they are. Their precise chemical compositions, too, are a closely guarded commercial secret. The toxicological effects of such flavourings have been inadequately monitored, on the assumption that anything consumed in such small doses cannot do you much harm. However, evidence of unacceptable levels of toxicity have been found in certain flavourings. These have not been banned – manufacturers have simply been told to look for alternatives. There are moves to create a European register of permitted flavourings that have gone through a full scientific evaluation but this is not expected to be in place until 2004.

INDEX

THE FOOD OUR CHILDREN EAT

Joanna Blythman is Britain's leading investigative food journalist and an influential commentator on the British food chain. She has won three prestigious Glenfiddich awards for her writing, including a Glenfiddich Special award for her first book *The Food We Eat* in 1997, a Caroline Walker Media Award for 'Improving the Nation's Health by Means of Good Food', and a Guild of Food Writers Award in 1997, also for *The Food We Eat*. She writes for the *Guardian*, several other magazines and newspapers, and broadcasts frequently on food issues. She has two children.

Also by Joanna Blythman

The Food We Eat